The United States and the Americas

Lester D. Langley, General Editor

*This series is dedicated to a broader
understanding of the political, economic, and
especially cultural forces and issues that have
shaped the Western hemispheric experience—
its governments and its peoples. Individual
volumes assess relations between the United
States and its neighbors to the south and
north: Mexico, Central America, Cuba, the
Dominican Republic, Haiti, Panama,
Colombia, Venezuela, the Andean Republics
(Peru, Ecuador, and Bolivia), Brazil, Uruguay
and Paraguay, Argentina, Chile, and Canada.*

The United States and the Americas

Colombia and the United States

Stephen J. Randall

Colombia and the United States: Hegemony and Interdependence

The University of Georgia Press

Athens and London

© 1992 by the University of Georgia Press
Athens, Georgia 30602

Set in 10 on 14 Palatino

The paper in this book meets the guidelines
for permanence and durability of the Committee on
Production Guidelines for Book Longevity of the
Council on Library Resources.

Printed in the United States of America

96   95   94   93   92   C   5   4   3   2   1

Library of Congress Cataloging in Publication Data

Randall, Stephen J., 1944–
    Colombia and the United States : hegemony and
interdependence / Stephen J. Randall.
        p.   cm. — (The United States and the Americas)
    Includes bibliographical references and index.
    ISBN 0-8203-1401-3 (alk. paper). — ISBN 0-8203-1402-1
(pbk. : alk. paper)
    1. United States–Foreign relations–Colombia.
    2. Colombia–Foreign relations–United States.
    I. Title.   II. Series. E183.8.C7R35   1992
    327.730861–dc20   91-17739
                                                              CIP

British Library Cataloging in Publication Data available

Contents

Maps

Acknowledgments

I have accumulated many debts in the course of preparing this volume. The first, of course, is to Lester D. Langley, general editor of The United States and the Americas series, for requesting me to contribute to the series, and to the very professional staff of the University of Georgia Press, with whom he worked. Second, there are the many librarians and archivists in Colombia and the United States who have given their time and expertise over the past several years and earlier, since this study draws on work that was completed for previous as well as the current project. The staff of the diplomatic and military branches at the National Archives and of the Manuscript Division of the Library of Congress deserve particular appreciation for various forms of assistance, as do the staffs of the presidential libraries: the Hoover Library, West Branch Iowa; the Roosevelt Library, Hyde Park, New York; the Truman Library, Independence, Missouri; the Eisenhower Library, Abilene, Kansas; the Kennedy Library, Boston, Massachusetts; the Johnson Library, Austin, Texas; as well as the staff in the manuscript divisions of Princeton University Library and Sterling Memorial Library, Yale University. Archivists at the Rockefeller Archives Center in the Pocantico Hills, New York, made a pleasant location for research even more rewarding. At McGill, I was assisted in an early stage of the research by two conscientious students: David Goetz and Patricia Bollanos.

In Colombia, I must particularly express my appreciation to Lilia Sanchez Torres, then director of the Colombian Foreign Ministry Archives, Bogotá, and to Luis Ernesto Niño, secretary of the Archives, for their painstaking assistance and remarkable hospitality. Colombian academics who have added considerably to my understanding of Colombian foreign policy include Marta Ardilla, National University, and Juan G. Tokatlian, University of the Andes. I am endebted to the former foreign minister, Alfredo Vásquez Carrizosa, for his observations on my treatment of the post-1945 years and to Manuel Zapata Olivella for his insights into Colombian race relations and culture. Several scholars of Colombia, Latin America, and U.S. foreign policy have been for many years generous and insightful in their guidance: David Bushnell, who offered helpful suggestions at an early stage of the project and a thorough, critical reading at the end of the process; Catherine LeGrand, Charles Bergquist, Robert Freeman Smith, Randall Woods, Ronald Newton, and Kurt Levy, who have either read and commented on parts of the manuscript or offered timely advice on sources and interpretation. I deeply appreciate their guidance. The maps were prepared by William Mills.

The Social Sciences and Humanities Research Council of Canada provided the financial support that made possible the extensive research that this project involved. McGill University, my former institution, provided support at an early stage of the research and writing. The Council and the University of Calgary also made it possible for me to have an uninterrupted term for writing at the end of the research. To each of them, my gratitude for their unusually sensitive understanding and support for scholarly work.

On the most personal level I could not have completed this study without the encouragement and assistance of my closest friends in Colombia, John and Carmen Petan and Annie de Ortíz. Their prodding and coaching over the past twenty-four years have given me much of my still imperfect understanding of their country. Finally, to my wife, Diane, who first introduced me to Colombia, and to our daughter Alex, who has come to understand our long affection for Colombian society, a very special *abrazo*.

The United States and the Americas

Colombia and the United States

Introduction

Arthur Schlesinger, Jr., wrote some years ago in *Foreign Affairs* that foreign policy is largely an extension of national character, "the face a nation wears to the world." Robert Pastor, in a more recent study of Nicaraguan-U.S. relations suggested that "all nations project their style, political culture or character, and interpretations of recent history onto the international landscape." Akira Iriye, in his work on Japanese-U.S. relations and his presidential address to the Society for Historians of American Foreign Relations in 1978, has also underlined the importance of culturally determined differences in perception among peoples and nations, as well as the relationship between power and culture, in attempting to understand the dynamic of their respective foreign policies.[1]

This study of Colombian-U.S. relations is premised on the assumption that foreign relations must be viewed in a holistic manner that includes cultural links, trade, and investment, as well as general political and military relations between two nations. Historians of U.S. foreign policy have only in recent years begun to move away from a traditional concentration on political relations, and in a study such as this, in which almost two hundred years is traversed and a wide variety of issues addressed, coverage is by necessity limited and more suggestive than definitive. The concentration of the book is on the period since 1890, in part because of the richness of materials for the modern period, but also because E. Taylor Parks's 1935 study of Colombian-U.S. relations in the late-eighteenth and nineteenth centuries has very well withstood the test of time. From the outset, it was also the intention to complete a book that would be of value to the specialist as well as the general reader; scholars will note the gaps and hopefully move to fill them in the coming years; the general reader will learn something about the dynamic of unequal power relationships in international relations.

1

Given the disparity of power between the United States and Colombia since the mid-nineteenth century, to some extent it is inappropriate to study their relationship in purely bilateral terms; yet, in the early nineteenth century as both nations emerged from colonialism, leaders of the two nations were optimistic that their respective nations would play important roles in leading the hemisphere; certainly this was true of Simón Bolívar and Francisco de Paula Santander in Gran Colombia during and shortly after independence, and of Thomas Jefferson, James Monroe and John Quincy Adams, among others, in the United States in the early nineteenth century. Colombians began the inter-American movement in the 1820s with the first meeting of the American states at the Panama Congress; but in its aftermath the inter-American movement languished until rediscovered by the United States in the 1880s and developed as an instrument of U.S. foreign policy. By mid-century the unequal growth of the two countries had already taken its toll; U.S. filibusters and propagandists were trumpeting the inevitability of the expansion of the United States through the Caribbean and South America; the U.S. presence on the Isthmus of Panama was embodied in the development of road and rail transportation and the initial enthusiasm for an isthmian canal that would ultimately bring both grief and glory. By the early twentieth century, as Colombia slipped behind economically, militarily, and politically after a generation of destructive civil war, the United States emerged as a great power, and the first major manifestation of their apparent divergence was the conflict over the secession of Panama in 1903, events that deeply shocked Colombians and tainted their view of the United States in subsequent generations.

Within Colombian politics and popular culture, as the following pages suggest, there has been a persistent tension between advocates of a relationship with the United States that is independent, even antagonistic, in orientation, on the one hand and on the other advocates of a policy of realism, those who suggest that as a middle, regional power Colombia has no realistic choice but to accept its place within the American orbit. The latter approach did not emerge in Colombia until the late nineteenth century and is associated with Presidents

Rafael Reyes and Marco Fidel Suárez. The approach was never advanced as a policy of dependency, but dependency has been the reality since at least World War I, when U.S. capital investment and trade came to dominate the Colombian economy and economic culture, and when U.S. popular culture, especially in the form of film, began to make its first impact on the society. The major motif of Colombian-U.S. relations since World War I has been dominated by the Colombian effort to retain autonomy of action, pursue independent regional and international policies, diversify its trade and foreign investment patterns, and attempt to escape where possible from the limitations imposed by the East-West conflict of the cold war years.

U.S. policy toward Colombia has derived from several basic considerations of national security, self-interest, and ideological considerations. Certainly the chemistry of the different components of policy have evolved over the past two hundred years. In the nineteenth century, the main focus was on trade relations, the development of transportation links, and ensuring that Colombian policies did not provide an avenue for further European major power involvement in the hemisphere, as in the long debate over the role of French or British interests in an isthmian canal. As the United States industrialized in the course of the century, its search for markets for both manufactured and agricultural commodities and for sources of critical raw materials intensified. Agriculturally, Colombia was competitive with the United States rather than complementary, producing grains, cotton, animal products, until the expansion of the coffee industry on which the economy came to rely by early twentieth century. Industrially, there was also competition as Colombia developed a cotton textile industry and then a petroleum industry, but this also increased Colombia's strategic importance to the United States as a potential source of a critical raw material; platinum had the same role, especially from the time of World War I. By 1920 U.S. policy toward Colombia was firmly based on markets, access to sources of raw materials, sphere of interest considerations, and Colombia's strategic location at the gateway to the continent and adjacent to the recently completed Panama Canal.

Trade, investment, raw materials, political stability and the extension of American economic and political institutions were the main
U.S. objectives in the 1920s, with the concern about trade and the
repercussions of economic nationalism heightened during the depression years. Hemispheric security became a primary goal in Colombian
relations during the late 1930s and World War II years, when the
threat seemed to emanate from fascism, but the main external threat
from the time of the Russian Revolution was the fear of a spreading
global communism; although the threat in Colombia seemed minor
even into the cold war, that concern was a factor in shaping policy
in the 1920s and 1930s on Colombian labor relations, especially with
U.S. firms; anticommunism as a basis of policy increased during the
1945–1980s years, whether it related to Colombian trade ties to the
Soviet bloc economies or the threat posed by Cuban or Maoist inspired
guerrillas after 1960. Communism posed a particular problem, but the
issue itself remained hemispheric solidarity and the maintenance of
acceptable political institutions.

More important than communism as a determinant in the bilateral
relationship between 1919 and 1939 was the emergence of economic
nationalism, initially associated with the Conservative party and embodied in new petroleum legislation in the 1920s; economic nationalism was then absorbed by the Liberal party and advanced with some
vigor during the presidency of Alfonso López Pumarejo in the 1930s,
when the general issue of U.S. foreign direct investment acquired a
momentum of its own. During the interwar years the Colombian situation fit well into the larger pattern of U.S. efforts to combat economic
nationalism throughout Latin America and the Third World. In the
Colombian instance, those efforts were generally highly successful by
the time of World War II and the presidencies of Franklin Roosevelt
and Eduardo Santos.

The cold war, mutual security, hemispheric solidarity, the restructuring of the inter-American system, and a rethinking of economic
development aid were the critical issues of the 1940s, 1950s, and 1960s.
Although clearly a small power, Colombia had its own political agenda
in the cold war years, and thus reinforced rather than imitated U.S.

interpretations of the cold war issues. Colombia broke diplomatic relations with the USSR in the late 1940s; Colombia was the only Latin American nation to contribute militarily to the United Nations force in the Korean War; it cooled its ardor for Fidel Castro even more quickly than did the United States, and strongly identified with the United States during the Cuban Missile Crisis. Major Colombian leaders such as Alberto Lleras Camargo and Carlos Lleras Restrepo in the 1950s and 1960s contributed significantly to the movement that led to a modification in U.S. foreign aid policies in the late Eisenhower and Kennedy/Johnson administrations. The major area of departure from the United States for Colombian leaders in these years was over the perceived failure of the United States to work as effectively as desired through the inter-American system. There was widespread criticism of the United States for the Guatemalan intervention in 1954 and for the Dominican intervention in 1965, as there was consistently for any U.S. actions that seemed to be interventions in the internal affairs of Latin American nations. Colombian adherence to the inter-American system and multilateralism over unilateralism predated 1900, but the perception that the United States had occasioned the secession of Panama in 1903 made any other position toward the United States permanently unacceptable.

By the 1970s and 1980s the emerging crisis in international narcotics trafficking moved to the fore in bilateral relations, although there were also important developments in Colombia's role in the Caribbean and Central America during the Nicaraguan and El Salvadoran crises. By the time of the Reagan and Bush administrations in the United States, ideology and national self-interest combined to place considerable importance on curtailing illegal narcotics traffic through Colombia, especially undercutting identified linkages between some of the guerrilla groups and the developing narcotics cartels. Sadly, the narcotics wars, the internal crisis of the United States economically and socially as a result of the rise of narcotics abuse, and the role of the media in the United States in recent years have contributed to the creation of a highly negative, stereotyped image of Colombians and Colombian society as violent and politically unstable. Yet, that image is not a product of only the post-1970s; it existed with varying degrees of intensity in the nineteenth and earlier twentieth centuries as well. Indeed, the tension between the view of Colombia as a land of beauty, opportunity, and high culture or of violence and instability has been an important motif in U.S. thought, just as there has been a paradoxical perception in Colombia of the United States as economically successful and prosperous but culturally shallow and racially unjust. Colombian writer Manuel Zapata Olivella captured that darker side of the Colombian perception in his memoir of travel in the United States: *He visto la noche* (I have seen the night).

To return to Schlesinger's insights; there have been several layers to the Colombian-U.S. relationship during the past two centuries. One has clearly been the level of formal diplomacy, including the negotiation of treaties, resolution of disputes over losses of property, for instance, and diplomatic pressures to improve the climate for foreign investment, among other issues that have held the attention of diplomats and politicians of the two nations. On that level, there have been periods of intense disagreement and not always a fundamental meeting of minds on differing national interests. That has been the level of power—economic, military, and political power—an area in which Colombia has not been able to compete since the wars for independence. A second level has involved the close economic linkages of the private sectors of the two countries, including essentially U.S. direct and indirect foreign investment in extractive industries, manufacturing, agriculture, and the service sector. Here as well there has been conflict as well as consensus over different paths to development. On yet a third level, that of popular culture, the influence of the United States and of "American" culture was relatively slow in making inroads into Colombia, dating essentially from the 1920s on a small scale and on a much larger scale from the 1960s, with the advent of television. In the area of high culture, Colombia has been far more successful in maintaining its separate identity than it has in formal foreign relations with the United States. Four hundred years of European intellectual roots have been more resistant to U.S. influences than has the political economy. What has plagued the United States in its dealings with Colombia over these two centuries has been the U.S. failure to recognize that Colombians and their political representatives have not seen themselves as a weak, insignificant, Third World nation. Had Theodore Roosevelt, for instance, understood that Colombian perception, inter-American relations could have been spared one of the most unfortunate legacies of the twentieth century.

1   The First Half Century

Whole generations have passed away without living to see its close, whilst others have succeeded them, growing up from infancy to majority, without ever tasting the blessings of peace. (Henry Clay, 1825)[1]

By the early 1800s, the old order was crumbling. The French Revolution quickly followed the American Revolution. The wars of the French Revolution and then the Napoleonic wars swept like prairie fire through Europe in the early nineteenth century. Those wars had a dramatic impact on Spanish America. The diversion of Spanish power to the continent left a vacuum of power in the Western Hemisphere and created the preconditions for an independence movement. In northern South America and the Caribbean basin—the center of Spanish power—independence was achieved only after more than a decade of fighting Spanish forces and royalist supporters. That was the context in which modern Colombia gradually emerged from its colonial heritage and came into increasing contact with the United States, itself still experiencing the pangs of new nationhood.

At the onset of the independence movement, the viceroyalty of New Granada encompassed the area that would become modern Colombia, Venezuela, Panama, the Caribbean coasts of Nicaragua and Honduras, and Ecuador. During the shifting fortunes of battle, independence leaders in 1811 briefly formed the United Provinces of New Granada, only to be reconquered and restored to a viceroyalty from 1816 to 1819. In the immediate aftermath of independence, the states of New Granada (essentially post-1903 Colombia), Venezuela, Ecuador, and the Isthmus of Panama formed a decade-long union as Gran Colombia, which in turn gave way in 1832 to the Republic of New Granada. That endured until 1857. There were subsequent alterations in borders and constitutional arrangements among its political subdivisions, until the formation of the modern republic of Colombia in 1886. Thereafter, the major change came with the secession of Panama in 1903.[2]

The racial heterogeneity of this region, the absence of significant self-government prior to independence, and continued rivalries among the separate nations that once formed a part of the viceroyalty substantially influenced the political and diplomatic history of the nineteenth century. One must add to those factors the excessive degree of militarism that grew out of the lengthy wars for independence. The emergence of Colombia to nationhood and its early role in international relations has to be viewed within this context of imprecise national boundaries, a weak sense of national identity, which in these years exceeded U.S. sectional conflict. In the broader tapestry of international relations, Colombians continued into the 1830s to fear Spanish efforts at recolonization.

Opening Contacts

U.S.-New Granadian contacts in the late eighteenth and early nineteenth centuries were marginal until Spanish hegemony was eliminated. While Colombia was part of the Spanish Empire, there was limited trade between the two areas.[3] The United States was preoccupied with its own nation-building in the 1780s and 1790s, and its international power to effect change was extremely limited, even in the Caribbean basin. U.S. survival in the war with Great Britain in 1812 and French and Spanish preoccupations did enhance the U.S. position in the region, enabling it to acquire the Louisiana territory and the Floridas. Still, the U.S. position never wavered from one of formal neutrality from the first stirrings of Spanish-American conflict until the United States recognized independent nations in 1822. Colombia (including Venezuela and Ecuador) was the first nation accredited in Washington that year. Although officially neutral, there was substantial empathy in U.S. administrations from the 1790s on for Spanish American independence. The United States never formally

COSTA
RICA
1821 *

C A R I B B E A N   S E A

Santamarta
Riohacha

Cartagena

Golfo de Urabá

RIOHACHA

SANTAMARTA

*PACIFIC
OCEAN*

Mompox

CARTAGENA

*Golfo
de Panamá*

PANAMÁ

Panamá

Ocaña

ANTIOQUIA

VENEZUELA
1830 *

Quibdó

Medellín

CHOCÓ

Bucaramanga

SOCORRO

Socorro

Málaga

PAMPLONA

*Bahía
de Buenaventura*

MARIQUITA

Muzo

TUNJA

Tunja

CASANARE

N E I V A

Popayán

Neiva

Santa Fé
de Bogotá

Macanal

S A N T A   F É

Pasto

P O P A Y Á N

E C U A D O R

1830 *

PERU
1821

From Colony to Nation:

COLOMBIA

1810

Political divisions

B R A Z I L

1 8 2 2 *

* Date of independence

Kilometres

0   100   200   300   400   500

0   100   200   300
Miles

wm

sanctioned support to the independence movements, but supplies nonetheless made their way from U.S. ports during the wars. Major figures such as Alexander Hamilton in the 1790s actively encouraged the independence movement and supported U.S. participation before his early death. Thomas Jefferson, James Madison, and James Monroe expressed support for Latin American independence; diplomats in their administrations persistently sought to advance U.S. interests in the area, especially in commerce, and when the Adams-Onís Treaty ended uncertainty over Florida in 1821 Monroe took the lead among the international powers in extending recognition. Henry Clay of Kentucky, one of the dominant Whig politicians of the first half of the nineteenth century, pressed in Congress for a policy of recognition, which he presented as a policy of principle rather than expediency.

Politically and intellectually, creoles from the coastal regions of Venezuela appear to have been more drawn to the experience of the United States for inspiration than were Santa Fé de Bogotá leaders. Tom Paine's *The Rights of Man,* for instance, was published in translation in Caracas in 1811 but does not seem to have appeared in Bogotá. Antonio Nariño, the leading figure among the precursors of the revolution in Bogotá, was more influenced by the ideas of Voltaire, Montesquieu, and Rousseau than by North Americans in the 1780s. Nariño produced the first local Spanish translation of the Declaration of the Rights of Man; he also later admitted working on a constitution similar to that of the United States and confessed to Spanish authorities that he had sought supplies in Philadelphia for a revolution. When his property was seized by Spanish officials, his library contained a portrait of Benjamin Franklin, but there is no clear evidence of Franklin's intellectual influence. Nariño, like others of his contemporaries, recognized that the most essential support had to come from the British navy not the United States. Politically, though theoretically attracted to federalism, Nariño in practice supported centralized power, advocating the control of Bogotá over the other provinces in the short-lived United Provinces of New Granada. Nonetheless, Miguel de Pombo published the Constitution of the United States in Bogotá in 1811, and the Constitution had sufficient symbolic value to prompt one New Granadian independence leader to advocate that their own declaration of independence should be issued on July 4 to coincide with the U.S. anniversary.[4]

The Caracas-born creole Francisco de Miranda was considerably more influential in U.S. circles during the revolutionary wars. He was involved in the Pensacola campaign of the American Revolution and toured the United States in 1783 and 1784, meeting George Washington, Alexander Hamilton, Tom Paine, and later Secretary of War Henry Knox. Afterwards he was a constant and persistent supplicant for U.S. support of Colombian-Venezuelan independence. Hamilton became a close confidant and likely his strongest advocate until his death in 1804. By contrast, Miranda made no inroads with Thomas Jefferson; this was ironic given Jefferson's intellectual sympathies with republicanism and revolution. A policy of support for the Spanish Americans meant siding with the British over the Spanish, and Jefferson was unprepared to support British interests. Miranda persisted in courting Knox, John Adams, Hamilton, and Rufus King, the U.S. minister to Great Britain in 1798. Yet, he failed to alter the American policy of neutrality. U.S. officials offered personal encouragement and expressed optimism about the future, but policy remained unchanged. King could write Hamilton from London in 1798 that the "destiny of the New World" was in American hands, but the United States merely watched while destiny unfolded.[5]

Miranda anticipated an improvement in the prospects for independence when Britain went to war with France in 1803 and Spain the following year. Still unable to obtain support from England, he returned to the United States in late 1805. He was warmly received by New York merchants and Rufus King; he met in Washington with President Jefferson, Vice-President George Clinton, and Secretary of State Madison. Armed once again with no more than expressions of sympathy, Miranda returned to New York to acquire a ship, the *Leander*, some two hundred American crewmen, and munitions. He set sail for Venezuela, acquiring reinforcements en route, but in an ill-fated attack on Spanish forces, he lost most of his vessels and men. Those who were not executed were imprisoned at Cartagena.

With rumors swirling that the United States had supported Miranda's attack, the Jefferson administration denied, especially to the Spanish minister, any complicity in the affair; Madison insisted that Miranda had been received only as a courtesy. The surveyor of the port of New York was dismissed for allowing the vessel to leave his port carrying munitions and volunteers on what was a treasonous venture, and Congress refused to appropriate funds for the Americans incarcerated in New Granada on grounds that to do so would be an admission of involvement.[6]

The United States continued its policy of cautious neutrality when large scale revolt erupted in New Granada in 1810 and 1811. Europe's preoccupation with its own crises diverted attention and power from the Americas, leading to the first real declarations of independence in the area and the formation of a fractious and ill-organized confederation among the main cities and regions. That first confederation included Santa Marta, Antioquia, El Chocó, Socorro, Casanare, Neiva, Pamplona, Tunja, and ultimately Bogotá. Under Nariño's guidance, Bogotá officials pressed for a centralized state until briefly forced into the loose confederation by Simón Bolívar. "Independence" enjoyed a brief moment of glory before royalist resurgence forced Bolívar to flee to Jamaica.[7]

During the brief lifespan of the United Provinces of New Granada, the United States moved to strengthen its commercial presence in the area in competition with Britain. The focus of U.S. activity was in what became Venezuela rather than Colombia. In 1810 a U.S. commercial agent, Robert Lowry, reached La Guayra and for a decade pressed Washington for U.S. naval support to improve the U.S. position. Lowry had limited success because of the changing fortunes of contending forces in the wars for independence; when there was a royalist resurgence, he was forced to withdraw. There was no formal U.S. representation in Bogotá until 1820 when Charles S. Todd arrived as a confidential agent.[8] Todd, like Lowry in Guayra, was most concerned with trade and piracy in the Caribbean. To strengthen the U.S. position, he advocated increasing the naval force in the region. Washington officials, reluctant to risk confrontations with either side in the wars, did not follow his advice; but the losses of American property and life during the conflict led to years of often fruitless legal and diplomatic action to obtain compensation.

U.S. administrations adhered to a policy of strict neutrality, but they also insisted on their rights as neutrals to engage in commerce in the area without confiscation or attack. In 1816, as the Spanish tightened their control of the Caribbean coast in a last effort to retain a disintegrating empire, Secretary of State Monroe protested the Spanish intention to apply a blockade to several hundred miles of coast from Santa Marta to Puerto Bello; although the two ports themselves would remain open to neutral shipping, neutrals found within the blockade area were to be seized.[9]

During this first phase of independence under the United Provinces of New Granada, before royalists forces regained power, the individual provinces sought U.S. support, in particular weapons and ammunition. The ruling junta at Bogotá also appealed directly to President Madison for guidance on the formation of new governmental institutions. The argument advanced in an effort to win U.S. favor was, significantly, the similarity of political ideals and institutions that bound Colombian rebels to the U.S. model.[10] Others, such as Cartagena representatives, stressed the commercial advantages the United States would enjoy in Colombian ports.[11] These and other appeals failed to alter U.S. insistence on strict neutrality, and the resurgence of royalist control reaffirmed Washington in that stance.[12]

Although the policy of neutrality remained in force, prominent U.S. leaders, including Thomas Jefferson, expressed strong verbal support for the idea of Spanish-American independence. U.S. representatives in Colombia saw independence from Spain as inevitable in the region. J. Robertson, the American agent in Caracas in 1813, predicted that given the widespread hostility to Spanish rule, Spain could never hold its colonies.[13]

There were slight signs of policy movement in Washington; Jefferson in 1816, influential though now out of power, indicated that the colonies had a "right to be free" and the United States had a "right to aid them." President Monroe moved toward an acceptance of the Spanish-American wars for independence as a civil war rather than rebellion, and two years later requested Secretary of State John Quincy Adams to attempt to obtain British cooperation to promote the independence movement. Adams discouraged the initiative; in his view it would have moved the United States away from strict neutrality at a time that U.S. relations with Spain were delicate. The administration sought to promote recognition by the major powers not to risk a rift; consequently, for the moment it backed away until negotiations with Spain over the Floridas could be completed and the U.S. latitude of action improved.

A military victory by antiroyalist forces in Colombia was the critical turning point. In August 1819, Bolívar led his troops into Bogotá, following the defeat of royalist forces at Boyacá after an arduous and spectacular march through the Pisba Pass of the Andes from Venezuela. Francisco Antonio Zea, vice-president of the hastily formed Republic of Colombia, stressed that amicable relations with the United States, which had inspired them in their revolt, was a priority of the new administration, and a few months later John Quincy Adams expressed similar sentiments to Manuel Torres, long-time resident of the United States and an "official" spokesman for "Colombian" interests during the wars for independence.[14] Northern Spanish America was effectively liberated except for pockets of resistance.

Manuel Torres pressed vigorously from 1818 to 1820 for U.S. recognition, weapons, and a reciprocal commercial agreement; Colombian officials saw an agreement with the United States as the route to prosperity as well as independence. Torres also obtained information concerning the Lancastrian system of education for possible adoption in Colombia and to provide the rules of debate for the U.S. House of Representatives and Senate, further indication of the degree of interest in U.S. political and cultural institutions. Interestingly, given the persistence of black slavery in the United States, Torres used as one of his arguments in favor of the struggle against Spain that the Spanish constitution denied citizenship to blacks, who were in his view "industrious and active people."[15]

The Colombian interest in the United States was tempered by fear of U.S. competition. The Foreign Ministry informed Torres that the Liberator opposed conceding special privileges, commercial or other, to any foreign power; there was concern in the ministry that the United States would totally dominate Colombian trade at the critical moment that it was taking its place "among the society of nations." The United States was not sufficiently industrialized at that time to meet Colombia's need for industrial imports, and the two nations were competitive in the production of tobacco and cotton. The Colombian government was nonetheless eager to attract skilled immigrants, including artisans, mineralogists, and farmers, and there was no doubt that, as Torres phrased his sentiments, the Colombian view at this stage was that the United States and Colombia were "natural allies" against the concert of Europe.[16]

Although the Monroe administration remained cautious, even before extending recognition it began to explore the possibility of a commercial agreement. Adams and Torres discussed trade negotiations in late 1820, and Torres met with President Monroe shortly before the latter's annual message to Congress, when Monroe called on Spain to grant independence to its former colonies. It was not until Spain ratified the Adams-Onís Treaty in 1821, however, that the United States was prepared to move decisively on recognition. In March 1822 the House of Representatives Committee on Foreign Affairs recommended recognition on grounds that Colombia had attained a free and well-organized, sovereign government; on 19 June Monroe received the seriously ailing Torres as the first official Colombian and Latin American representative to the United States. The following year the first official U.S. diplomat, Richard Anderson, was sent to Colombia. More than a decade of uncertainty had come to an end.[17]

The Monroe Doctrine

There was a temporary convergence of interests between Colombia and the United States in the 1820s. Bolívar sought to maintain Latin American cooperation forged by the demands of war, and the United States moved to define its own foreign policy goals. Consequently, as Bolívar made preparations for a congress of Spanish American states to meet at Panama in 1826, President Monroe and Secretary of State John Quincy Adams were putting the final strokes on the Monroe Doctrine. The Monroe-Adams and Bolívar initiatives derived from differing visions of leadership in the hemisphere; but they also recognized the reality of U.S. and Spanish American interdependence to resist European incursions into their former colonial territories. Thus, Colombian leaders greeted the Monroe initiative favorably in the mid-1820s. Not until the intensification of U.S. ambitions in the Caribbean and Central America in the 1840s and 1850s, as the United States gradually challenged British dominance in the region, did Colombian leaders reassess their relationship with the United States.

A sense of "American" isolation from the affairs of Europe was not unique to the U.S. statesmen in the 1820s. Bolívar and Santander both desired a strong American front against Europe, but Bolívar was considerably less enthusiastic than Santander in the mid-1820s about the involvement of the United States in any Pan-American movement. Santander, who had earlier been cool to the possibility of U.S. aid, referred to Monroe's position as befitting the "land of liberty" and saw as feasible an alliance with the United States as a defense against European designs. In early 1825 he wrote to Monroe expressing appreciation for Monroe's support of independence for former Spanish colonies. Colombian officials in Bogotá and Washington quickly learned that the United States was unreceptive, in spite of official anxiety in Bogotá that the collapse of the Constitutionalists in Spain would result in an effort of the Holy Alliance to reimpose colonialism in Spanish America. Foreign Minister Pedro Gual believed that Britain would prevent such action in the event diplomacy failed. A similar sentiment, combined with a pragmatic assessment of British naval power led Bolívar to prefer to tie the Colombian future to the British star.[18]

Formalizing Trade Ties

In the 1820s, indicative of its early leadership role, Colombia rapidly moved to formalize commercial links with the United States, trading actively through the ports of New Orleans, Charleston, Savannah, Baltimore, Boston, and New York. By 1824 or 1825 Colombia ranked second to Mexico among Spanish American countries as a market for U.S. exports and was the leading exporter to the United States. Curiously, the perception in the United States was that Britain was strongly entrenched and favored throughout Colombia. The bilateral commercial agreement (ratified in 1825) established commerce on a most-favored-nation basis, provided for freedom of religion (reflective of the U.S. desire to ensure the protection of Protestants).[19] There was no success in dealing with the thorny issue of the international slave trade, however. Colombia made more rapid progress toward emancipation and manumission than the United States did in these years, and in the immediate aftermath of the divisive Missouri Compromise of 1820 (in which Missouri entered the Union as a slave state and Maine as free), U.S. officials were loathe to address slavery questions in international agreements.

The Panama Congress

Bolívar's leadership and vision in hemispheric relations were evident in the initiative that led to the 1826 Panama Congress meetings. The calling of this congress underlined differences between Santander and Bolívar over the place of the United States in inter-American relations and revealed the continuing ambiguity of U.S. commitments toward Hispanic America. The political jockeying for position within Colombian ranks represented very distinct philosophies about the place of the United States in hemisphere affairs. Plans for a conference of emerging American states as well as a vague notion of a confederation of states had been under consideration for several years. Colombian authorities proposed U.S. participation in a congress to Richard Anderson shortly after his arrival in the Colombian capital at the end of 1823. John Quincy Adams seems to have found the concept of a defensive confederation visionary but impractical, yet he did not dismiss the idea. The Monroe message to Congress in late 1823 indicated that the administration preferred to exercise unilateralism. Nor was there enthusiasm in Congress or the administration for participation even in a broadly defined conference. Anderson argued that the U.S. presence would enable Washington to press its policy on neutrality, to "fix some principles of international law," provide an opportunity to discuss the means of resisting further European colonization, and to deal with such thorny issues as the international slave trade.[20] An additional issue of pressing importance was the U.S. concern that Colombia, perhaps in alliance with other Spanish American nations, would attack Spanish forces in Cuba and Puerto Rico, possibly triggering European intervention.

Bolívar's initial invitations in late 1824 for a general congress did not include the United States. He was clearly jealous of his own leadership position; he was also aware of U.S. opposition to Colombian liberation of Cuba and Puerto Rico, preferred an all-Latin nation conference, and, moreover, thought Colombian interests would be best served by courting Britain rather than its trade rival in the Caribbean. He also objected to giving the Panama Congress any power to negotiate agreements. The view in Bogotá differed. In the fall of 1824 the Colombian foreign minister, Pedro Gual, later a delegate to Panama along with General Pedro Briceño Méndez, wrote enthusiastically to Salazar expressing admiration for Monroe's message to Congress. He stressed that the basic principles contained in the Monroe statement provided a basis for much closer alliance between the United States, Colombia, and its Latin allies. Gual indicated that Colombia "ardently" sought U.S. participation at the proposed Panama conference. The Colombian minister in Washington sounded out the United States to ensure acceptance of an invitation. Santander specifically suggested in early 1825 to Bolívar that the United States be invited, and Bolívar reluctantly yielded. Thus, Colombia and Mexico extended a belated invitation to the United States to attend the Panama Congress the following year.

With the understanding that Congress had the power of final approval of the mission, Henry Clay accepted the invitation and named as delegates Anderson along with John Sargeant of Pennsylvania. Clay stressed in his instructions to Anderson and Sargeant that the administration was interested in reaching agreements on questions of commerce, neutral rights, and maritime law. He stressed the opposition of the administration to any involvement in a military alliance or military action against Cuba or Puerto Rico; there was to be no departure from the policy of neutrality between Spain and her colonies, even though recognition had been extended and the nature of U.S. reaction in the event of military action by the Holy Alliance was yet to be determined. Clay added that although the administration had no desire to interfere in the internal affairs of other nations, the government preferred that Latin America adopt a system of government similar to that of the United States and certainly reject monarchism, especially if the intent were to place a European prince on an American throne.[21]

Colombian overtures to Britain in early 1826 to send an observer to the congress met a cautious response. The main Colombian objective was to preserve peace in the Americas, something they feared they could not do alone. After discussing the invitation with the king, Foreign Secretary George Canning determined to send an observer, indicating that the British objective was to "maintain harmony between the several States of America, to restore peace (if possible) between these countries with Spain." At the same time, Canning noted that British policy was not as opposed as was that of the United States to Spanish American control over Cuba and Puerto Rico.[22]

Slavery and race relations also provided a point of friction between the United States and Colombia before the Panama Congress met. This was an important area of divergence, one that helps us understand later relations between the two societies. Colombian leaders then and later prided themselves on their more "liberal" approach to race questions. If the United States found abhorrent the establishment of monarchism in the hemisphere, Colombian leaders expressed concern about the establishment of relations with nations that held strong racial views without risking internal political, social, and political strife in Colombia. Pedro Gual, for instance, observed that in the United States "Africans" and their descendants lacked all participation in public affairs but were legally protected; in Europe blacks had no standing and were objects of hatred. Gual was anxious to obtain an international agreement controlling the slave trade and promoting abolition.[23]

The issue of a possible Colombian military campaign against the Spanish Antilles formed an important part of the context in which the Panama Congress met. There were expressed concerns in the Adams administration about the continuing militarism of Colombian society, a concern that would plague later years as well; there was particular opposition to any military expedition against Cuba and Puerto Rico. The Colombians, for their part, faulted Spain for its failure to negotiate peace and recognize the independence of its former colonies. What Colombia hoped to gain through U.S. assistance was either a final peace treaty with Spain or a Spanish commitment not to strengthen its garrisons in Cuba and Puerto Rico. Much of the policy initiative in this delicate, transitional period sprang from a strong sense of insecurity on all sides. Whether for Colombia, Spain, or the United States, national self-preservation was the first priority.[24]

Colombian overtures to Britain and the United States, and U.S. efforts to gain Russian assistance in negotiating with Spain provided an important part of the international context in which delegates from Colombia, Peru, Mexico, and Central America and observers from Britain and the Netherlands, gathered in the sweltering heat and rains of Panama in 1826.[25]

The congress was singularly unsuccessful. The United States effectively did not participate, since Anderson died before reaching the conference and Sargeant reached Panama only after the meetings had adjourned in mid-July to meet again in Tucubayo, Mexico, later in the year. The Colombian and Peruvian delegates actually began their talks in Panama in December 1825 and were joined in late June 1826 by the others. The discussions did produce four treaties, which only Colombia approved: the first was a strongly Bolivarian concept, involving permanent union, league, and confederation; a second provided for military cooperation; the third was a confidential agreement outlining the movement and organization of naval and land forces to meet any European threat; finally, participants agreed in principle to hold subsequent meetings. This was an inauspicious beginning to a Pan-American movement, which would not catch fire until the end of the century. With an end to the first decade of independence on the horizon, Colombia's status as a member of the community of nations remained uncertain and fragile. At the same time, the United States was gradually gaining its stride in the decade following the War of 1812.

The Post-Bolívar Generation

By the late 1820s there was growing disillusionment in U.S. circles with Colombian political and economic developments. In 1827, three years before the dissolution of Gran Colombia into New Granada, Venezuela, and Ecuador, Clay wrote Bolívar expressing disappointment in Colombian progress in establishing free political institutions. Clay's correspondence in this period revealed that he and President Adams had become increasingly pessimistic and also skeptical about Bolívar's capacity and sincerity.[26] In the waning years of Bolívar's power, U.S. minister William H. Harrison concluded that both Bolívar and his Council of Ministers were monarchists, though the Colombian people were not. Harrison gained a reputation as an opponent of Bolívar, was implicated in the opposition to the ailing president, and nearly deported for his orientation.[27]

Bolívar's time had in any event expired. In 1830, dying of tuberculosis, Bolívar left the inhospitable political climate and drizzle of Bogotá, in a final journey to death in Santa Marta, captured so evocatively by Gabriel García Márquez in El general en su laberinto (The general in his labyrinth). Though empathetic toward Bolívar, Harrison's successor Thomas Moore was less sanguine about Colombian capacity for republican government and free institutions. He found Joaquín Mosquera's new administration supportive of the United States and favorable to republican institutions; but Mosquera was politically too timid to resist the pro-British faction. In his view, since the mid-1820s Britain had enjoyed a monopoly of Colombian commerce, and British subjects were well entrenched in Colombian mining. In 1831 a short-lived new government modified Colombian trade policy; it reduced import duties on flour and high duties on imported biscuits in favor of American commercial interests. Moore urged the conclusion of a commercial agreement to take advantage of the favorable political climate.[28] That did not occur for another decade, but in the interim Colombian-U.S. trade enjoyed some vitality. In spite of the paucity of data for the 1820s, and significant discrepancies between Colombian and U.S. trade information, both William McGreevey and Luis Eduardo Nieto concur that Colombian-U.S. trade was active from the 1820s until the recession of 1837. U.S. exports to Colombia lagged behind imports throughout the pre-1840 years, with U.S. imports reaching a peak value in the late 1820s of approximately $2 million, and Colombian imports valued at less than half a million dollars in 1830. By 1840 U.S. data indicate that U.S. exports (and re-exports) to Colombia had fallen to $135,000. There was no significant recovery until 1854.[29]

The British and Americans were commercial rivals in the region, yet it was Americans who seemed most preoccupied with the nature of Colombian political institutions. U.S. disapproval of the Colombian orientation did not diminish when in 1832 exiled former Vice-President Francisco de Paula Santander returned as president of New Granada. It was ironic that the Jackson administration should have found Santander and his government unappealing; Santander was a pragmatic liberal, not unlike Andrew Jackson; on trade matters Santander as president was a protectionist, at a time when the Jackson administration was embroiled in conflict with low-tariff Southern Democrats. Santander limited military power, emphasized the rule of constitutional law, and continued to promote state-supported secular and liberal education, with a strong dose of the ideas of British liberal Jeremy Bentham. He preferred a more centralist political structure in the 1830s.[30] Although it was premature in the 1830s to speak of political parties, those differences of political philosophy between centralists and federalists lay at the basis of emerging conservatism and liberalism. Each of Santander's views in the 1830s should have endeared Santander, and what constituted an embryonic Colombian Liberal party, to the Jacksonians.

The State Department in the Jackson years would also have preferred the continuation of a strong, united Gran Colombia, rather than the weaker states that resulted from the 1830 dissolution, if only because such a nation would have been a more effective defense against European efforts at recolonization. Yet, the U.S. chargé in 1835 thought it impossible to attain a reunification of Gran Colombia; even the effort would result in great bloodshed and would require despotism because the "habits, prejudices and views of the leaders are totally dissimilar." Ironically, in 1833, in the midst of the South Carolina nullification crisis, the State Department was at considerable pains to reassure New Granadian authorities about U.S. political stability. Yet, U.S. governments in the years leading up to the U.S. Civil War demonstrated little tolerance toward another nation experiencing problems of unification.[31]

Jacksonian suspicion of Santander in the mid-1830s was ill-placed; his election in 1832 ushered in a five-year period of comparative prosperity in New Granada with economic growth, educational expansion, and reform and political stability. Progress was made on the freeing of slaves; in science, the national astronomical observatory was established, and the National Academy founded, and a population census conducted in 1834 and 1935. The New Granadan Congress also showed prescience in passing enabling legislation for isthmian road transit in 1834. This was greeted with some skepticism in Washington. Chargé Robert McAfee advanced the view that would dominate American policy on isthmian traffic. It should be a project that involved the "governments of the continent," not one left to a single enterprise or nation, unless that nation happened to be the

United States. McAfee nonetheless praised New Granada for "the most enlightened and liberal policy," which would be to its "imperishable honor."[32]

Progress or not, McAfee continued to find New Granadan society "backward" in its attitudes toward commercial development, with Colombian officials adhering to outmoded concepts of mercantilist systems, including the granting of monopolies for the mining of salt and tobacco cultivation. Differences aside, in 1835 New Granada seems to have hinted at a military alliance with the United States in return for a reduction of duties on U.S. imports. With one and a half million people, New Granada was the third most populous nation in Latin America; though a substantial portion of its people lived in subsistence-level poverty outside the monied economy, the country still constituted a potentially important market for the products of American farms and factories and a source for raw materials.

U.S. efforts to develop that market lacked imagination; Washington even relied on British subjects as consuls in these early years. In an effort to protect New Granadan artisans, Santander resisted liberal imports of inexpensive manufactured goods; he personally dressed in New Granadan "homespun" fabrics to demonstrate his encouragement of local manufactures, though neither impressed the American (or British) minister. In McAfee's views the undue influence of the Roman Catholic Church was a further impediment to the capacity of the society to achieve economic and political progress, but Santander and other Latin American liberals generally shared that assumption.[33]

U.S. interest in the development of isthmian transportation remained one of the persistent themes in the bilateral relationship in the nineteenth century. Clay and Adams had earlier expressed interest in an isthmian route, as did private capitalists in the United States. In 1834 New Granada passed legislation encouraging that development, and the following year sent Charles Biddle as a special agent to Central America and New Granada. Biddle was empowered only to make observations and enquiries.[34]

In Panama on route to Bogotá, Biddle detected what would prove to be a constant theme in isthmian–New Granadan politics—secessionist sentiment. He predicted that New Granada would not endure another two years, at least not with control of the isthmus. Only a combination of capitalists would, in his view, be able to arrange the substantial funding required to link Atlantic and Pacific. Biddle himself soon took a personal interest in the project. To the dismay and chagrin of Washington in 1836, Biddle obtained a contract, held jointly with a Bogotá group, from the New Granadan government for the construction of a combination of steamboat and road transport in Panama. He further sought a concession for the construction of a railroad from the mouth of the Cauca River to Cartagena. The Jackson administration immediately denied official support for the initiative and reprimanded the chargé for supporting Biddle with New Granadan authorities; yet, Biddle was entirely correct in his assessment that transportation development held the key to Colombian economic progress. He was also optimistic about the Colombian future. The wars for independence had created too many ambitious military officers with little regard for productive civilian employment, in his opinion; but, the new generation that was emerging was more highly motivated and also acquiring education in the United States and Europe. At the time, however, Biddle was in advance of government policy.[35]

The Mallarino-Bidlack Treaty

During a decade that witnessed a growing U.S. interest in overseas commercial expansion, with American merchants increasingly testing Asian markets and sources of goods for the West, it was not surprising that there would be efforts to improve the commercial relations with one of South America's major nations. America's outward thrust in this period, involving not only trade expansion, but war with Mexico, the consolidation of continental borders through treaty with Great Britain, unofficial filibustering expeditions into the Caribbean and Central America, and the rhetorical muscle flexing embodied in Manifest Destiny were all part of the context in which the two nations turned to commercial negotiations. In the 1840s the Democratic administration of James K. Polk sought to breathe economic life into rhetorical expansionism.

Generally stable political conditions in New Granada during the 1840s presidencies of Pedro Herrán (1841–45) and Tomás de Mosquera (1845–49) provided an opportunity to normalize commercial relations between the two countries. Fragile New Granadan control of the Isthmus of Panama, the possibility of rail, road, and canal construction through either Central America or northwest New Granada to link Pacific and Atlantic placed New Granada in an important strategic position that went beyond its market potential. New Granadans saw themselves still to have a bright future in spite of the yet unfulfilled political and economic promises of independence, and the Isthmus of Panama was viewed as one of the keystones of that progress. The Polk administration was more energetic in its pursuit of isthmian interests than had been President Harrison and Secretary of State Daniel Webster, although there seems to have been U.S. consideration of recognizing an independent Panama during the 1837–41 New Granadan civil war. At that time the provinces of Panama and Veragua on the isthmus separated from the other states of New Granada and requested recognition by the United States as the State of the Isthmus. The United States was on the verge of despatching a special agent to negotiate when the end of civil war brought Panama back into the fold.[36]

U.S. isthmian policy underwent one major change in the course of these years. Contrary to later U.S. policy, the Harrison administration was prepared to accept construction of a canal by a non-U.S. enterprise, as long as there were no restrictions on access. The U.S. representative was informed on leaving Washington: "It is of great importance to the United States that the rail-road or canal . . . should be constructed and that we should have the free use of it upon the same terms as the citizens or subjects of other commercial nations."[37]

Commercial relations and isthmian transit thus formed an integral part of mid-century negotiations. So did Anglo-American rivalry in the region. Efforts to contain British ambitions came from New Granada as well as the United States; indeed the New Granadans sought to play the two other powers' ambitions and anxieties against one another to the Granadan advantage. In early 1837, well before formal commercial and transit negotiations got under way, the New Granadan chargé in Washington, Domingo Acosta, praised a Washington *Globe* article regarding New Granadan protests to Britain for the alleged political activity of a British commercial agent in Panama. Acosta stressed to Secretary of State John Forsyth that it was suspected Britain planned to gain control of the isthmus, and he urged the United States to resist British designs. In 1839 the Van Buren administration appointed John L. Stephens to retrace the failed Biddle mission.[38]

With British inroads into the Mosquito coast, which New Granada claimed, and the failure of New Granadan diplomats to bring Britain and France into an agreement for the multilateral development and protection of an isthmian canal, Bogotá naturally inclined toward the United States in search of a balance of power. In late 1843 New Granada proposed a treaty to Britain and France for cooperation in the construction and defense of a canal. New Granada offered to support the canal enterprise with access to isthmian coal and forest resources and the grant of some three hundred thousand acres of land to be used for construction and also for immigrant settlement. The only major caveat was New Granadan insistence that its own troops defend the area.[39] Lord Aberdeen rejected this overture from New Granada for the establishment of French, British, and American protection for the isthmus, guaranteeing its neutrality for international commerce and New Granadan sovereignty. The French reaction was equally negative. Thus, Bogotá's turn to Washington for an agreement was inevitable unless New Granadan military and economic capacity changed.[40]

Benjamin Bidlack, Polk's new minister, reached Bogotá in 1845 as New Granada's prospects for support in Europe were ebbing. Secretary of State James Buchanan's instructions to Bidlack stressed the importance of obtaining a settlement of outstanding claims questions and a commercial agreement as a prerequisite for the expansion of commerce between the two nations and the economic development of Colombia. Buchanan left no doubt that it was a high U.S. priority to ensure that the isthmus not fall into European hands and that British designs on the Mosquito coast should be discouraged.[41] In general the initiatives of the period underlined the economic motivation of policy, although it is difficult to make a meaningful distinction between commercial motivation and strategic considerations where control of isthmian transit was concerned. Colombian Foreign Minister Manuel Laria Mallarino, however, attempted to place a different face on the nature of U.S. policy, appealing to the higher "moral" objectives of the United States against the crass materialistic motivation of the European countries who would take advantage of the weakness of the new Latin American nations.[42]

Bidlack's initial inclination was to try to keep commercial and canal negotiations distinct, but largely on the insistence of President Mosquera he accepted the idea of a more comprehensive treaty. Significantly, the treaty Bidlack and Foreign Minister Mallarino ultimately signed would in fact be the most comprehensive U.S. agreement in the nineteenth century until the end of the Spanish-American War in 1898.[43]

The coincidence of U.S. desire to obtain an end to New Granadan commercial discrimination against American products, fear of increased European influence on the isthmus, and New Granadan desire to obtain international guarantees of its jurisdiction in the isthmus contributed to successful though hasty negotiations in Bogotá in late 1846. These negotiations occurred in a mood of apparent equality between the two nations, very unlike the situation that prevailed in the post–World War I years. Though confronted by ongoing economic and political problems, the Granadan generation of the first half of the nineteenth century still anticipated Colombia's potential greatness, and they approached negotiations with the United States and European powers believing they held leverage, unrealistic as that may have been.

The Bidlack-Mallarino Treaty, which was ratified in 1848 after much political hesitancy in both the White House and Congress as the United States emerged from the Mexican war, provided for the equality of treatment of U.S. products by New Granada. The agreement did not remove trade protection on the New Granadan mainland

coast for the products of the Granadan interior, an issue that continued into the 1850s as a problem in Colombian-U.S. trade relations;[44]
the treaty contained an important guarantee of freedom of worship
and liberty of conscience; the critical Article 35 granted the United
States, its goods, and its citizens equality of treatment in the Isthmus of Panama with New Granadan citizens; the article guaranteed
that isthmian transit would be open and free to the United States and
its citizens. In return the United States guaranteed the "perfect neutrality" of the isthmus, "with the view that the free transit from the
one to the other sea may not be interrupted or embarrassed in any
future time while this treaty exists"; further, the treaty required that
the United States "guarantee . . . the rights of sovereignty and property which New Granada has and possesses over said territory."

    Controversial as these terms were in Washington, Bidlack informed
Buchanan that he could not have obtained the commercial agreement
the Polk administration sought without the guarantees to New Granadan sovereignty on the isthmus. Bidlack detected that there had been
an improvement in Granadan attitudes toward the U.S., which had
been hostile during the Mexican-American war but had eased during his term in Bogotá. "This people," he observed, "[would] much
rather fight for us than against us, but God forbid that there shall
ever be occasion to put them to the trial."[45] The final terms of the
agreement were to be the source of ongoing tensions, disagreement,
and ultimately rupture during the next sixty years of Colombian-
American relations. Though the treaty had something of a stormy
passage through Congress, with the eye of the hurricane centering on
Article 35, Buchanan was able to inform Bidlack of the ratification in
July 1848; in his view the agreement would be of "great and lasting
advantage" to both countries. Both sides achieved their main objectives, though the Polk adminstration remained anxious that in signing
such an agreement it had departed from the tradition of not entering
into formal alliances.[46]

The Isthmus in U.S.-Granadan Relations

The discovery of gold in California in 1848 rapidly made the agreement of vital importance to U.S. trade and security. American and European migrants streamed through the isthmus on their way to California, to fortune for some and despair for many. Steamship companies quickly expanded their services from New York to Chagres on the Atlantic coast of the isthmus and from Panama City to San Francisco on the Pacific, bringing not only an influx of capital and people to Panama but nationality, class, and racial tensions that spilled over on more than one occasion into violence.[47]

Increased Isthmian traffic and the growing international significance of the development of transportation in the area led the United States to intensify its efforts in the 1850s to offset British influence in the area. When it became likely that U.S. interests would construct a railroad though the isthmus, the United States worked to cooperate with Granadan authorities in Europe to obtain a British guarantee that the isthmus would be neutral territory in any international conflict, similar to the U.S. guarantee in the Mallarino-Bidlack Treaty. The result was the vitally important 1850 Clayton-Bulwer Treaty between the United States and Great Britain; it was designed to neutralize the isthmus as a point of friction between the two nations by stipulating that neither side would build and fortify any isthmian canal against the interests of the other.[48]

While Britain and the United States negotiated, American entrepreneurs were active in developing the transportation system on the isthmus. In late 1848 three New York entrepreneurs, William Aspinwall, John L. Stephens, and Henry Chauncey completed their negotiations for the construction of a railroad across Panama with the Colombian minister in the United States, former president Pedro A. Herrán, a strong supporter of the political institutions of the American republic. The agreement provided a grant of a forty-nine year exclusive concession, payment to Colombia of 3 percent of revenues per annum, the Colombian right to regain the property after twenty years, and a requirement that construction be completed within six years.[49] The company was chartered in New York and the contract approved less than two years later in Bogotá, not coincidentally in the same year as the Clayton-Bulwer Treaty.

The negotiations in the 1846–50 period underlined the vulnerability of the New Granadan position. Herrán, for instance, was convinced that American entrepreneurs would develop an alternate route if New Granada failed to come to terms. He has also feared that U.S. defeat of Mexico would provide the United States with an alternate route through the Tehuantepec region. Nonetheless, the U.S. need for a rapid route for the movement of troops to consolidate control in Oregon territory and for the colonization of the West combined with the conclusion of the Mallarino-Bidlack Treaty and the Clayton-Bulwer Treaty to move New Granadan fortunes to the forefront and to enhance U.S. interests in the region.[50]

The construction of the Panama Railroad began a new chapter in U.S.-Colombian relations and marked the first major American corporate presence in Colombia. One company official also predicted that "uniting of the two oceans" would "change the commerce of the world."[51] The railroad company ultimately contributed substantially to shaping the diplomatic relationship of the two nations and the course of Colombian history, as the isthmus became increasingly isolated and alienated from Bogotá power, politics, and economic policies. Although inevitability may have no place in historical analysis, there was every indication as early as mid-nineteenth century that Panama's ultimate links would be to the United States rather than to mainland Colombia. The history of the next half century in Panamanian-Colombian-U.S. relations served to cement those ties as the United States rose in international power and Colombia declined.

As with the later construction of the Panama Canal, building the rail link drew thousands of workers into Panama, most of them imported from other areas of the Caribbean. Many lost their lives in the dangerous working conditions and disease-ridden environment. Once completed in 1855, the railroad significantly increased the traffic and business activity in the region, since it was only one of many U.S. business-sponsored transportation improvement projects at the time.

Its operation occasioned increased prosperity, but its presence also intensified racial, class, and political tensions in Panama and exacerbated already strong Colombian regionalism. The city of Colón was itself a byproduct of the growth in isthmian traffic. The railroad was also an instant financial success for both the company and Colombia. It produced constantly high dividends for its shareholders and was the single most important revenue source for the Colombian treasury from the turbulent 1850s until the contract was revised in 1867.[52]

Construction work on the railroad and the conclusion of the Mallarino-Bidlack Treaty also quickened official U.S. interest in New Granada, not only in Panama, as a site for canal construction. Negotiations over the railroad and Mallarino-Bidlack Treaty contributed to the U.S. desire to obtain a declaration of British neutrality toward the area. In 1849 Secretary of State William Clayton informed U.S. representatives in Bogotá and London that the British guarantee of neutrality was essential to the ability of the railroad company to raise the venture capital to complete the project, which was "of great and obvious importance to the United States."[53] The Clayton-Bulwer Treaty between the United States and Britain the following year was the logical culmination of the diplomatic efforts to achieve parity in the area. Colombian Minister Rafael Rivas saw the agreement as an unexpected victory for the United States, and a blow to the British "lion," which had to retract its "claws." Rivas also claimed credit for the inclusion in the agreement by Bulwer of the clause guaranteeing the neutrality of any isthmian route. To Rivas, that guarantee of neutrality by Britain would also free Central America from annexationist activity by the United States, which was just as much to be feared as British imperialism.[54]

A reduction of British influence in the area was of interest to both the United States and to New Granada, the latter seeking to undercut British penetration into the Mosquito coast.[55] In the early 1850s the United States also demonstrated more active interest and involvement in surveying possible routes for canal construction. In 1850 the U.S. Chargé at Bogotá, Thomas Foote, urged Washington to pay more attention to the possibility of developing a canal through the Atrato route in northwest New Granada, since the Atrato was a deep river emptying into the Pacific that could be connected to the San Juan River running to the Atlantic by a short canal; it had the advantage, in his view, of being less expensive than the anticipated Nicaraguan route and of being no greater distance from California than the Panama route. In early 1854 the first of several official U.S. exploration groups, headed by Naval Lieutenant J. G. Strain, surveyed the Isthmus of Darien with the strong support of the Colombian minister to the United States, Victoriano Paredes, who presented the initiative to the governors of Panama and Cartagena as of "immense" importance to New Granada and for the "national interest of the entire world." [56]

Unfortunately, New Granada failed to make effective use of its new resource. During the period that he remained in the United States as New Granadan minister, Herrán urged the adoption of a range of development projects, including the active encouragement of immigration from Western Europe, particularly Spain, England, and France, along the lines of the U.S. experience, even employing some of the American immigration companies. Herrán stressed to the Colombian Foreign Ministry in 1848 that immigration, especially of families, would encourage industrialization, the development of New Granadan natural resources, and the opening of new lines of communication. Family based immigration, he contended, would facilitate integration and minimize social conflict between immigrants and established populations.[57] Bogotá politicians, however, feared a significant change in the composition of New Granadan society, although that change came in any event. Herrán's successor as consul general in 1849, Rafael Rivas, although not strictly anti-American, saw the United States as a growing threat to New Granadan interests, especially in the isthmus; yet he was more antagonistic to Britain, referring caustically in his correspondence to "los ingleses." The range of issues with which Rivas dealt while in the United States also underlined the importance of Central American questions in New Granadan–U.S. relations at mid-century: the Nicaraguan canal; Panama railroads and canals, border settlement issues between Panama and the Mosquito coast, and a postal convention with the United States.[58]

Crisis at Mid-Century:
Peace and Security in Panama

From the beginning of U.S. involvement with transportation de-velopment on the isthmus, the capacity of local and national New Granadan authorities to maintain peace in the area, to protect U.S. property and citizens, and to maintain uninterrupted traffic was the main area of friction between the nations. The combination of weak New Granadan authority, tensions between Panama and Bogotá, the visible symbol of American power that the railroad company came to represent in the eyes of Panamanians, and the often lawless, unruly travelers who crossed the isthmus on their way to the California coast created a volatile social situation. There were concrete disputes as well, over the legality of a head tax on passengers, the use of land allotted to the railroad company, and the power of Granadan authorities to determine freight rates. However, the most volatile tensions were the result of popular confrontations between the Panamanian population and American interests on the isthmus. Four years before the Panama Railroad was completed, the U.S. consul in Panama, S. B. Corwine, demanded that the governor of Panama deal officially with the fre-quent violence—robbery, murder, and assault—against U.S. citizens in transit. Particularly objectionable to the consul was Panamanian use of convicts as police and military guardsmen.[59]

These tensions derived in part from strongly divergent political cultures and differing perceptions of one another. In 1850 the U.S. chargé in Bogotá reflected on the nature of Latin American culture. He found Latins antagonistic to easy assimilation with other cultures, dis-trustful of strangers, lacking cohesive political powers. "The motives that in our country cause combinations of political parties . . . here cause revolutions." To the chargé the lack of racial homogeneity in New Granada militated against social cohesion. Political faction and strife reflected family disputes, undermining any orientation toward a strong sense of nationality. Regardless of the accuracy of this view, the perception itself was an important ingredient in shaping policy. Latin Americans were by nature undisciplined, antagonistic to foreign interests, and inclined to violence. When conflicts emerged on the isthmus in the course of the 1850s and New Granadan authorities had difficulty maintaining order and stability, they were simply fulfilling the stereotype. This image of New Granadan incompetence and unreliability ran through the U.S.-Colombian relationship from mid-century until at least the Panama Canal crisis in 1903. Strikingly, the Colombian self-perception at mid-century differed radically from that held by American officials. Victoriano Paredes, the New Granadan chargé at Washington in 1852, informed Daniel Webster that Colombia had in the past several years made impressive progress in establishing political institutions based on modern concepts. There is no doubt that Peredes sincerely believed that Colombians were basically devoted to "liberal and democratic" ideas, to humanism and to the idea of progress and determined to introduce U.S. political philosophy and institutions in Colombian society.[60]

Tensions in Panama were also clearly exacerbated by the substantial black Panamanian population and the application of U.S. racial prejudices and practices whether by travelers or residents in the area. New Granada formally freed its few remaining slaves in 1852, more than a decade before the United States. Although both racial hierarchy and prejudice survived slavery in New Granada, the relationship between black and white was far more fluid than in the United States. American travelers in Panama in the 1850s arrived at a time when sectional tensions were at their peak in the United States, when sensitivities over race relations were heightened by the racism that underlay the proslavery argument in the U.S. South, and with the debate over manumission still strong within New Granadan society.

Significantly, Consul Corwine in Panama blamed racial differences for many of the social and political tensions and held responsible the white population, "among whom were the dissolute and lawless of our own and other countries." He recommended that U.S. warships with a marine force be permanently stationed at the termini of the railroad to cooperate with local authority in maintaining order. Local English language newspapers, the *Panama Echo* and the *Panama Star*, vigorously criticized the behavior of American travelers and the

American government for failing to support law and order on the isthmus. The U.S. vice-consul in Colón, A. B. Boyd, placed more blame on Panamanian blacks in the aftermath of full emancipation in New Granada. He contended that "year after year the blacks have been gaining in power until they have at last gained supremacy over the white native population," which, he claimed, they were plotting to exterminate.[61]

New Granada's credibility suffered from its failure to establish a capable and adequate military presence in Panama. There were complaints of U.S. interference with New Granadan sovereignty. Yet the lack of military and police security in a region that had substantial volumes of wealth moving through it each day made it inevitable that Americans would contract for their own protection. In the early 1850s New Granadan authorities formally objected to the right of U.S. interests to recruit a military force in Panama. Insurance and express companies began raising their own private forces to protect life and property. Advertisements in the local press calling for recruits to work in such a capacity underlined the public dimension of the crisis.[62]

In 1852, when six hundred U.S. soldiers crossed the isthmus without prior approval, New Granadan authorities protested. There followed a series of sharply phrased exchanges over the meaning and intent of Article 35 in the Bidlack-Mallarino Treaty. The Pierce administration was adamant that Article 35 provided the express right for the U.S. government to move its troops through the isthmus and that inclusion of such a guarantee had been vital to Senate ratification of the agreement. At the time the treaty reached the Senate, Oregon had just been organized; it was sparsely settled and "filled with savages"; the Treaty of Guadalupe-Hidalgo with Mexico was under consideration, and its likely extension of U.S. territory on the Pacific increased the strategic need for troop mobility. Secretary of State William Marcy thus concluded with a definitive insistence on American "right" to convey troops in its service across the isthmus and that "no unnecessary impediment" would be imposed by the government of New Granada. The New Granadan authorities sought a face-saving solution by noting that they were considering a similar clause in a commercial treaty with France, permitting the transport of troops as long as New Granadan authority was not violated.[63]

The isthmian situation deteriorated with more general political instability in Bogotá in the early 1850s. This decade saw the revival of Colombian liberalism, in part paralleling the European movements of 1848. Between 1851 and 1856 seven new presidents and the Liberal semifederalist constitution of 1853 were recognized. In the midst of the 1854 dispute with the United States over the Bidlack-Mallarino Treaty, General José María Melo established a brief military dictatorship. Melo's coup had the support of the artisan classes of the interior who had opposed the liberal reforms of the decade, including lowered tariffs, the expansion of tobacco cultivation the opening of the Magdalena River to steamboat traffic. Those reforms had undercut New Granadan producers by facilitating imports, but they also opposed the democratization implicit in the adoption of universal manhood suffrage. Factions of the Liberal party, with some conservative support, soon drove Melo from power, but central authority in Panama continued to decline. In 1854 a constitutional amendment recognized Panama as a self-governing state, except for matters of defense and foreign policy, for which it remained at least nominally dependent on Bogotá.[64]

Panama became increasingly estranged from Bogotá and linked to U.S. economic interests. By the mid-1850s traffic through Panama was extremely heavy; between January and June 1855 alone forty-eight American vessels, involving almost twelve hundred crewmen and forty-four thousand tons of cargo, arrived from the U.S. and Cuba.[65] It was in the context of this swelling traffic that in April 1856 an altercation over payment for a slice of watermelon touched off a large-scale riot in Panama city. The conflict began between an intoxicated white American traveler and a light-skinned black fruit vendor in Panama; within fifteen minutes of the initial incident, church bells sounded in the black quarter of town, and a large crowd of some six hundred men gathered; in the rioting that followed there was widespread destruction of property. An estimated eighteen Americans and two Panamanians were murdered, including women and children according to the U.S. consul in Panama. Shortly after the riot, the Department of State appointed two special agents to determine whether the riot was premeditated and if the attacks resulted from hostility to the United States and its citizens. Although the extensive testimony and systematic reports collected by both American and Granadan authorities cannot be reconciled on many basic points of fact, there is little doubt that the specific incident led to large-scale conflict because of long accumulated frustrations on the part of the Panama population, many of whom felt abused and exploited by the foreigners using the Panama Railroad route. There is also little doubt that Granadan police and military sided with the attackers against those Americans who took refuge in the railroad company offices. In the confusion of the moment, Granadan officials appear to have believed they were firing on an armed group in the railroad company offices. The U.S. consul in Panama confirmed that the railroad company agents had made a "great display of useless arms" shortly before they were attacked, and he also indicated that the railroad officials had refused his request to move his men inside the building.[66] Regardless of the intent of Granadan officials, reliable eyewitness accounts implicated the governor and chief of police for supplying gunpowder to the attackers and encouraging them. American officials, with logic but without clear evidence, denied the allegation that the American passengers had been armed, arguing that had they been, the death and injury toll on the other side would have been greater.[67]

Colombian Foreign Secretary Lino de Pombo vigorously refuted American allegations that there had been any premeditation on the part of Panamanians, although he agreed there had to be an investigation of the role played by the governor of Panama and the Panamanian police force. What he believed was necessary in the long term was the establishment of a reliable force in Panama to reduce lawless behavior on all sides. However, he also saw the need to "check the attempts to treat like a savage tribe, a horde of malefactors, an essentially friendly, kindly, and hospitable people . . . because in a moment of excitement . . . they have allowed their passion to lead them to reprehensible extremes." He continued to believe and to argue that the main problem was the undisciplined behavior of American passengers in transit. The foreign secretary was visibly more concerned with the implications for New Granadan and Central American relations in these months of the actions of William Walker, the American filibuster in Nicaragua, than he was with the Panama riot.[68]

From the perspective of the U.S. chargé in Bogotá, James Bowlin, the main problem was not a lack of good faith on the part of Bogotá officials but the absence of impartiality in the reports that reached Bogotá. Central Granadan authority lacked the power more than the will to act against Panama; Bogotá possessed neither "army, fleet nor arms, nor money, nor credit, to procure either." Granada had great resources if there were integrity enough to manage them with justice. Under the circumstances, he recommended that the U.S. sloop *St. Mary*, one of the vessels ordered to Panama during the rioting, be retained in Panama harbor as a reminder of the seriousness of U.S. intent. Bowlin commented presciently, although he was by no means alone in this vision at the time, that the future of the isthmus depended on U.S. military and political power and that the day might come when "they drive us to the necessity of governing it, whether we ought to govern it under the shadow of their power, or seize it and protect it, as it should be protected for the uses of mankind. . . . This idea is more to be regretted as it presupposes a change in our foreign policy."[69]

The Pierce administration believed that the original idea of defending neutrality on the isthmus had not been intended to deal primarily with domestic disturbances but rather with the threat of foreign powers to the control of the isthmus. It seemed reasonable to expect that New Granada station an adequate military force along the route of the railroad and in the two major cities, Aspinwall (Colón) and Panama City.[70] The Department of State specifically insisted on financial compensation for the loss of life and property. The administration also raised the stakes of negotiation, pressing for a new convention that would have effectively transferred sovereignty in Panama to the United States during periods of crisis. Employing the example of the British at San Juan de Nicaragua and in the Bay Islands of Honduras, the United States proposed that it be given effective control over several islands in Panama harbor, including Taboga. Further, it requested a transfer to the Panama Railroad Company of the reserved rights of New Granada in the 1846 treaty. In return the United States proposed to pay New Granada $1.2 million and release New Granada from its obligations to protect the isthmian route or to pay damages in the event of failure to do so. Marcy stressed that if New Granada were unwilling to negotiate on these terms it would have to be reminded that the Nicaraguan route was a viable alternative.[71]

Confronted with Washington's diplomatic threat, Bogotá now sought to use Panama's strategic importance as leverage to gain international assistance. Herrán traveled to London and Paris in search of either military support or diplomatic intervention on New Granada's behalf in order to prevent war, occupation, and dismemberment. New Granada hoped, however vainly, to obtain an international agreement guaranteeing the permanent security and neutrality of the isthmus. Such an approach, it argued, would serve European interests against the United States.[72] When the overtures failed, the New Granada government of Mariano Ospina Rodriguez had to find accommodation with the United States, including consideration of possible annexation to the Polar Star.

The process of negotiation and ratification of a settlement of the Panama riots took several years to complete. In both nations there were other pressing domestic issues, impending civil war in the United States during the Democratic administration of James Buchanan; in New Granada a return of Conservatives to power led to the adoption of a new Constitution in 1858, this one even more strongly federalist. In 1860 Liberals, with the aid of such former Conservatives as Tomás C. Mosquera, returned to power through civil war. Ironically, New Granadan instability echoed that in the United States, with the Liberal-Conservative civil wars taking place shortly before Abraham Lincoln's election and the eruption of civil war. The mutual suffering from civil conflagration might have made for mutual empathy, but the United States never equated its own civil rupture with what Americans viewed as the petty tyrannies of its southern neighbor and ally.

Nonetheless, as both nations slipped toward civil war and national reconstruction in the 1850s, they managed to reach agreement on the many outstanding claims questions that had plagued relations for a generation. In 1860 Bogotá finally ratified an accord that included New Granadan acceptance of responsibility for the Panama riots, although actual resolution of those claims did not come until late in Lincoln's presidency.[73]

On the eve of civil war in the United States, New Granadan–U.S. relations were at their lowest point in a half-century. From a promising beginning based on shared ideals and mutual respect during the wars for independence, affairs between the two nations had deteriorated to the level of bitter recrimination, hostility, suspicion, and, at times, open contempt for the other society and its political culture. Although individual Americans and New Granadans continued to share those ideals, the diplomatic record of that first half-century did not augur well for the future.

2 An Era of Civil War and National Reconstruction, 1861–1886

> Resistance to our ambition daily grows more and more impossible. (William Seward, 1860)

> The confusion into which Colombia has unfortunately fallen . . . because of the imperfections of its institutions, requires new and precise affirmation of the most elementary principles of political science. (Rafael Nuñez, 1885)[1]

Although one would not want to make the analogy too strict, there were some striking similarities between the course of Colombian and U.S. history in the two decades after 1860, in part because they reflected some broader historical patterns in the West in those years. This was a generation of national unification, often following decades of regional and local factionalism, sometimes, as in the case of the United States and Colombia, accompanied by bitter and vicious civil wars. Modern Germany and Italy emerged as part of the unification process at this time; Canadian confederation occurred in 1867; Argentina moved toward political unification with a reformist liberal national president in Domingo Sarmiento from 1868 to 1874; Porfirio Díaz, for all the repression of his government, contributed to the unification of the modern Mexican state, to cite only a few examples.

In the United States the political efforts to contain the forces of sectionalism and the debate over slavery and slavery extension finally collapsed in 1861 with Lincoln's inauguration as the first Republican party president. Four years of civil war followed, years that not only

43

COSTA
RICA

CARIBBEAN SEA

David

Colón
Chagres
Panamá

Golfo
de Panamá

PACIFIC
OCEAN

PANAMÁ

Golfo de Urabá

Barranquilla
Sabanilla
Cartagena
Santa Marta
Ciénaga
Riohacha

MAGDALENA

Mompox

CAUCA

BOLÍVAR

ANTIOQUIA

Antioquia

Medellín
Quibdó

VENEZUELA

Rionegro
Bucaramanga
Socorro
Pamplona

SANTANDER

Manizales

Cartago
Muzo
Chiquinquirá
Ambalema
Tunja

Buenaventura
Cali
Ibagué
Bogotá

CAUCA

Popayán
Neiva

Pasto

TOLIMA

BOYACÁ

Villavicencio

CUNDINAMARCA

ECUADOR

CAUCA

PERU

The United States of

COLOMBIA

1864

Political divisions

BRAZIL

Kilometres
0   100   200   300   400   500
0   100   200   300
Miles

wm

temporarily destroyed a substantial portion of the Southern cotton economy and decimated its young white male labor force but that also left a legacy of racial and political tension that has yet to be fully overcome in either its symbolic or substantive forms. Slavery ended by constitutional amendment in 1865 with the military defeat of the Confederacy, and the task of rebuilding a nation began in earnest amidst radically differing visions of what the postwar world should be. This was a significant period in American constitutional history, with changes resulting through both amendment and judicial review. Amendments addressed not only slavery but also civil liberties more generally, the rights of property, the protection of male suffrage, and the assertion of national authority. All strengthened central political power. Following a period of bitter "radical" reconstruction in the late 1860s and early 1870s, there was shift to moderate and then conservative national reconciliation, with an emphasis on capitalist economic development, unfettered free enterprise, and the enshrinement of laissez faire individualism. The 1870s justly earned the title Mark Twain coined—the Gilded Age. The United States in those years moved into the modern age, with rapid industrial expansion in such heavy industries as steel, almost breathtaking expansion of its railroad network through the 1880s, and the first emergence of large-scale industrial violence and unionization. Although the conservatism that cloaked itself in nineteenth-century classical liberalism seemed triumphant, one of the main themes of the late nineteenth century was the emergence of conflicting visions of individualism versus commonweal.

Colombia underwent some parallel changes in these two decades. An extended civil war between Liberal and Conservative factions from 1857 to 1861 gave way to the reestablishment of Liberal dominance until 1884. In that year a split in Liberal ranks enabled a resurgence of Conservatism led by former Liberal Rafael Nuñez, one of the outstanding political figures of the late nineteenth century. Nuñez established a Conservative party rule that was essentially unbroken until 1930. The differences between modern Colombian Liberal and Conservative were crystallizing, although on some issues, such as economic policy, the distinctions were muted. The former tended to be more supportive of diversified economic development, educational reform, anticlericalism, scientific advance, and an outward-looking foreign policy. Conservatives, for the most part, were more introspective, strongly committed to the continuing power of the Roman Catholic Church, traditional education under the Church, limited economic diversification, with an economy and value structure that was more rural and agricultural than urban and industrial. On the issue of a federal versus a centralized state, the two parties wavered. Whichever held power was inclined toward greater centralization.

During the Liberal era in the 1860s, the nation acquired a new constitution, establishing the United States of Colombia as one of the most decentralized and, at least on paper, liberal nations in Latin America. Each state controlled its own defense and conducted its local affairs. The national presidential term was limited to two years, with no immediate reelection; each state had one vote for president, with suffrage determined by the individual state. The liberal provisions in the constitution included a bill of rights, which ended capital punishment, granted virtually unlimited freedom of speech, and guaranteed every citizen the right to bear arms. Subsequent Liberal governments promoted free, secular education and employed German educators. Thus civil war in Colombia, in contrast to the American experience, in the late nineteenth century produced greater decentralization rather than a stronger, national government, which came in the backlash against the Liberals in the 1880s and with Nuñez's rise to power. He presided over the adoption of the 1886 constitution, which created the modern Republic of Colombia.

Economically, Colombia experienced a degree of continued economic growth, if not full prosperity. The tobacco-fed boom of the 1850s continued into the 1870s, then went into relative decline with the growing importance of cotton cultivation, the production of quinine, and the emergence of coffee. Colombian producers in these years were uncompetitive in overseas markets; there was no sustained economic growth and little transportation development until coffee production took off in the twentieth century. A substantial proportion of the labor force remained beyond the money economy. Once considered a major Latin American country, Colombia lagged behind the continental leaders—Chile, Mexico, Argentina, and Brazil—in the late nineteenth century.

The Civil War Years

The legacy of the Panama riots of 1856 and the claims questions that arose out of that conflict combined with continuing debate over the place of the isthmus to form the main motifs of Colombian-U.S. relations in the 1860s.The Cass-Herrán Treaty late in the Buchanan administration provided for the appointment of a claims commission to determine the amount owed to the United States as a result of the Panama crisis and longer standing claims from the wars for independence. The commissioners appointed under the terms of the treaty agreed to accept seventy-three cases, carrying a dollar value of over $490,000. Since the Colombian minister in Washington refused to accept the umpire's ruling on claims amounting to over $300,000, that left accepted claims of slightly more than $135,000, which included an amount compensating for the Panama riots.[2]

In both nations a disruptive change of government occurred in mid-negotiations. The Lincoln administration for two years declined to recognize a Liberal revolution led by Tomás C. Mosquera, which erupted in 1860. To strengthen his position on the isthmus, Mosquera appealed to the United States to establish order under the 1846 treaty. Secretary of State William Seward refused to choose sides in the Colombian conflict; he wisely stressed that the U.S. government would act to ensure that transit on the isthmus remained open and neutral and that U.S. citizens and property would be protected. U.S. ambassadors in London and Paris were instructed to determine European attitudes toward possible U.S. intervention on the isthmus to preserve peace. The British reaction was firm. Lord Russell informed Charles Francis Adams that there was no need for "interposition" at that time. Russell contended that the Colombian civil war was just another example of what was "happening all the time in

South America" and that on the main issue, isthmian traffic, there had been no disruption in service. In the event that traffic were disrupted, Britain was willing to cooperate with the United States to restore tranquillity. The reply from Paris was identical, and it was evident that the French and British had been consulting fully on the matter. The French foreign minister, who was clearly highly informed on the domestic situation in Colombia at the time, emphasized that the issue was the neutrality of the isthmus and that that had not been compromised by either side in the Colombian civil war. He indicated that France had not recognized Mosquera because he was not yet firmly in control militarily or politically, and he further questioned the status of Herrán in Washington, since he did not have the confidence of Bogotá.[3]

Representatives of competing Colombian political factions in Washington further complicated matters. The "official" Colombian minister, Pedro Herrán, by 1862 opposed President Mosquera, to whom he referred as a "revolutionary chief engaged in subverting the Granadine Confederation." Herrán requested U.S. intervention in Panama to defend Panama against the government that he formally represented. Since Mosquera was also his father-in-law, Herrán's position contributed neither to national nor domestic harmony! When Colombia's new representative in the United States in early 1862, Francisco Párraga, found that Herrán refused to turn over the Colombian legation or its records to him and that Herrán had the support of the Lincoln administration, which he had convinced that the Mosquera government was a dictatorship unlikely to survive. The result was that both men continued to report to Bogotá in this period, until matters moved toward reconciliation with the arrival in Washington of Manuel Murillo, himself shortly to become president of the United States of Colombia in 1864.

Even during this dispute over U.S. recognition, however, Párraga reported very favorably on the North's successes in the Civil War, in particular in mid-1862 on the initiative taken by General John C. Fremont in freeing slaves in Louisiana and the Port Royal experiment with freed slaves in South Carolina. He criticized Lincoln for overturning Fremont's action and the Union for suppressing freedom of the press in the North on war-related matters. Murillo, when he arrived in New York, did not press his position with Washington, deciding not to present his credentials for fear of rejection; interestingly, Murillo expressed the view that the independence of the South was an accomplished reality and that it was only a matter of time before France extended recognition to the Confederacy. Murillo remained convinced, nonetheless, of the justness of the northern cause, which he presented as a "moral force," a "Christian task," although he saw Lincoln as overly timid and pragmatic on emancipation, having been pushed by European public opinion rather than moral conviction to issue the Emancipation Proclamation, and he noted the extent of racism in northern society.[4]

At the end of 1862 Seward still declined to meet with Murillo on grounds that official U.S. policy was neither to recognize nor to have any dealings of an official nature with any government resulting from revolutionary transfers of power. The situation was not improved by the continuing efforts of Herrán and J. M. Hurtado to raise funds to purchase weapons for the anti-Mosquera forces, using the receipts of the Panama Railroad Company as collateral. When Lincoln reported to Congress early in 1863 on the state of relations with Colombia, he stressed that there was no present power in Colombia to which recognition could be granted. At the same time the fortunes of Herrán and Hurtado in Washington went into decline, since Lincoln opposed their efforts to raise military funds on American soil; in addition, Senator William P. Fessenden introduced a motion in Congress calling for an investigation of Herrán's activities. To Murillo, Seward remained the impediment to recognition of Mosquera's government, but at least Herrán's position was in decline. In May, Mosquera was declared the constitutionally elected president of Colombia, however, and by July 1863 Murillo was officially accredited by the Lincoln administration.[5]

Recognition cleared the way for a continuation of the claims negotiations. When they did initiate a resumption of talks, both sides agreed on a reconsideration of the claims that had been rejected by Pedro Herrán two years earlier. The U.S. Civil War altered the position of

William Seward's State Department, making the administration more sensitive to the vulnerability of the United States for similar claims arising from the Civil War, the naval blockade of the South, and possible injury to neutral third parties who might be foreigners residing in the United States. The Lincoln administration indicated as early as 1862 that citizens of the United States who had taken up long-term residence in New Granada were subject as were Granadans to the laws of that country. Although the United States sought to alter that position at the end of the Civil War, Colombia objected to the U.S. position. In fact Colombia in 1865 passed a motion through Congress specifying that foreigners in the country were subject to all Colombian laws except military service and war loans; a second law established the primacy of national Colombian courts as the locus of first appeal; although this was not pleasing to the State Department because of a lack of confidence in Colombian courts, it had little choice but to accept what was an established principle in international law. Seward had to acknowledge that American businessmen had to assume a certain risk in establishing themselves abroad.[6]

Thus, the political and legal context had altered somewhat when Colombia and the United States sought to complete the claims issue. In early 1864 they agreed to a new convention establishing another mixed claims commission, this time with a neutral, the British minister in the United States, serving as umpire, and the agreement was ratified the following year as the American Civil War drew to a close. Ultimately, Colombia paid to the United States on behalf of American claimants more than $400,000, some $60,000 of which was compensation for lost American lives and property at Panama in the bloody melee of April 1856. This brought to a close one of the most divisive chapters in Colombian-U.S. relations.[7]

It is very difficult with limited sources available to determine the full spectrum of Colombian views on the U.S. Civil War. Even the volume of documentation in the Colombian Foreign Ministry Archives drops off sharply for the U.S. Civil War years, likely as a result of the frequent changes in personnel that appear to have occurred during the Colombian civil war of these years. To some extent the Liberal revolt led by Tomás C. Mosquera, who served as president of the short-lived United States of New Granada in 1862 and 1863, as president of the United States of Colombia from 1863 to 1864 and 1866 to 1867, diverted attention from developments outside the country. In mainstream political circles, however, Colombian sympathies seem to have been with the Union and against the Confederacy. That view was in part pragmatic, including the need for recognition by the United States in 1863 of the Mosquera government; but Colombians also held a genuine hostility to slavery and believed that it was southern slaveholders who posed more of an expansionist threat in the Caribbean and Central America than did the North.

The pro-Mosquera Bogotá newspaper *El Tiempo*, edited by Lorenzo María Lleras, consistently presented the United States in 1864 as a nation of liberty and constitutional freedoms, in which the people reigned supreme. The paper associated American economic growth and prosperity in the previous half-century as a byproduct of that liberty. Although many of the paper's actual reports on the Civil War were summaries based on the New York *Herald* or *World*, that coverage reflected a clear northern bias. Economic news related almost exclusively to New York markets, and there was a regular feature entitled "Revista del mercado de N.Y." (Review of the New York market); there was considerable interest in Lincoln's Emancipation Proclamation and early reconstruction plans as well as in the course of military events on the battlefield. The general view of *El Tiempo* was that even if Lincoln achieved no more than the emancipation of slaves that accomplishment would be sufficient to earn Colombian admiration and support. Although there is no doubt that this pro-Mosquera and pro–Manuel Murillo paper had pragmatic reasons to praise the United States in order to reinforce efforts to gain recognition of those governments in the United States, there is no reason to doubt the ideological affinity for Lincoln and the Republicans over the Democrats, who were associated in Colombian circles purely with proslavery forces. Consequently, *El Tiempo* took a distinctly antiMcLellan position in the 1864 election. The paper also drew an analogy between the debate then current in Colombia over the extent of the suffrage and what it considered the unfortunate consequences of extending the vote in the United States to semiliterate immigrants; El Tiempo portrayed immigrant Irish as "more ignorant than our Indians" and as misled, through the influence of the Democratic party and the Roman Catholic Church, into supporting antidemocratic forces in the United States. Universal suffrage in the United States was, nonetheless, considered more justifiable than in Colombia because of the higher level of education among the common man.[8]

Lincoln's assassination brought forth an outpouring of sympathy in the pages of El Tiempo. The crime was presented not as an act of an isolated man but as the product of the "slavery spirit," a fanatical group who had placed "guns and daggers in the hands of the new Ravaillacs," and which was a futile act of revenge that could not erase Lincoln's and the war's accomplishments.[9] One of the few expressions of empathy for the plight of the South came at the end of the war in expressions of respect for General Robert E. Lee, but that did not extend to the Confederacy more generally.

The possible emancipation of American slaves occasioned consideration of and in one instance a concrete proposal for colonizing freedmen in Colombia. That initiative grew out of the larger entrepreneurial operations of Ambrose Thompson, an American who since the 1850s had been engaged in acquiring and developing properties in the Chiriqui region of Panama through the Chiriqui Improvement Company, which was chartered in Pennsylvania. The Buchanan administration had even negotiated a contract with the company to use the harbor facilities developed by the company as well as land on both the Atlantic and Pacific coasts for naval installations. The contract was not approved by Congress, and New Granada was not even consulted on the project before Buchanan and the Democrats gave way to Lincoln and the Republican party in early 1861. Although the Lincoln administration did not revive the project, Thompson himself proposed to Colombia in 1862 that he import black American labor to his Chiriqui properties to work the mines, roads, and other facilities. Each family head was to receive eighty acres of land and each adult twenty acres on condition that the land be improved. Thompson sought U.S. government financing to assist with the opening of coal mines, with the advance to be repaid in coal and by providing access to Colombian and American naval vessels. Thompson was neither racially blind nor philanthropic in this initiative; he contended that the Panamanian climate was "eminently suited to the African race," and he sought a Colombian government grant of an additional three million acres on which to colonize an estimated fifty thousand emigrants.

The Colombian minister in Washington, Murillo, indicated his support for the project to the Colombian Foreign Ministry. He agreed with Thompson's assessment of the suitability of black labor to local conditions, suggested that this was an opportune means of obtaining significant immigration into the area, and rejected as unfounded the fears of those who opposed black immigration on racial grounds; Murillo was convinced that the white population would retain its dominance and that miscegenation would further alleviate potential conflict. Párraga further claimed to Thompson that Latins had never felt the revulsion toward Africans which had been the case with Anglo-Saxons; in short he was prepared to recommend positive action to Bogotá as long as there were assurances that there would be no challenge to Colombian sovereignty in the area and provided that there was adequate provision for the survival of the colonists during their first year.[10]

The Civil War in the United States, the sensitivities of other Central American governments, the fact that there was no American recognition at the time of a Colombian government, and fear in various quarters of Colombian society that American black immigrants would give the United States an entering wedge all militated toward the failure of the scheme. The Lincoln cabinet discussed the idea, and there was some support in Congress, but Lincoln was unwilling to take any initiative until there had been formal agreement with Colombian authorities, an impossible task in 1862 and 1863. Although there were further proposals and some expressions of interest after the Civil War, there was no concrete development.[11]

The Lincoln administration and Colombian governments held common views of the French imperial intervention in Mexico, the over-

throw of the reformist government of Benito Juárez, and the installation of Archduke Maximillian of Austria on the throne of Mexico. Both
the United States and Colombia vigorously opposed the initiative,
although the United States was both preoccupied with the Civil War
and apprehensive about possible French recognition of the Confederacy, in particular with the difficult early military course of the war.
The Lincoln administration protested the French initiative, sent arms
to Juárez during the occupation. In 1866 the Johnson administration
pointedly asked the French to leave Mexico.

Colombian Liberal sympathies were strongly with Juárez and the
Mexican Liberals, with whom they identified political sentiments akin
to their own orientation in the Colombian civil war of the early 1860s.
The Mosquera government in Bogotá never accepted the French contention that a French presence in Mexico would serve to offset Anglo-
American power and provide a "Latin" racial barrier against Anglo-
Saxon advances. Colombia opposed the use of the Panama Railroad
by French troops and sought assurances that the United States would
be firm in its defense of the concept of neutrality of the isthmus embodied in the 1846 treaty. The Panama Railroad Company was also
cooperative, indicating to the French government that it would not
transport French troops without the consent of the Colombian government. Whether this was deference to Bogotá or to Washington
was another matter. Also, in return for Colombian diplomatic support
against the French, the Mexican Liberal representative in Washington
campaigned on the Colombian behalf during the debate over recognition of Mosquera's government, but the Mexican effort had little
impact. Indeed, Seward was angry with Mexican interference and denied that the Lincoln administration sought to intervene in the internal
affairs of the American states.[12]

By the end of the American Civil War the American economic presence in Colombia was considerable, although it was concentrated on
the isthmus. An American, A. B. Boyd, owned the major English language newspaper in Panama, the *Panama Star and Herald*, founded
in 1852; the Boston Ice Company made significant investments after
1866, not only in ice sales but also in lumber and general merchan-

dise. In 1867 New York and Colón were connected for the first time by telegraph cable under a concession granted to the New York firm, the International Ocean Telegraph Company. Another New York firm, the Central and South American Telegraph Company, laid the cable that joined Panama City and Colón. The Pacific Mail Steamship Company of New York was the main shipping interest in the New York–Colón run, but even within Panama the steamship company owned by William Nelson, a former U.S. consul, not only provided coastal service but also owned considerable property near Panama City. Nelson was also a commercial agent of the Panama Railroad Company in the 1860s. In terms of communication, Panama was now the main point of contact between the United States and Colombia, with steam navigation to other major Colombian ports, including Cartagena, far less frequent.[13]

American investments and economic activity in Colombia in this period concentrated in transportation activity, although judging by travelers' descriptions and the reports of local U.S. consuls, American manufactures were found widely in Colombian society. It was not until after the turn of the century that a marked shift of investment to extractive industries occurred, notably petroleum. American interests had significant investments in gold mining operations in the Chocó region in the late nineteenth century. The Eder family began its plantation developments in the Cauca Valley following the Civil War. One of the largest investments in the Civil War era was in dredging and navigation of the Magdalena Canal (Canal del Dique), joining Cartagena with the river and providing an outlet to the Caribbean, by the New Granada Canal and Steam Navigation Company of New York. This enterprise began as a British operation, and its shift to American capital and enterprise was indicative of the gradual U.S. displacement of Britain as the main power in the area, although that transition was not dramatic until World War I. This was also reflected in the shift of the Magdalena Steam Navigation Company from European to American control after its initial establishment in 1846.

In railroad development, Colombia that was starved for transportation links. In the late 1870s the New York and South American Contract Company obtained a concession to construct a line from Cali to the Pacific, although financial and political problems delayed completion until World War I. Such delays also characterized railroad construction to link Bogotá with Girardot on the Magdalena River, Puerto Berrio with Medellín, and Puerto Colombia with Barranquilla on the Caribbean coast; in each of those projects a Cuban-born American, Francisco Cisneros, was the driving force. Railroad links between Barranquilla and Sabanilla were established in the 1870s as well, improving the trade access for the region. In street railway construction and operation, American entrepreneurs were dominant in Bogotá, forming the Bogotá Street Railway Company of New York and quickly bringing the lines into operation in the early 1880s. In total, U.S. investments in Colombia by 1881 had reached an estimated $14 million, the bulk of which was represented by the Panama Railroad.[14]

Actual investments represented only a fraction of American entrepreneurial activity; for every company that obtained a contract there were many others interested in such operations.[15]

Isthmian Canal Negotiations

The main issue in Colombian-American relations during the two decades following the American Civil War was the possible construction of a canal between the Atlantic and Pacific oceans either through the Isthmus of Panama or via Darien. U.S. policy throughout this period remained firmly based on the principle that any canal constructed should involve the United States. There was considerable objection and resentment when Colombia turned to France and Ferdinand de Lesseps.

As early as 1862 Colombian authorities were prepared to delay consideration of canal construction applications from American firms because of exploration work by European interests in the Darien area. Two years later, a Paris organization was established to obtain a Colombian canal concession. During debates in Bogotá over a U.S.

canal treaty, the French organization wrote to President Santos Gutierrez applying for such a concession.[16]

The United States moved quickly after the Civil War in an effort to
consolidate its position. In 1868 President Andrew Johnson appointed
Caleb Cushing as a special U.S. emissary to negotiate with Colombian authorities for the construction of an interoceanic canal. Cushing's prominence as a former negotiator on commercial questions with
China in the 1840s indicated the seriousness of the mission to Colombian officials. Seward had gradually become convinced the project was
highly significant and wished to complete the negotiations before the
end of the Johnson administration. In the early 1868 negotiations the
Colombian government insisted that all costs of construction be born
by the United States. It required the consent of the Panama Railroad
Company for any canal. It wanted any canal grant to be exclusive to
the United States, with Colombia not permitting another interoceanic
canal in its territory. Colombian authorities were not prepared to compromise on Colombian sovereignty in any canal concession, with the
result that the government maintained that Colombia would be responsible for the police and security of the canal, though the canal
company would pay the costs of military protection. Colombia was
prepared to grant a one hundred year concession in return for 6 percent of gross revenues, with a minimum guarantee of six hundred
thousand pesos annually.[17]

The two sides came to terms in some haste in early January 1869,
but the Colombian Senate voted decisively against ratification, and
the U.S. Senate let the agreement die without a vote. One source of
opposition in Colombian political circles was the fear that the United
States, once having acquired the concession, would delay building the
canal in order to defend the exclusive privilege of the railroad company. Miguel Samper, former Colombian foreign secretary, lamented
to Caleb Cushing that there was ignorance in Bogotá of how much the
United States desired and needed an isthmian canal, especially with
the Suez Canal nearing completion.

The terms of the failed agreement reflected the critical issues that continued to divide the two nations on a canal treaty. Colombia accepted in the 1869 agreement exclusive U.S. control over a twenty-mile strip of territory in which the canal would be constructed, though there was lip service to Colombian retention of sovereignty. Of equal significance was the agreement that U.S. troops, not Colombian, would defend the canal, although they were to be under a cumbersome joint command.[18] The issues of defense and sovereignty thus remained critical.

President Ulysses S. Grant took a personal interest in an isthmian canal and pressed for the renegotiation of the failed agreement. Grant's objectives were clearly strategic in nature, and he was less inclined than his predecessors to consider multilateral agreements pertaining to construction or defense. Grant considered any canal "an American enterprise." Secretary of State Hamilton Fish expressed his regret over Colombian rejection of the 1869 canal treaty. The tone of the U.S. position seemed threatening, and the Colombian minister cautioned Bogotá not to underestimate the willingness of the United States to obtain by force what it could not gain by diplomacy: "The expansionist spirit of this nation has not died," he warned, "and with slavery, which galvanized the entire North against territorial expansion, now abolished . . . the spirit has taken on a new energy among all social groups."[19]

With a canal treaty identified as a high priority, the Grant administration immediately sought to bring new negotiations to a successful conclusion. The administration provided "secret service" funds to Stephen Hurlbut in Bogotá to improve American public relations through the pages of prominent Bogotá newspapers, including the *Diario Oficial* and *El Liberal*. Initially Hurlbut sought terms based on a possible internationally controlled canal, but the Grant administration remained firmly attached to an American enterprise. Hurlbut's agreement with Colombian officials in early 1870 was essentially the treaty of 1869 but contained provisions more favorable to Colombia. One of the major alterations was a clause in which the U.S. government guaranteed to meet the annual obligations of the Panama Railroad to Colombia if the company failed to do so. Hurlbut lamented that it was only the "political and military advantage" of the canal which would justify U.S. acceptance of the burdens of the treaty. President Grant promptly submitted it to the Senate. A survey team under Rear Admiral Charles H. Davis was already in Central America to study alternative routes, and in the course of 1870 additional missions were sent to conduct surveys of the Tehuantepec and Nicaraguan routes.[20]

The U.S. Senate, despite the Colombian Senate's favorable action, failed to bring the treaty to a vote in 1870, partly because of its financial implications, and, perhaps, because of congressional hostility toward the Grant administration's reckless and irresponsible initiative to annex Santo Domingo. American inaction in Panama and American private and public consideration of alternate routes drove the Colombians into the arms of Europe.[21] Had the 1870 treaty been ratified, much of the delay, expense, and possibly the crisis of 1903 might have been avoided by both sides. In 1871 Hamilton Fish wrote to the Colombian minister that Colombia remained "custodians of the only open way across the Isthmus."[22]

Acceptance of the treaty in the Colombian Senate in 1870 masked considerable opposition to the canal project, and the debates in the Senate revealed the frequent ambivalence of sentiments toward the United States. The Liberal administration of Santos Gutierrez even had difficulty appointing a balanced team of negotiators. Senator Carlos Martín, for instance, who was a Liberal, refused even to serve as a negotiator because he found a treaty repugnant. Senator Miguel Samper, a member of the Senate committee charged with reporting on the treaty, expressed concern that the canal would make Colombia a target for international attack but that any attacks would have to be repelled by the United States, thus seriously undermining Colombian sovereignty in the area. Samper also strongly objected to American warships using the canal in wartime. Senator Ezequiel Rojas opposed the treaty but expressed sympathetic views toward the United States as it moved toward the displacement of Europe in economic importance to Colombia; Rojas noted that canal development would provide considerable revenue to Colombia and the economy itself could be rejuvenated, converting largely worthless lands into productive enterprise, especially in those states that were directly associated with the canal—Panama, Cauca, Magdalena, and Bolívar. Senator Justo Arosemena, one of the negotiators of the agreement, argued that the United States was entirely sincere in its intention to construct a canal and was not seeking to prevent other nations from developing the area. Senator Antonio Ferro shared Rojas's opinion; the treaty itself was an excessive delegation of power to the United States over Colombian affairs and should not be approved, but the United States was nonetheless the "first nation of the world . . . [where] are united the highest degree of intellectual and moral qualities. . . . If there is one nation," he concluded, "that satisfies all the aspirations of those who seek the indefinite progress of mankind, then it is the North American people." [23]

Canal negotiations made little progress until the end of the 1870s. In the interim Colombia passed through another devastating Liberal-Conservative civil war in 1875 and 1876, disrupting commerce and economic growth. As peace was restored throughout the country, the U.S. consul in Panama predicted that Colombia "for years to come [will] deplore in sack cloth and ashes this madness." The nation had been making economic and political progress until the fresh outbreak of civil disorder. The return of peace would lead to further growth. The consul contended that there had been little change in Panamanian agriculture since independence, except in Chiriqui, where a number of Americans had migrated to cultivate coffee. Significantly, the consul urged the U.S. government to devote more attention to building its merchant marine to improve its world commercial status. There was increased traffic on the isthmus, which now had a population of approximately 150,000, with considerably more produce passing through Colón, but most of that merchandise was destined for Europe. Echoing sentiment in official circles in Washington, he emphasized that no nation would derive as many advantages from the construction of a Panama canal as the United States. Until the completion of a canal he urged that the United States could expand its commercial opportunities by establishing a commercial exchange at Panama to facilitate the movement of U.S. manufactures to South

America in return for agricultural and mining imports. A strong advocate of liberalized trade, he urged tariff reduction to undercut competition from Europe and facilitate imports from South America; he also advocated government subsidization of exports in order to gain access to markets.[24]

For the remainder of the 1870s there was little progress either on a canal project with the United States or with U.S. satisfaction with political stability on the isthmus. Even as Damaso Cerrera was inaugurated in early 1880 as president of the State of Panama, the U.S. consul predicted that with the unsettled state of affairs "their perennial revolution will without doubt take place within the next thirty or forty days." Given the substantial American interests in the area, the consul advocated stationing a U.S. warship at Panama or Colón to restrain the "turbulent and excitable element of this country."[25]

Colombia Turns to France

During the U.S. Civil War, with Louis Napoleon Bonaparte seeking means to restore the glory of the first French Empire, there was a quickening of French interest in the Western Hemisphere. The ultimately tragic and ill-considered Mexican venture with Maximilian was one manifestation of that ambition; French interest in an isthmian canal was another, although the Second Empire was defeated before any canal enterprise took concrete form. Early in the 1860s Colombian minister in Paris, José M. Samper, reported extensively on French entrepreneurial interests in Panama and the formation of several exploration activities. While there were active negotiations with the United States, Colombian Liberal governments generally demonstrated little interest in a French company, and it appears that the Colombians were genuinely opposed to any initiative that might involve the French government. With the failure of the United States to act on the 1870 canal treaty and with evident U.S. interest in a Nicaraguan route, however, Colombian sentiments took a new tack. By 1876 a French group, including Ferdinand de Lesseps, was investigating a

Panama project, and the same year found Anthony de Gorgoza (an American citizen who had earlier conducted personal surveys of the isthmus), in Bogotá representing French interests. He gained a concession to survey and construct a canal. Two years later French Lieutenant Lucien Napoleon Bonaparte Wyse managed to obtain a revised concession from Colombia and to interest de Lesseps and the International Scientific Congress meeting in Paris in early 1879. In mid-1879 Wyse transferred his concession to de Lesseps for several million dollars, and de Lesseps organized the canal company that would become in the next two decades the focus of much international intrigue.

De Lesseps himself arrived in Panama in late December 1879, dispelling any lingering American doubt about the seriousness of the project. The survey began with great fanfare. "The Colombian and Panamanian Governments," the U.S. consul reported, "are disposed to grant any concession to Mr. de Lesseps that he may desire. The general line of public sentiment here is unfavorable and antagonistic to the United States." Strikingly, even the English language *Panama Star and Herald* editorially asked what business it was of the U.S. Congress where and whether a canal was built; the very idea of control over the canal by another government, it suggested, was "arrogance and outrage."[26]

The French engineer and entrepreneur rapidly set about the task of acquiring the capital and international support necessary to the project, a project that became the largest single foreign investment in Latin America in the century. In New York, in spite of a warm personal welcome afforded de Lesseps, he received no formal endorsement from the United States for a canal project. Undaunted, and riding on the crest of his reputation from the Suez Canal and the inflow of capital from anxious investors, de Lesseps managed to begin actual work on a canal in February 1881. After decades of diplomatic, political, and scientific controversy over alternate routes, the way now appeared clear for a practical engineering achievement.[27]

The U.S. reaction was immediate. When Colombia approved the contract with Lieutenant Wyse, the Republican administration of Rutherford B. Hayes reopened the legation in Bogotá after two years

of inactivity and appointed a new American minister, Ernest Dichman. Dichman was instructed to report on the French initiative. His
despatches simply confirmed what Washington officials believed, that
the de Lesseps project was ill-conceived but would result in the establishment in Panama of a veritable French colony if brought to completion.[28]

A former senator and Colombian minister to the United States,
Justo Arosemena, bore the full brunt of U.S. anger with the French
agreement. Arosemena had underestimated the U.S. opposition and
perhaps misled Bogotá as a result; he informed the Foreign Ministry
in October 1879 that he did not think that either the U.S. government or American public opinion would be hostile to someone as
distinguished as de Lesseps.[29]

American reaction was much stronger than he anticipated. The New
York *Tribune* editorialized that the United States could not permit
another nation to block the movement of its commerce and military
between the oceans. The *Herald*, more cautious in its reservations,
suggested that de Lesseps could do little without American capital.
Secretary of State William Evarts criticized the Colombian government
for failing to consult the United States before concluding an agreement with the French interests, although Arosemena assured him
there was no danger to the United States and that the contract guaranteed the neutrality of the canal and its accessibility for all nations.
The Colombian minister indicated that only from 1848 to 1850, when
the United States had seemed to threaten Colombian sovereignty on
the isthmus, had Colombia approached Britain and France for support. Arosemena was partially sympathetic to the U.S. position and
realistic about the need to avoid a major rift with the United States,
and he recommended to the foreign minister that the 1846 treaty
be renegotiated to include a reference endorsing the Monroe Doctrine. He was also sufficiently concerned about U.S. opposition to the
canal project to urge de Lesseps to move the canal company's head
office to New York in order to minimize the effects of U.S. antagonism. De Lesseps understood what was at risk; later in the year he
approached the U.S. secretary of the navy, Richard Thompson, to

serve on the American Committee of the company, but there is no indication that the Colombian government wavered at this stage in its commitment to completion of the canal by the French company.[30]

The Hayes administration adopted a hard, arrogant position on the canal question during 1880, making it clear that the U.S. objective was not only to ensure that there was international stability and neutrality for a canal zone but that the only acceptable canal would be U.S. built and controlled. Hayes was partly prodded by Congress. Congress in the course of 1879 had debated the applicability of the Monroe Doctrine to the situation in the isthmus, and in late December the House of Representatives created a special committee to conduct hearings on the canal. Those hearings, at which de Lesseps testified, produced no concrete result except to reinforce the Hayes administration's inclination to take a firm position. Thus, in March in a tightly worded message to Congress, Hayes stressed that American canal policy was unchanged; any canal constructed would be an American canal.[31] The House of Representatives Foreign Affairs Committee in late April adopted a resolution suggesting the abrogation of the Clayton-Bulwer Treaty of 1850, clearing the way for a strictly U.S. canal venture.

President Hayes provided a fuller statement in his annual message to Congress in December. That message underlined the premises of U.S. canal policy and perceptions about the relationship between private capital investment, whether American or foreign, and state action twenty years before the crisis of 1903. "The United States cannot," Hayes admonished, "consent to the surrender of this control to any European power or any combination of European powers. . . . The capital invested by corporations or citizens of other countries in such enterprise must, in a great degree, look for protection. . . . An interoceanic canal will be virtually part of the coastline of the United States."[32]

Consistent with Hayes's position, the U.S. minister in Bogotá, Ernest Dichman, issued a strong protest to the Colombian Foreign Ministry during the first presidential term of Rafael Nuñez; Dichman's protest stressed that U.S. commercial interests and sovereignty were at issue in the Panama canal question and that the United States "cannot consider itself excluded from any arrangements between other powers or individuals to which it is not a party." U.S. rights and obligations under the 1846 treaty were unambiguous—to defend the neutrality of any interoceanic communication across Panama—and the United States had every intention of fulfilling that obligation with "scrupulous fidelity." The Hayes administration missed the element of contradiction between the assertion of American responsibilities under the treaty, insistence that any canal be a U.S. canal, and the fact that it was *Colombian* sovereignty under the 1846 treaty that was to be defended. In fairness to Dichman, he informed an unreceptive Washington that the French government had maintained an entirely neutral position and that the French consul in Panama had been reprimanded by the French government during the de Lesseps visit for inappropriate remarks.[33]

The American consul in Panama, following the conclusion of the de Lesseps survey of the Panama route, sent different signals to Washington, warning that de Lesseps had exploited anti-American feeling in Colombia and Panama and that if the canal were constructed as planned it "would be only a matter of time before the entire Isthmus were under French influence and control and American supremacy would be a thing of the past." Not only American commerce but also the American form of government was being threatened by the completion of a major project "under any other auspices than our own." It was in response to such claims that the Colombian minister in Washington, Ricardo Becerra, felt compelled to write to the *New York Times* in late 1884, denying the contention that the "French element" had a preponderance in the affairs of Panama. Becerra stressed what was the reality of Colombian policy, that the canal was for the benefit of all nations and the exclusion of none.[34]

A lack of cooperation by Panama Railroad officials with both local American and Colombian officials exacerbated tensions. American consul John Wilson reported from Panama that the company seemed to think it its right to be exempt from all consular control as well as fees required by government. "The only privilege," Wilson lamented, "they willingly grant the Government is the right to protect their vessels and cargos." Sale of the railroad company to the Panama Canal Company the following year did not end tensions with local authority, however. While the debate over the canal development escalated, the United States made an ill-timed decision to send a naval expedition into the Bay of Chiriqui and Golfe Dulce in early 1880 to survey for coaling stations, evidently assuming that the old concessions granted to Ambrose Thompson were still valid. There was public criticism of the U.S. actions in Panama among Panamanian officials as well as the Panama *Star and Herald*. When the Colombian government protested the presence of American warships in Colombian territorial waters without consultation or consent (the U.S. consul in Panama was also not notified), Secretary Evarts defended the action on the grounds that the waters of friendly nations were always open to a friendly visit, but he noted in closing that the ships had nonetheless been ordered to a U.S. harbor. The matter was viewed with sufficient concern in Washington that Dichman was ordered from Bogotá to Panama to investigate, with little concrete result. In fact the following year, again without informing the local consuls, the Hayes administration requested a congressional appropriation of $200,000 to establish coaling stations on the isthmus.[35]

Clearly anxious about the series of events, the Nuñez administration increased its military presence on the isthmus, sending four additional battalions of federal troops under the command of General Trujillo in mid-July 1880. President Nuñez himself made an unprecedented trip to Panama in October. If various Colombian governments had consistently shown this degree of initiative to maintain a visible presence on the isthmus, the history of the region and the canal might have been different; but again by mid-decade revolution once again compromised Colombian sovereignty on the isthmus.[36]

The 1885 Revolution

The unsuccessful radical Liberal revolution against Rafael Nuñez and his moderate Liberal and Conservative supporters ended twenty years of progressive Liberal reform, led to the drafting of a radically new, highly centralized constitution, and ushered in more than forty years of Conservative rule. Reacting against the excessive degree of state autonomy under the 1863 constitution, the principal architects of the 1886 document, Miguel Antonio Caro and Rafael Nuñez, sought to eliminate the factionalism, that they believed resulted from extreme localism and personalism in politics. Caro and Nuñez thus sought to strengthen the central government and the executive branch and to move away from the liberal economic and social policies of the previous decades. Such changes had several implications for relations with the United States. Panama, for instance, lost its autonomous status. This alteration might have created the basis for enhanced central control over Panama; but Bogotá did not follow the constitutional modification with the economic and military policies that would have made constitutional ideal into political reality. The reduction in status of Panama, the absence of adequate central military presence to ensure stability and free transit on the railroad and the floundering Panama Canal Company under de Lesseps combined with continued economic uncertainty in the country as a whole to increase secessionist support in Panama. Second, trade with the United States was further hindered by the shift under Nuñez toward greater tariff protectionism and support for agricultural exports and local manufactures.

The 1884–85 crisis was precipitated by a number of factors: prosperity associated with the expansion of tobacco cultivation and exports had fallen severely in the course of the 1870s with a decline in exports; coffee production and exports, which were just beginning to gain significance in the Colombian economy, experienced problems because of price instability in the 1870s and 1880s, resulting in at least a 50 percent decline of exports between 1874 and the mid-1880s. U.S.-Colombian trade declined steadily in the 1870s and 1880s, from a value in excess of $16 million in 1875 to $7.9 million in 1885, and efforts during the Republican administration of Chester Arthur to negotiate a reciprocity agreement, while they achieved positive results in Mexico and the Dominican Republic, failed to reach fruition in the Colombian case. The Colombian minister in Washington had pressed for such an agreement in 1884, arguing that tobacco from Ambalema and Cauca as well as sugar produced in Bolívar would benefit from such an agreement, in return for which Colombia would likely need to increase its imports of U.S. petroleum products. One reason for the evident failure of Colombia to press Becerra's position, however, was disagreement over whether Colombia could gain. The consul in New York, Comacho Roldán, contended that Colombian tobacco could not compete with American produce and that American iron and steel products were already admitted largely free of duty.[37] The increasingly evident problems of the Panama Canal Company, which moved toward bankruptcy in the mid-1880s, served further to discredit the central government in many quarters.

There were also fundamental philosophical differences between radical Liberals and Conservatives in these years, based on attitudes toward religion and the role of the Church in Colombian society, toward economic development and progress, the role of the individual versus collective interests in a political community, and relations with the international community. Colombian Liberals had looked to Britain and the United States and to France for political models and institutions as well as ideas on economic development and progress, liberalization of trade, and the role of the state in economic development. They placed a higher emphasis on individualism than did the Conservatives, who looked to a more corporate and Hispanic model.[38] This ideological/political dichotomy not only shaped domestic Colombian history but also clearly had significant implications for relations with the United States, although there appears to have been little appreciation for this among American statesmen of the time.

The political and military crisis of 1884 and 1885 also brought another American intervention to assist Colombian forces in maintaining order on the isthmus. In the course of 1884, the Nuñez government fought an alliance of nine Colombian states, necessitating a concentration of government forces on the mainland. Although some Colombian scholars maintain that Colombian forces adequately controlled the isthmian situation, and the Colombian minister in Washington objected after the fact to the intervention, U.S. and Colombian officials in Panama at the time viewed the threat to stability in different terms; even the U.S. minister in Bogotá was cut off from communicating with Panama for a period of two months. The less expansionist Democratic administration of Grover Cleveland, however, was considerably less aggressive than his Republican predecessors had been toward the isthmus and more sensitive to ensuring that the United States adhered closely to the letter of the 1846 treaty guaranteeing neutrality on the isthmus.[39]

In January 1885, however, the Panama executive, General Ramón Santo Domingo Vila, informed U.S. officials that he could not guarantee order and safe passage on the isthmus and requested U.S. military assistance. U.S. Consul Anderson reported in February that Panama was the only Colombian state not in revolt at the time, its greater stability largely explained by continued employment opportunities with the canal company. Yet, he also cautioned: "we sleep on the brink of a volcano." The danger came not from Colombian revolutionists but from a vacuum of power which could give free rein to the "vile characters attracted here by the works of the Canal Co." Shortly after this report, Santo Domingo Vila left Panama to command government troops at Barranquilla, leaving Pablo Arosemena in command. The situation continued to deteriorate in March, when there were three contending armed factions in Panama: government forces; the former Liberal president of Panama; and Pedro Prestán, identified by officials as a Haitian who led a force of Radical Liberals.

Unable to contain these factions and the threat to American lives and property, the Nuñez government in April requested U.S. intervention, with the result that during the next month more than one thousand U.S. troops from six warships occupied Colón and Panama City, under Commander Bowman McCalla. They restored order, but not before Prestán had set fire to Colón. Order was maintained by U.S. and Colombian government forces while the latter were strengthened. The U.S. consul did fear an overreaction by Washington, however, with the result that Commander McCalla was instructed not to interfere with the landing of Colombian government forces.

Anderson's position was important, because it was clearly a reflection of the view that the 1846 treaty obliged the United States to defend Colombian sovereignty not to prevent national forces from establishing order over rebellious factions. That the administration concurred with Anderson was reflected in the reprimand McCalla received from the secretary of the navy in late April for allegedly interfering with local authorities. "Keep in mind," he was instructed, "that we desire no interference with functions of local government not necessary for protection of transit and wish your withdrawal at earliest moment stable government is re-established." Secretary of State Thomas Bayard followed this instruction with a cable to the consul indicating that "interference with landing or movements of Colombian forces wholly unauthorized. No infringement on their sovereignty intended by United States." By now prominent Panamanians seemed willing to countenance an American protectorate.[40]

The Cleveland administration was cautious and legalistic not only on application of the 1846 treaty to the isthmus but in its interpretation of international law concerning blockades. The administration rejected the Colombian government's declaration of a naval blockade and the closure to international commerce of the ports of Sabanilla, Santa Marta, and Barranquilla on grounds that a legitimate blockade required sufficient naval presence to enforce that blockade, noting as precedent the New Granadan blockade in 1861, which had been rejected by both the United States and Great Britain.[41]

In the course of the civil war, work on the canal made little progress. There was low morale among the largely Jamaican and costeño labor force; the death rate from accident and disease was high, and rumors, ultimately inaccurate, of American preference for a Nicaraguan route at one stage in early 1885 led more than one thousand men to leave their positions. Even before the U.S. occupation of Colón and Panama City in April, the U.S. consul was predicting that the canal company would be unlikely to endure another year. Although he exaggerated the problems, the American consul criticized the "incompetence, blundering, lack of foresight and of supervision in essential details, gross favoritism, reckless extravagance, and key bargains which appear to have the taint of corruption" on the part of canal company and Colombian government officials. To that he might have added that official American opposition to the project had undermined it in international diplomatic and financial circles. Regardless of causation, in 1888, after an expenditure of more than $400 million and with less than two-fifths of the canal completed, the first Panama Canal Company, Colombian aspirations to assume a more prominent role in hemisphere leadership, and the reputation of Ferdinand de Lesseps came crashing down with the economic bankruptcy of the company.[42]

Relations between the two nations continued to move toward crisis during the next decade, with the vortex of that controversy centered on the canal and Panama. As he left his tour of duty in Panama City after the 1885 civil war, American consul Thomas Adamson prophetically wrote from Philadelphia: "That narrow neck of land is to us what the Isthmus of Suez is to England. It is there that almost every question arises which is the subject of diplomatic controversy between our government and that of Colombia."[43] Adamson's position may have underestimated the significance of other aspects of Colombian-U.S. relations, but his vision of the central focus on Panama could not have been more accurate as events unfolded at the turn of the century.

3   Nations in Crisis:
The Loss of Panama, 1890–1921

> If according to President Roosevelt . . . the recognition of Panama
> was an act justified by the interests of civilization, that theory
> neglects the principles which govern the conduct of nations and
> thus undermines the fundamental bases of civilization. (Luis
> Carlos Rico, 1904)[1]

The government of national regeneration and the constitution of 1886 established an uneasy alliance between traditional Conservatives and moderate Liberals from the late 1880s until 1899, when
depression in the emerging coffee economy undercut the alliance
and exacerbated natural differences among the parties. From 1899 to
1902, the War of a Thousand Days between Liberal rebels and the
Conservative government convulsed the nation. The civil war further
undermined central power in Panama and contributed to the crisis on
the isthmus, which led to Panamanian secession, recognition by the
United States of an independent Panama, and U.S. construction of
the Panama Canal.

The 1890s

In the decade prior to the civil war there was comparative prosperity in Colombia and relative harmony in U.S.-Colombian relations.
Trade between the two nations improved after a decline of the 1870s
and 1880s, with the United States continuing to enjoy a favorable balance of trade with Colombia. Between 1886 and 1891, U.S. exports to
Colombia were valued at $26,208,767. Although total trade increased
from $6.1 million in 1890 to $6.3 million in 1895 and $7 million in

1900, the value and volume were below that of the 1870s. New U.S. investment appeared, most significantly in the banana export interests of Minor C. Keith. Keith was one of the founders of United Fruit in 1899. He gained control of the British-owned Colombia Land Company in the Santa Marta region, along with banana properties in the Bocas del Toro area held by the New Jersey–based Snyder interests. By 1900 United Fruit controlled more than thirteen thousand acres, a small percentage of its ultimate holdings in Colombia during the next several decades. Boston interests in the 1890s developed Cartagena's harbor facilities and constructed a portion of the Cartagena-Calamar railroad. The Pan American Investment Company held a concession to exploit coal and sources of petroleum on the Atlantic coast; the West India and Colombia Electric Company owned and operated the telephone systems in Barranquilla and Santa Marta. The Bogotá Street Railway Company held a monopoly on tram traffic in the capital. Beyond capital interests, the presence of two private American schools in Bogotá, the American School for Girls and its male counterpart, was indicative of the existence of an American community in the city.[2]

Colombia played an active and positive role at the first Washington-initiated Pan American meeting in 1889. The main objective of the conference was trade promotion and the encouragement of closer inter-American relations. The range of issues addressed underlined the economic objectives of the conference, including tariffs, weights and measures, the creation of an international monetary union, banking, the establishment of a commercial office for the American republics, the surveying and construction of an inter-American railroad, and health improvement. Colombian delegate Carlos Martínez Silva further proposed the establishment of what became the Pan American Union Library. The conference approved the establishment of an inter-American bank (which failed passage in the U.S. Congress), and a Commercial Bureau of the American Republics, which was rapidly approved in Washington and Bogotá.

The conference committee on railroads, in which the United States was prominently represented by Andrew Carnegie, in 1890 recommended completion of a feasibility survey for an inter-American railroad. Congress quickly endorsed these recommendations, and during the next several years survey and construction teams made progress on sections of line within each country. In the Colombian case progress was dismal until well into the twentieth century. Colombia was one of those countries which presented the most serious obstacles to the completion of an inter-American line, in part because of its key location at the entrance to the continent, but also because of the vast territory from its northern border to Ecuador. Nonetheless, Colombia was one of the few nations that made its first $4,000 (gold) payment to help finance the survey work in 1891, and by April of that year two survey teams, under the U.S. Department of War, left to work on the Colombian, Ecuadoran, and Peruvian routes. By January 1892 the survey team had reached Cali, working north from Ecuador, and by September was in Cartagena.

This was a beginning to the development of a desperately needed transportation network in Colombia, where access to the Caribbean was limited to the Cauca and Magdalena rivers and mountainous mule trails. Indeed, one of the bitter complaints made by more development-minded and market-oriented coffee interests in the 1890s was that this system was inadequate for their needs.[3] Unfortunately, construction was minimal before civil war brought political and economic catastrophe to the nation, but significantly, even during the more stable years in the 1890s, there was little American capital involved in the railroad development required by Colombian export-import interests.

Secretary of State James G. Blaine had hoped to use the 1889 conference to stimulate trade between the United States and its southern neighbors, but the protectionist orientation of the Regenerationists (and their Conservative allies who dominated politics after 1886) left little opportunity for trade liberalization. There was consequently commercial conflict between the two countries during the Harrison administration, in part because of the reciprocity provisions in the 1890 McKinley tariff. That provision was a trade weapon, providing not positive incentive for Colombia and other nations to encourage trade but rather the threat of commercial retaliation in the event that they did not grant reciprocity to U.S. goods. The Harrison administration in early 1892 threatened to end reciprocal trade, unless Colombia dropped "discriminatory" duties on American imports.

The Colombian reticence was natural; of Colombian exports, only sugar was competitive with U.S. producers; hence U.S. interests sacrificed little by admitting Colombian goods free of duty. The situation was entirely different for Colombian producers, who could not hope to compete with U.S. cotton, tobacco, sugar, or wheat. By the late 1880s U.S. products dominated almost 90 percent of the import market in Colombia for breadstuffs, meat, dairy products, sugar, tobacco, and vegetables, although Colombians naturally preferred Spanish and French wines. Most imported wood, iron, and steel products from the United States entered duty free. Colombia imported twice as much iron and steel from the United States as it did from France or Spain and 30 percent more than from Great Britain. All imports into Colón and Panama City, which had been free ports since the mid-nineteenth century, were duty free, and U.S. merchandise imported into the isthmus for consumption represented over 35 percent of all Colombian imports. Colombian duties were relatively minor; but Blaine firmly argued that Colombian tariffs were "a serious impediment to the enlargement of our trade relations."[4]

Efforts by former President Nuñez, President Carlos Holguín, and Foreign Minister Marco Fidel Suárez to placate the U.S. government were to no avail.[5] The retaliatory proclamation went into effect in March 1892, imposing duty on key Colombian exports. Restrictions continued until 1894, when the Cleveland administration implemented the Wilson-Gorman tariff. That tariff improved Colombia's position by restoring hides, coffee, and tea to the free list.[6] In the interim, however, the decree hurt Colombia; the Colombian minister in Washington reported a two-thirds decline in coffee sales since March 1892.

This tariff dispute underlined the vulnerability of a predominantly agricultural export-oriented economy, although Colombia had the advantage of a more varied economy, with agricultural diversification, significant gold exports, rich coal deposits, emeralds, tropical woods, and hides. The debate also indicated the strains within Colombian politics and the growing importance of coffee planters and export- ers and their links to the international commercial community. The civil war at the end of the decade resulted from the political frustra- tion of the Liberals as well as from conflict between those tied to the international sector and those more traditional, neo-feudal Colom- bian political groups associated with the National Conservatives, who were neither economically committed to the export market nor intel- lectually part of the more dynamic, capitalist Atlantic world. Like Americans of the South before 1860, they were temporarily able to slow down the march of economic change as the world and worldview they represented became increasingly anachronistic.

The Canal

Nothing in the history of Colombian-U.S. relations looms larger than the secession of Panama from Colombia in 1903. It was a period of high drama, tension, and conflict involving strong, colorful, and manipulative personalities: Theodore Roosevelt, John Hay, and New Panama Canal Company attorney William Nelson Cromwell on the American side; on the Colombian, the scholarly President José Manuel Marroquín, Colombian Minister Tomás Herrán, Manuel Amador Guerrero, the Panamanian doctor who headed the Panamanian revo- lutionary junta, and his compatriots on the junta, including Tomás and Ricardo Arias, Federico Boyd, José Augustín Arango, and C. C. Arosemena. Several of the Panamanian rebels were associated with the New Panama Canal Company or Panama Railroad; Amador was a company physician; Arango was a company attorney. They were assisted by other company officials, primarily superintendent James Shaler and freight agent James Beers. The wild card among the person- alities was Philip Bunau-Varilla, formerly chief engineer of the Panama Canal Company under Ferdinand DeLesseps and a vital force in the formation of the new company in 1893. Bunau-Varilla (depending on whose account one consults) was either the critical figure in financing the revolt in 1903 and negotiating the treaty with the United States or a pompous self-promoter, with William Nelson Cromwell of the U.S. law firm Sullivan and Cromwell the real power behind the revolt.

The events of 1903 were at the core of diplomacy between the two countries until the early 1920s, when there was at least the formal resolution of the dispute, but the political and cultural legacy of the Panama episode was of both greater duration and depth, shaping Colombian perceptions about the nature of the imperialist threat that it was believed the United States had come to pose to Colombian sovereignty and self-respect. As recently as the 1960s the distinguished Teatro Candelaria in Bogotá produced a play on the "taking" of the Canal Zone, in which Theodore Roosevelt was cast in the role of villain. *Semana*, a prominent weekly Bogotá magazine with international circulation, in 1989 featured an article on the events; thus the legend lives on.

The timing of the Panama crisis contributed to anxiety in Colombia and Latin America more generally, since it followed by only a few years the Spanish-American War, with the U.S. acquisition of Pacific and Caribbean territories, events that seemed to mark the arrival of the United States as a major actor on the world stage. There was a note of irony in the U.S. role in the "liberation" of Cuba from Spanish control, since that was a Colombian objective U.S. governments had opposed in the 1820s and 1830s; the final end to the Spanish imperial presence in the Caribbean consequently was bitter-sweet for Colombians. There was neither irony nor ambiguity about Colombian views on events in Panama; the loss of what was generally considered its richest province after a generation of extended civil war throughout the country seemed a particularly cruel blow to national pride as well as a sad reflection of the impotence of Colombian power in international relations in the early twentieth century.

The loss of Panama had symbolic importance, but its real significance was the exercise of power in the Caribbean basin—economic, military, and political power. At a time when U.S. policymakers in Congress and in the McKinley and Roosevelt White House were debating alternate routes for the construction of a canal and negotiating with the nations involved, Colombia had reached the nadir of its capacity to influence the course of its own international affairs. Isolated Bogotá politicians, a crippling civil war, the desire of a Panamanian elite to tie their future to the Polar Star, and the U.S. desire for strategic and commercial advantage ensured that Panama would be the Colombian Achilles' heel.

The War of a Thousand Days accelerated the loss of Bogotá's authority on the isthmus and made secession possible, regardless of the actual role played by the Roosevelt administration. By 1898 opposing political forces, led by Liberals and many historical Conservatives, those seeking tariff and paper money reforms and improved transportation, besieged the fragile Nationalist government of Manuel Antonio Sanclemente, in which the real power was held by José Manuel Marroquín. In October 1899 revolt began in the depressed province of Santander under the leadership of Rafael Uribe Uribe, a leading Liberal lawyer, landowner, and military figure. The Liberal party for the moment officially opposed civil war, and the Historical Conservative leadership remained aloof, while the Nationalists prepared for war and rank-and-file Conservatives rallied to the government side. Historian Charles Bergquist has thoroughly documented the factors that led to the party alignment during the conflict. Liberals and Conservatives, as contemporary Jorge Holguín suggested, split along political, social, and ethical lines. The Roman Catholic Church played a significant role in the split, encouraging mass Conservative support for government forces.[7]

The civil war rapidly spread through the country from Santander. It was the revolt on the isthmus and the power of antigovernment forces there that most significantly affected Colombian-U.S. relations. Panama stood to gain more than any other area of the nation from economic development and closer ties to the United States. So desperate was the Colombian government situation by late November 1901 that the governor of Panama notified the U.S. Consul in Panama that Colombian troops could not maintain order. He thus requested the aid of the USS *Iowa* to ensure that trains could operate and to prevent attacks on American investments, such as the Caribbean Manganese Company at Nombre de Dios.[8]

U.S. officials acted with a reasonable degree of restraint, though they did use military force. When Colombia requested aid in 1901, the American consul informed the Panamanian governor that the State Department was not disposed "to land troops unless necessary. Such action is of such serious character that it is to be hoped that it may be avoided." On the mainland, the American consul in Barranquilla, Irwin Shaw, delayed requesting a warship to protect Americans at Santa Marta and Barranquilla until there was major fighting. In a similar vein, Captain Thomas Perry, commander of the USS *Iowa*, stressed that the United States was obliged to intervene only "after the Colombian government has exhausted its means to maintain the transit and to prevent interference." Thus Perry occupied the rail line with his forces only after there was a resumption of heavy fighting that Colombian troops could not contain.[9]

By 1902, as government forces brought the revolt under control in other parts of the country, in Panama Liberal forces under Benjamin Herrera remained powerful. Herrera could not gain control of Panama City or Colón without risking U.S. intervention, however; with the surrender of insurrectionists on the mainland in late 1902, he saw little viable option but to negotiate a settlement with government representatives. The country's economy seemed in ruins by that time. There was a smallpox epidemic on the isthmus and high unemployment, and Colombian forces could not guarantee safe transit across Panama for international traffic. Symbolic of U.S. power in the area, the civil war combatants reached peace terms on board a U.S. warship, the USS *Wisconsin*.[10]

In 1903–after years of secessionist sentiment, agitation, and political intrigue in Panama, debate in Washington over the most appropriate location for an isthmian canal, and the inability of the Colombian central government to maintain military control in the region—local political elites simply seized power in Panama in a bloodless coup. Colombian forces sent to restore order in Colón and Panama City were outmaneuvered by Panamanian rebels, officials of the Panama Railroad Company, and canal company officials anxious to bring their project to a conclusion after so many years of frustration. The actions of the Theodore Roosevelt administration in the crisis of 1903 rightly earned Colombian wrath. U.S. encouragement of secessionist leaders, the almost immediate recognition of the rebel government as an independent republic, the immediate conclusion of a canal treaty with representatives of that government, and interference with Colombian military forces attempting to suppress insurrection made impossible Colombian retention of the isthmus.

During the War of a Thousand Days in Colombia, officials of the McKinley and then Roosevelt administrations pressed forward in their efforts to open the diplomatic channels for the construction of an isthmian canal. Crucial to that objective was renegotiating the 1850 Clayton-Bulwer Treaty with Britain. The treaty prohibited either nation from constructing a canal on its own or fortifying a canal. The first revision in 1900 by Sir Julian Pauncefote, then British ambassador to the United States, and John Hay removed the requirement that any canal constructed would have to be completed jointly by the two nations but did not alter the fortification provisions. U.S. congressional opposition (and New York Governor Theodore Roosevelt) believed this omission was a fatal flaw and pressed successfully for renegotiation. The second Hay-Pauncefote Treaty erased the previous century of British dominance and prepared the way for an American canal.

The U.S. Congress had for several decades muddled over the most appropriate route and method of acquiring a canal. John Hay stressed in early 1900 that a canal was more imperative than ever; the United States had to act. "Nothing," Hay wrote, "will finally prevent the building of the canal. As soon as Congress is convinced that the people of the country demand the construction of the canal it will be done."[11] In 1902, with Roosevelt president, the Walker Commission, which had initially supported construction of the canal through Nicaragua, reversed its conclusion after brilliant lobbying by William Nelson Cromwell, Bunau-Varilla, and their congressional supporters. Congress then approved an administration measure, the Spooner Act, authorizing the Panama route if satisfactory terms could be arranged with Colombia.

Bunau-Varilla pressed President Marroquín to accept reasonable terms in order to secure the Panama route, stressing that it was the long-term economic advantage that would prove most important to Colombian development rather than any short term financial gain. He emphasized that once the Nicaraguan canal was begun, the value of the Panamanian canal properties would plummet, since no European nation would risk alienating the United States in constructing a rival canal, even if it remained economically viable.

From the Colombian perspective the major objective was defense of its sovereignty in Panama. A difficult task in peacetime, it became almost impossible in the context of civil war. Bogotá seriously neglected canal negotiations during the civil war. The Colombian minister in Washington, Martínez Silva, impatiently cautioned Bogotá that the Nicaraguan lobby was very strong. Colombia risked losing a treaty and the canal in the process. "The moment has arrived," he chastised his superiors in Bogotá, "for Colombia to make a definite resolve." The Colombian minister thus pressed ahead on his own in an effort to salvage the situation, attempting to convince John Hay that the canal company's concession price was negotiable and that the Colombian government was "well disposed to facilitate the construction of the proposed interoceanic canal through its territory." [12]

By 1903 the Roosevelt administration had come to the conclusion that it might not be possible to reconcile Colombian and U.S. national interests or for Colombia to maintain tranquillity in the region. From 1901 through the secession crisis in 1903 Colombian officials, isolated in the capital, overestimated their capacity to reach terms with the United States as well as to control the course of events in Panama; but they did not underestimate the significance of the canal to Colombian development. Foreign Minister Antonio José Uribe in 1901 instructed Colombian diplomats to obtain an agreement by any means possible; Colombian leaders generally accepted the fact that the New Panama Canal Company was incapable of completing the project and only U.S. entrepreneurship and capital could salvage twenty years of frustration. There was also understanding of the alternatives. Martinez Silva wrote that the United States, with its "acquisitive, imperialistic tendencies," could acquire the canal by fomenting a secessionist and pro-U.S. annexationist movement in Panama. Rather than suffer the fate of Spain, he believed, it was necessary to turn American ambition to Colombian advantage. The real threat to Colombian sovereignty in Panama was not U.S. ambition, but Colombian weakness.[13]

José Vicente Concha, a major figure in Colombian politics during his generation, replaced Martinez Silva in early 1902. The latter urged his successor to accept the U.S. request to station troops in the canal territory, still a major impediment to agreement, but for Martínez Silva this was simply a recognition of the power reality. Clearly he resented U.S. attitudes: lack of respect for Colombian law, judicial procedures, or political process; lack of appreciation of the importance to Latin Americans of public honor. North Americans, he observed, found South Americans to be procrastinators, overly sensitive, inefficient, and liable to violate their own laws. Yet, he believed they were correct in their assessment. Still, he believed that Colombia had itself to blame for its dilemma. The nation badly needed to broaden its horizons, to welcome foreign capital and ideas, to come more directly into contact with outside "civilization," to reduce the level of intolerance and eliminate Colombia's "byzantine" internal feuding. The canal could bring Colombia into the twentieth century.[14]

The Marroquín administration shared his sense of urgency. Foreign Minister Miguel Abadía Méndez instructed Concha to place the highest importance on the canal negotiations. He failed, however, to understand U.S. policy and the significance of the Hay-Pauncefote Treaty when he attempted to have Britain, France, and other European powers guarantee the neutrality of the canal. Washington would not tolerate further involvement of European powers in the canal. A Colombian cabinet meeting also reaffirmed the position that the canal company could not transfer its concession without approval in Colombia. That was the context when the U.S. House of Representatives in June 1902 authorized President Roosevelt to attempt to negotiate for the rights and properties of the New Panama Canal Company, with the proviso that a satisfactory treaty with Colombia had to be concluded. The die were cast.[15]

Concha worked feverishly to repair Colombian credibility in Washington. He informed Hay that Colombia had no "lust of gain through the construction of the canal in its territory," and that pecuniary considerations would not delay an agreement. Colombia wanted the canal completed as much as did the United States; for Colombians the international waterway represented the "ideal of universal peace and progress." Concha wrote Roosevelt that the "consummation of such an event will be the fulfilment of the prophetic intuition of Columbus" and the "opening of a new highway to the heralds of peace and progress, among whom the American people deserve a place of honor."[16]

Negotiations finally bore fruit. In January of 1903 the Colombian chargé d'affaires in Washington, the experienced and able Tomás Herrán, concluded a treaty with John Hay providing the United States with the right to construct the canal in Colombian territory and to hold a lease on a six-mile-wide strip of territory as a canal zone for a period of one hundred years. In return, Colombia would receive an initial payment of $10 million, with annual payments of $250,000.[17]

The U.S. Senate approved the treaty in mid-March 1903, but it became mired in politics, economic difficulties, and national anxiety in Bogotá. When the Marroquín administration attempted to renegotiate the terms of the agreement, Roosevelt balked, personally giving vent to his frustration: Colombians were not demonstrating good faith in the negotiations; they were "contemptible little creatures" with whom it was more difficult to deal than it was to "nail currant jelly to the wall." Hay, equally frustrated, accused Colombians of graft and "folly."[18] Roosevelt respected power and efficiency, both of which he found wanting in Colombia. In what was interpreted locally as an act of national self-preservation, but which was seen in Washington as incomprehensible political arrogance, the Colombian Congress by unanimous vote in August rejected the Hay-Herrán Treaty, thus returning the initiative to the Roosevelt administration.[19]

In his subsequent account of the events in Bogotá, Bunau-Varilla was as scathing as was Roosevelt of the Colombian political process; he criticized President Marroquín for replacing the realistic Martínez Silva as minister to the United States. To Bunau-Varilla Bogotá politicians were cut off from the real world: "the Panama Canal issue was debated as astronomers would debate the nature of canals on Mars," he caustically remarked. He was especially critical of the role played by General Joaquín Vélez, the Conservative president of the Senate. Yet, Vélez did not stand alone in his opposition to the treaty, receiving support from *El Nuevo Tiempo* and Miguel Antonio Caro, former president and author of the 1886 constitution.[20]

There were foreign policy realists in Bogotá as well as in Washington. Foreign Minister Luis Carlos Rico, for instance, frustrated with the Conservative-dominated Colombian Senate, stressed the practical significance of the canal. In a losing cause, he argued that the commercial prosperity of both Colombia and the United States depended on completion of the canal. Rico stressed that the de Lesseps effort had clearly failed, leaving Colombia with no option but cooperation with the United States if the project were to be realized and cautioned that the Nicaragua route would be chosen if Colombia failed to reach agreement. Pablo Arosemena, a prominent Liberal, later wrote: "There are erudite men of great talent and vast learning in Bogotá," but they failed to comprehend the major world developments that had profoundly altered the international context. European powers "bowed in the presence of the American eagle." Colombia, divided, discredited, and financially weakened, was simply an obstacle in the path of the American people. "Destiny," he concluded, "decreed this separation."[21]

U.S. officials weighed their options in the aftermath of Colombian rejection of the Hay-Herrán Treaty. Philip Bunau-Varilla contended subsequently that Roosevelt and Hay believed the 1846 Colombian-American Treaty provided the solution to the impasse with Bogotá. If, as seemed likely, a further revolt against Colombian control were to occur in Panama, the United States was obliged to maintain open transit; if primary emphasis were placed on that provision rather than the defense of Colombian sovereignty, then a revolt might succeed, and the United States would be free to renegotiate a new treaty with an independent Panama.

The evidence strongly sustains Bunau-Varilla's interpretation. In a position paper prepared for Hay and Roosevelt by international law expert John Bassett Moore in August 1903, Moore went considerably beyond legal niceties in his analysis; he stressed that the Panama route was "the one that we should have," and that a private enterprise could not build the canal without the support of a major nation. "The United States," he observed, "now holds out to the world a certain prospect of a canal. May Colombia be permitted to stand in the way?" Moore traced the history of American involvement in maintaining peace on the isthmus, stressing that although the sovereignty of the states occupying the region had always to be respected, sovereignty also had its responsibilities. Moore also cited Hamilton Fish's remark in 1871 that an attack on Colombian sovereignty on the isthmus had on several occasions been averted by warnings from the United States. American forces had frequently acted to maintain or restore internal peace, normally at the request of the Colombian government. Previous U.S. governments had honored the maxim expressed by former Secretary of State William Seward: "The U.S. will take no interest in any question of internal revolution in the State of Panama or any other state of the United States of Colombia, but will maintain a perfect neutrality. The United States will nevertheless hold themselves ready to protect the transit trade across the Isthmus against invasion by either the domestic or foreign disturbances of the peace of the State of Panama." Moore concluded that existing treaty provisions required American protection of transit on the isthmus, which could mean American completion of the canal. "The United States in constructing the canal would own it, [and] the ownership and control would be in their nature perpetual." [22]

Roosevelt admired Barrett's logic. He wrote Hay in August 1903 that, although it might be best to do nothing at present, under the 1846 treaty the United States had the right to build the canal and that was what should be done. "I do not think that the Bogotá lot of Jackrabbits should be allowed permanently to bar one of the future highways of civilization." He further elaborated that by October they could either opt for the Nicaraguan route or "in some shape or way to interfere when it becomes necessary so as to secure the Panama route without further dealing with the foolish and homicidal corruptionists in Bogotá." Even the hyperbolic Bunau-Varilla did not claim that Roosevelt, during their meeting on 10 October, made any verbal commitments to intervene in Panama. Bunau-Varilla claimed that Roosevelt had shown no more than interest in what he anticipated would follow a revolt in Panama.[23]

The secessionist cause was bolstered by news of Hay's communication to Bunau-Varilla less than one week later that U.S. naval forces were steaming toward Panama. At the end of October Bunau-Varilla cabled Manuel Amador Guerrero, one of the secessionist supporters in Panama, that the USS *Nashville* would arrive within two days. Although likely not known beforehand by the secessionists, well before the actual secession Roosevelt ordered the Navy to hold warships ready within striking distance on both the Atlantic and Pacific coasts. The USS *Boston* was sent to San Juan del Sur, Nicaragua; the *Dixie* prepared to sail from League Island as soon as marines could be placed on board, and the *Atlanta* was ordered to proceed to Guantánamo in Cuba. Certainly the movement of the *Nashville* was known in Panama, and this news, combined with Bunau-Varilla's earlier assurances to Amador of funds for the revolutionary forces, would have raised the spirits of secessionists.[24]

When Colombian government reinforcements under General Tovar reached Colón on 3 November in an effort to suppress the Liberal revolt, the *Nashville* was already in place. The U.S. Navy did not interfere with the Colombian landing, but it subsequently prevented Colombian troops from crossing the isthmus by rail to liberate Colombian officers arrested in Panama City by the revolutionary junta. The American logic was clear. The U.S. consul in Colón estimated that the revolutionary junta in Panama City had the support of the "entire population," and that any Colombian effort to suppress the revolt would lead to widespread civil war and inevtiable disruption of isthmian traffic. Finally, when Colombian forces threatened to kill Americans living in Colón unless Tovar were released, the *Nashville*'s captain landed troops to maintain order and assisted junta forces in returning Colombian troops to Cartagena.These actions were not the isolated decision of a U.S. military commander but Roosevelt administration policy.

Colombian forces held Roosevelt and the United States responsible for the secession; Daniel Ortíz, the Colombian general at Barranquilla, on 23 November issued a circular to soldiers in Panama in which he stressed the challenge the "Colossus of the North" posed to Colombian liberty. "It is preferable," he indicated, "to see the Colombian race completely extinguished than to submit ourselves to the infamous policy of President Roosevelt. It is well enough proved that the Chief of the American Union does not know how to interpret the boasted Monroe Doctrine, and that he does not comply, either in the spirit or the letter, with international treaties."[25]

Local U.S. officials revealed a cavalier attitude toward Panamanian opinion. Consul Oscar Malmros informed Washington that all the municipalities along the railroad line had declared their adherence to the Republic of Panama. The failure to hear from other towns was simply the result of "poor communications." In a telling observation, he noted: "The population of these towns (those having publicly declared support) is not very numerous, but considering the political sentiments and local patriotism of a majority of the intelligent population of the towns and other settlements not yet heard from, and in view of the influence the U.S. cannot fail to exercise upon the inhabitants, it is highly probable that those towns would also support the Republic of Panama." Malmros indicated that he believed he was thus justified in entering into official relations with the new republic, and the United States extended recognition.[26]

Hay immediately entered into negotiations with Bunau-Varilla on a new canal treaty. Both U.S. officials and Bunau-Varilla were anxious to expedite the process, Bunau-Varilla because he feared for his own position with the revolutionary junta in Panama and anticipated that Colombian General Rafael Reyes would shortly arrive in Washington in an effort to negotiate a settlement. The Roosevelt administration accepted Bunau-Varilla's credentials as Panamanian minister and hurriedly prepared a draft treaty for his consideration. Hay's draft was in essence the rejected Hay-Herrán agreement. The United States pledged to pay Panama the amount originally offered to Colombia for the canal rights, guaranteed Panamanian sovereignty and the neutrality of the Canal Zone, but insisted on U.S. jurisdiction within the zone. Bunau-Varilla proceeded to sign the treaty prior to the arrival of the other Panamanian officials, with the result that when two other Panamanian representatives reached Washington the next day, they were presented with a fait accompli. The Roosevelt administration ignored Panamanian objections and sent the Bunau-Varilla Treaty forward, gaining U.S. Senate approval on 23 February 1904.[27]

Throughout the dispute, Colombia was a frustrated spectator. Its commissioners met with Panamanian delegates in late November, but the Panamanians, bargaining from strength, insisted that independence was irrevocable. When Rafael Reyes finally reached Washington, Hay extended the courtesy of a brief, cool interview. Roosevelt advised the Colombians to follow the U.S. lead and recognize the independence of Panama. Although Reyes won some support in Washington for the Colombian cause, U.S. public opinion appears to have supported the administration's position. Colombian writer-diplomat Ismael Arciniegas concluded: "The Americans are against us. What can we do against the American navy?"[28] Colombian legal efforts in France also realized no success, and Cromwell by early 1904 made preparations for the work of the canal commission. The commander of the U.S. Caribbean squadron at Colón further reported that a planned Colombian invasion had "collapsed."[29]

The Quest for a Negotiated Settlement

The diplomatic efforts to negotiate a settlement occupied the remainder of the Roosevelt administration, that of his successor William Howard Taft, the Woodrow Wilson administration, and reached a conclusion only in 1922. Four American presidents, eight secretaries of state, as well as several Colombian presidents and foreign ministers at some stage of their administrations sought to resolve the dispute. American diplomats in Bogotá reported that little progress in such areas as foreign investment, trade, and cultural relations could be expected until the issue was settled. As long as Roosevelt lived, however, the majority of his party was not prepared to countenance any agreement that implied complicity in the secession of Panama. Only the Democrats remained committed to finding a solution, and there was thus optimism in Colombia when Woodrow Wilson took office in 1913.

During the twenty years that separated the secession from the Thomson-Urrutia Treaty there was considerable frustration, anger, and obstinance on both sides, although on a more personal level both Colombian and American diplomats, businessmen, and academics made considerable progress in improving the relations of the two nations. Elihu Root paid a courtesy visit to Cartagena in 1906 and was received with warm hospitality; the American minister to Bogotá from 1905 to 1907, John Barrett, was a dedicated Latin Americanist who went on to become director general of the Pan American Union. Barrett's genuine love of Latin America, of travel, and his human skills made him a highly regarded figure in Colombia and did much to counteract some of the damage caused by the events in Panama. Barrett's accounts of his travels, his observations on such themes as popular culture, economic conditions, and architecture, represent an important legacy of his comparatively brief assignment in Colombia. He was also able to lay the foundations for an initial though unsuccessful effort to negotiate a treaty resolving the dispute.[30]

In subsequent years the State Department consistently refused to submit the Panama issue to international arbitration, preferring to negotiate a trilateral agreement with Colombia and Panama to settle boundary difficulties and gain Colombian recognition of Panamanian independence. An early Colombian draft of a possible agreement with Panama underscored the intensity of Colombian views and determination to set the record straight on the events of 1903; it specified that secession was not the result of Colombian tyranny or mismanagement, that there was no concerted action by the majority of the Panamanian population in favor of secession, that the revolt was the work of the Colombian garrison in Panama City; that the Colombian government had been prevented from attacking the rebel forces by the action of U.S. agents, and that the real motivation for the secession was the expected benefits to be gained from the seizure of the railroad and canal.[31]

President Reyes himself sought a peaceful settlement and resisted the more jingoistic elements in his own government and party. A well-educated member of the elite, Reyes was an internationalist in outlook and training, and that background shaped his more realistic approach to the United States. He attempted to impress on his contemporaries the necessity of recognizing the reality of U.S. power: "As a navigator has to study the maritime charts to determine a true position," he cautioned Congress, "so we must study to understand the exact character, position and power of the American nation." Reyes attributed the serious errors made by Colombia at the time of the Hay-Herrán Treaty to the Colombian failure to understand the United States, its ideas, motives, and the ideosyncracies of its government and people. He also cautioned against provoking the United States. Colombia had to accept U.S. hegemony and work within its sphere of influence.[32]

Obstacles aside, the desire for settlement and a gradual change of actors paved the way for movement on the diplomatic front. Root and Colombian foreign minister General Alfredo Vásquez Cobo signed a memo of agreement at Cartagena in 1906 in an effort to initiate basic negotiations. Root and Colombian minister Enrique Cortes reached agreement in 1908 on a potential treaty. Although this treaty was ultimately rejected by the Colombian Congress as inadequate compensation for the loss of Panama, the basic outlines of the accord formed the basis for the Thompson-Urrutia Treaty that finally resolved the matter in the early 1920s. The Root-Cortes Treaty provided for the payment of a modest indemnity to Colombia of $2.5 million in compensation for material losses, including the loss of Panama Railroad Company revenues, and the recognition of a Colombian-Panamanian border that from the Colombian perspective represented a further loss of territory. The treaty, though a failure, indicated the desire of both administrations to normalize relations.

Colombian domestic politics again led to the failure of the treaty. The Reyes administration in February 1909 submitted the Root-Cortes Treaty and the Panama-Colombia Treaty to Congress for approval. *El Nuevo Tiempo* had already criticized the terms, in what American chargé Paxton Stibben described indelicately as "a characteristic appeal to the blind pride of these people."[33] The visitors gallery was crowded for the first day of debate in open session; the foreign diplomatic corps in Bogotá watched in anticipation as the Colombian congress passed the treaties through first reading and referred them for study to a special committee. The U.S. Senate had given its consent to the agreements. In Bogotá, delay followed delay. The opposition in Colombia mounted, pushing the Colombian government to request that new treaties be negotiated, a request that was refused.[34] So strong were opposition sentiments in Colombia that in early 1910 as Enrigue Cortes returned to Colombia, the former minister to the United States and his wife were confronted by a hostile mob outside their hotel in Barranquilla. Government troops escorted them to a train for Puerto Colombia, from which they sailed for France.

Anti-American feelings ran high in this period. There were frequent attacks on Protestants in Colombia, whether American or Colombian. In 1910 a mob attacked and stoned the American school in Bogotá and the U.S. legation. The American minister's son and the clerk of the legation were attacked on the street in Bogotá and had to be rescued by the police. In 1909, during antigovernment military agitation, there was vigorous dissent to a courtesy visit by the USS *Tacoma* to Barranquilla, and officers cautiously canceled shore leave.[35]

The Taft Years

The passing of the presidential mantel from Theodore Roosevelt to his former secretary of war, William Howard Taft, marked no significant transition in foreign policy on issues relating to Colombia. Taft was more cautious, less belligerent, but much of the Roosevelt foreign policy establishment remained intact and committed to defend the course of events in Panama.

Acrimonious debate over Panama exacerbated the problems of other U.S. interests in Colombia, but they also masked progress in other areas of the bilateral relationship. Trade, for instance, expanded. The U.S. share of Colombian imports arriving at Barranquilla from 1901 to 1905 was 34.5 percent, well ahead of Britain's 27.5 percent and Germany's 18.9 percent.[36] One area of U.S. investment, however, became a target of attack as a symbol of the U.S. presence—that was the Bogotá City Street Railway Company, a New York incorporated company, which had provided horse drawn trams for Bogotá since its original concession in 1882. The company was the largest single U.S.-based investment in the country before the war, with annual profits in excess of $60,000. By 1910 the company was constructing a hydroelectric generating plant to supply the lines.[37]

In March of 1910 tensions between an anti-American public and the company boiled over into violence and a boycott of the trams by Bogotá citizens. After prolonged negotiations the company agreed to sell its operations to municipal authorities, but the level of acrimony aroused during the incident reflected a deep underlying anti-Americanism in Colombian popular culture.[38] There was considerable press and public comment. *El Nuevo Tiempo,* for instance, used the occasion to raise the issue of the Monroe Doctrine, contending that "Yankees" pretended to be "lords and masters" of the hemisphere and that the company manager's "brutal" conduct was typical of his "race." Other comments stressed instead the problems of Colombian employees of the company. One otherwise pro-American public letter from Emilio Ruiz Barreto (it began by praising the virtues of George Washington and Benjamin Franklin) that was published as a pamphlet and as an open letter to the U.S. Minister, contended that the company's employees were poorly paid and were recruited from among the "coarsest" elements in Bogotá society, thus discouraging Bogotanos of more refinement from using the trams at all.[39]

U.S. minister Elliott Northcott was not surprised by these developments. With candor but lack of empathy, he observed: "It must be remembered that the very foundation of the Colombian character is hatred for the United States" because of the Panama affair, a basic resentment of the "success and progress" of the United States, and a perception that Americans were an "alien race." When Colombians used the term "race," they appear to have been speaking in terms of nationality rather than the genetic-racial typology current in the early twentieth century. Nonetheless, this distinction did not reduce the vehemence of the antagonism to the United States. So strong was anti-Americanism at the time, Northcott concluded, that any show of U.S. naval force to intimidate Colombia would result in the "massacre" of Americans in Bogotá.[40]

The Panama Debates Continue

American minister James T. DuBois, reaching Bogotá in 1911, rapidly gained Colombian respect for his forthright and positive approach. DuBois became a Colombia booster, stressing its rich natural resources and potential for economic development and trade. He noted that Colombia possessed important strategic location on both oceans and adjacent to the future Panama Canal; he also argued that the Hay-Herrán Treaty had been rejected in 1903 by an unrepresentative Colombian Congress. This interpretation enabled him to see Colombia as a potential ally of the United States and worthy recipient of investment. DuBois also developed a close personal affection for President Reyes; he spent time with him on his hacienda, swimming and horseback riding, and praised him to Washington as "broad, liberal and fearless," giving Colombia the first real constitutional government after decades of political strife. Washington gently reminded him that he was to advance the American point of view.

DuBois was nonetheless highly regarded in Washington, with the result that the terms of a treaty that he outlined to the department and President Taft gained considerable support. DuBois supported the Colombian claim to substantial indemnity; he urged the inclusion of preferential rights for Colombia in the use of a canal, except in the event of a Colombian war with Panama, but he also recommended that Colombia should renounce all claims in connection with the canal, except for the claim to fifty thousand shares of the capital stock in the New Panama Canal Company. Taft indicated to Secretary of State Philander Knox in 1912 that although the indemnity of more than $16 million appeared high: "I believe that the advantage of settling the questions is so great that I would not hesitate to recommend such a treaty to the Senate for its ratification."[41] Before World War I heightened security considerations and prior to the development of Colombian oil, Taft was unlikely driven primarily by narrow economic considerations, but he did want improved trade, investment, and national security.

Tensions remained. In 1911 Theodore Roosevelt's *Outlook* magazine article, "How the United States Acquired the Right to Dig the Panama Canal," was translated and published in a number of Bogotá newspapers. Combined with Roosevelt's alleged remarks to a Berkeley audience that he had "taken" the canal, the article created a potentially explosive situation. Colombian Foreign Minister Enrique Olaya Herrera, however, anxious to avoid further tension, was able to have some critical U.S. press comments published in Bogotá, creating the impression that Roosevelt's views were not widely shared. There were no public demonstrations in Bogotá and little hostile comment.[42]

Even the well-intentioned Taft failed to gain a Panama settlement during his term. Indeed, there were new strains on relations during 1912, in part because the State Department was determined that the Root-Cortes agreement of 1909 should be ratified by Colombia as a basic condition of negotiation. For Colombia that would have required acceptance of the U.S. interpretation of events in 1903. The State Department firmly held to the view, which it defended before the U.S. Congress, that the main question was whether Panama had the right to secede in 1903. Root had advanced that position in early 1906 to the Colombian foreign minister: "We assert that the ancient state of Panama, independent in its origin and by nature and history a separate political community, was subjugated by force." This was, of course, a subject of constitutional debate in Colombia; the U.S. position and intervention was analogous to Colombia siding with the constitutional arguments of the Confederacy in 1860 and 1861, recognizing it as independent and preventing U.S. troops from reinforcing Fort Sumter.

Du Bois's efforts to promote agreement in Bogotá were to no avail. Frustrated with the hostile Colombian public reaction, DuBois wrote to Ismael Arciniegas, director of *El Nuevo Tiempo,* shortly before his departure from Bogotá, stressing that his proposals had been informal, "honorable," and with "friendly" intent. Failure still stalked an agreement, in part because Colombians anticipated better terms from a Democratic administration. Both sides clearly sought a reconciliation at this stage to improve trade and investment, but neither side was willing to make major concessions of national interest or pride.[43]

The Democrats Seek Reconciliation

Colombians were optimistic with Woodrow Wilson's election in late 1912. The "party of Roosevelt" was out of the White House, the Democrats further enjoyed a substantial majority in Congress, and Colombians anticipated a favorable settlement of the Panama question. Wilson added to his esteem in Latin America in his selection of the outspoken anti-imperialist William Jennings Bryan as secretary of state. *El Republicano,* for instance, referred to Bryan as a "ray of hope." The President gained further praise for his late 1913 address to the Southern Commercial Congress in Mobile, Alabama, when he pledged adherence to principle and morality and constitutional liberty rather than expediency in foreign policy, claiming that the United States would never again seek by conquest "one additional foot of territory."[44]

Colombian domestic politics nonetheless remained unstable and the atmosphere unfavorable to a settlement. In late 1912 the Senate elected as president an ultraconservative and leader of the historical wing of the party, José Vicente Concha. The conservative General Jorge Holguín was elected president of the House of Representatives, and all other officers selected were Conservatives. The Medellín-born President Carlos E. Restrepo (1910–14) feared he could expect no support from the small Liberal bloc led by General Uribe Uribe, leaving the president and his Republicans isolated and weak. In 1914 Concha was selected as the presidential candidate of one wing of the Conservative party and was swept into power with Liberal as well as Conservative support. Concha was considered brilliant but erratic. More importantly he was considered favorably disposed to settlement with the United States.[45]

The Wilson administration, though preoccupied by Europe and Mexico, pressed forward with efforts to improve relations with Colombia. Wilson appointed to Colombia Thaddeus Thomson, a noncareer Texas Democrat and friend of Postmaster General Albert Burleson and Wilson adviser Colonel Edward M. House.[46] Thomson served until June 1916, the longest term of any minister since L. F. McKinney in the mid-1890s. He devoted much of his tour of duty to negotiating a new treaty.

Colombian officials promptly approached the Wilson administration; to pave the way to agreement the Colombian government dropped its former insistence on arbitration.[47] Yet, as Colombian Foreign Minister Francisco José Urrutia stressed, the basic issue for Colombia was the belief that the United States had violated the 1846 treaty. If the U.S. government encountered political obstacles to a settlement, observed Urrutia, Colombians also had strong feelings about the circumstances surrounding the secession of Panama.[48]

Thomson received assurances that president-elect Concha would support the Restrepo administration's effort to resolve the dispute before he took office the next August, and there was support from such influential politicians such as Marco Fidel Suárez. Although Suárez remained critical of the U.S. role in Panama in 1903, he preferred direct negotiations to arbitration, and argued, in terms indicative of his own values, that any indemnity received should be used to improve Colombian primary education; establish high quality normal schools, schools of agriculture, mining, and natural sciences; as well as improve transportation and harbors. For a man who had been born in poverty and illegitimacy, these were understandable goals.[49]

Optimism was premature, and a year elapsed before an agreement was signed and several more before it was approved. Thomson anticipated continued difficulties because of the sensitivity of the question, the "quixotic nature of the people," and the tendency of politicians to make capital from the issue. The American Consul in Cartagena indicated that public opinion in Colombia could be divided into distinct groups: the business community and government officials, who were very favorably disposed to a settlement; the press, which was well disposed toward the United States but made violent attacks on Theodore Roosevelt; and the general public, which shared the press view and was strongly anti-American. On 7 December students demonstrated in Cartagena, in a show of solidarity with Chilean students who had demonstrated against Roosevelt. Several prominent businessmen also gave speeches. The rally's poster was printed in the three colors of the Colombian flag, with black representing Roosevelt's "crime."

Thomson contended that any successful agreement would have to contain an indemnity, an expression of regret over the 1903 events in Panama, preferential treatment of Colombian trade through the canal, and clarification of the Colombian-Panamanian border.[50] Bryan sent Thomson's early despatches to the president's attention, with the notation: "The enclosed is very significant." He replied to Thomson, however, that the department required more precise information on the preferential trading rights; the department also insisted that Panama be consulted on the boundary dispute.[51]

Bryan worked closely with Wilson on the wording of a new agreement, in particular the expression of regret. Bryan suggested a preamble to the agreement that included a statement regretting "that anything should have occurred to mar in any way whatsoever the close and traditional friendship which so long existed." Wilson ultimately approved a treaty in principle and defended the administration's insistence on including an expression of regret. Yet, important opposition came even from among his own supporters; George Record, for instance, informed Wilson aid Joseph Tumulty and Wilson in May 1914 that he saw "practically unanimous opposition" on the street to the Colombian treaty. Record thought that most people would see the agreement as Bryan's personal attack on Theodore Roosevelt and that the William Randolph Hearst and Roosevelt supporters in the Republican party would exploit the issue.[52]

Final agreement remained elusive. The main obstacles were the amount of the indemnity, now tentatively fixed at $25 million, and the Panama border. Colombia requested an indemnity of $50 million and concession in the use of the canal when it opened in 1914. Bryan informed Thomson with some exasperation in March 1914 that it was impossible to go beyond $25 million, but that "rather than close negotiations we are willing to take up and consider anything further that they may have to offer on the subject."[53]

Colombian sentiment became more favorably disposed toward a settlement in the course of the spring of 1914, in part because of the desperate need for funds to acquire weapons to deal with a border war scare with Peru. On 6 April the Treaty of Bogotá was signed in the Colombian Foreign Ministry. Announcement that evening in the press met a mixed reception, with Liberal *El Tiempo* leading the critics.[54]

In spite of a challenge to the constitutionality of the treaty in the Colombian Supreme Court and the opposition of eight outspoken Conservative senators, Colombia quickly approved the agreement with overwhelming majorities in both houses of Congress on 8 June. Attention now shifted to the United States. Former President Reyes wrote Wilson optimistically from the Hotel Majestic in Paris, congratulating him on the success of the negotiations and for his "sound and just political opinions."[55] His optimism was premature. Theodore Roosevelt referred to the treaty as a "crime against the United States," thus fanning the flames of partisan loyalty.[56] With the war in Europe a more pressing issue, the Wilson administration allowed the treaty issue to fade from public attention, although with great international fanfare the canal opened in mid-August 1914. A century-long ambition had been realized, but at high cost to hemispheric relations.

For the next several years the treaty languished in the U.S. Senate, while Colombian politicians and newspaper editors beat their breasts against American inaction. The Wilson administration realized that passage of the treaty would be well received throughout Latin America, but domestic politics and more pressing international problems pushed the Colombian treaty temporarily aside. Wilson and his emissaries made occasional genuflections to assuage Colombian sensitivities. The president himself stressed that his "personal interest in that treaty has been of the deepest and most sincere sort" and that the agreement "constitutes a just and honorable understanding." Yet, there matters remained for the moment.[57]

In January 1916, Foreign Minister Marco Fidel Suárez warned that U.S. failure to ratify the treaty "prejudiced" commercial interests and "the respect of the other Latin American peoples to whom the ruin of the rights of a sister-nation cannot be a matter of indifference." Even so, Colombian press statements at this stage remained moderate, with the exception of what was considered the "yellow press," such as *Gil Blas*, which used the issue in an effort to embarrass the government.[58]

The War Years

With war in Europe, Colombia attempted to exploit U.S. concerns about security of the hemisphere to advance the treaty's fortunes. *El Diario Nacional*, for instance, proposed closer relations with Japan as a way to counterbalance U.S. power. *La Tribuna* and *Unidad*, both of which were considered pro-German (Thomson claimed both were in the pay of the German legation, and that *El Espectador* had also received funds), were outspoken in their criticism of the U.S. inaction. *El Tiempo*, on the other hand, which was just beginning to emerge as a major journal, warned of the dangers to Colombia of German expansionist ideology. Treaty opponents in the United States also attempted to exploit alleged connections between Colombia and Germany to undermine any support for ratification. The New York *American*, for instance, contended that Colombia was in alliance with Germany and would assist in attacking the canal in the event the United States entered the war. Given the volatility of the war issue in the United States, such rumors created an unfavorable atmosphere for the treaty. Thomson warned that its rejection by the United States would seriously jeopardize American interests and make Colombia more likely to be pro-German in its orientation. Suárez cautioned Thomson that the Colombian government could not long restrain public opposition.[59]

Wilson recognized the dilemma but found his hands tied and Secretary of State Robert Lansing not enthusiastic on the treaty. Wilson nonetheless urged Senator William Stone in February 1917 to push for ratification: "The main argument for the treaty," he insisted, "is that in it we seek to do justice to Colombia and to settle a long-standing controversy which has sadly interfered with the cordial relations between the two republics." More importantly, he added, "we need now and it is possible shall need very much more in the immediate future all the friends we can attach to us in Central America, where so many of our most critical interests center." Stone replied that he shared his concerns and would "test the Republican waters." Taft's minister to Colombia, James T. DuBois, lent unexpected support with a privately published pamphlet in 1917 endorsing the Colombian position. DuBois forecast that "the time is not distant when Latin America will have a hundred million of people, inspired by new conditions of national and commercial life. Those now living feel that the Panama incident is the only real injustice committed by the United States against the Latin American people."[60]

Lansing and department officials redrafted the treaty, when it was evident that the Senate would not pass the current version. Lansing wished to eliminate any expression of the "sincere regret" of the United States that "anything should have occurred to interrupt or to mar" the cordial relations between the two countries. Lansing's new draft specified that rights and privileges granted to Colombia in the use of the canal would not apply in the event of war between the United States and Colombia or Colombia and Panama; and that the $25 million indemnity would be made in five instalments over four years. Colombia would lease two small islands to the United States for a period of one hundred years for defense of the canal, and grant the right to construct another interoceanic canal through Colombian territory, possibly the Atrato route.[61]

Roosevelt himself lobbied vehemently against the treaty, and under fire from such prominent quarters, the treaty languished in the Senate.[62] U.S. entry into the world war made the Wilson administration more determined to ensure that Colombia assumed a pro-Allied position; but Colombia was not a sufficiently important military power to require Senators to put aside party and ideological differences to pass the treaty. On the Colombian side, the war, changing trade and investment patterns and a massive earthquake in Bogotá in September 1917 occasioned economic dislocation and a sense of increasing dependency on the United States. Criticism of the United States and of U.S. Senate inaction continued, but the passage of time, the German submarine campaign, and the possibilities of economic development improved Colombian patience. Wilson's open support for the treaty and his popularity in Colombia contributed to the Colombian willingness to be tolerant. *El Espectador* observed 11 December that Wilson recognized the need to give Colombia justice; *El Nuevo Tiempo* carried an article 17 November that was very favorable to Wilson; but, within elite Colombian diplomatic circles, there was criticism. The powerful and recently established Advisory Commission to the Foreign Ministry determined in late 1917 that Colombia had to maintain pressure on Washington.[63]

Colombia's strategic position near the canal, its deep water ports on both Caribbean and Pacific oceans, and its raw materials, especially platinum, made it important for the United States to counteract the influence of the Central Powers. Though the still-festering memory of the loss of Panama weakened support for the United States, the basic political and ideological orientation of the Restrepo, Concha, and Suárez administrations was sympathetic to the Allied nations. German businessmen were also prominent in Colombia, however, with the result that American and British blacklists of such firms were ill-received. The main U.S. concern was to prevent Germany from using

Colombian coasts as U-boat bases or for wireless operations. This was not idle fear. Prior to the war there had been considerable German activity on the Caribbean coast; in 1912, the German minister had spent several months surveying harbor facilities in the Gulf of Urabá area. The Hamburg-Colombia Banana Company also had extensive landholdings in the region; Germans held concessions to coal deposits in the area, and the managing director of the Hamburg-American shipping interests was a major shareholder in the company holding the concession. The fact that the concessions granted the right to develop harbor, telegraph, and railroad facilities gave reasonable cause for concern in Washington.[64]

In economic terms the war marked the clear dominance of the United States in trade with Colombia. By 1919 Colombia imported 72.4 percent of its commodities from the United States. American investment also increased. It was during the war that U.S.-based petroleum companies first entered the country. Henry Doherty in 1917 acquired title to a concession held by Virgilio Barco near the Venezuelan border. In 1918 the American Mercantile Bank of Colombia opened in Bogotá, with the approval of commercial groups concerned about the high lending rates of Colombian banks; and in the same year the Colombian Society of Agriculturalists sent representatives to the United States to obtain U.S. participation in Colombian land development.[65]

Prominent Colombians, Liberal as well as Conservative, appear to have shared the broader war aims of the Wilson administration. Liberal *El Tiempo* editorialized in early 1918 that Colombian foreign policy had to be based on realism. As people of the Americas, Colombians were part of the American political system, and the main objective of policy should be to attempt to consolidate their position within that system. One prominent Colombian, Esteban Jaramillo, suggested that in such a conflict there could be no real neutrals; he presented the conflict in Wilsonian terms as one between autocracy and democracy, between liberty and the spirit of conquest. The United States had treated Colombia relatively well commercially during the war by not curtailing shipping to Colombia and not controlling the price of coffee. The main damage to the Colombian economy from the war was the loss of European markets for Colombian goods, especially coffee, and the decline in imports because of scarcity and high prices, with the resulting loss of Colombian customs revenues.[66]

The newspaper *Gil Blas* editorialized 5 March 1918 that neither Colombia's moral nor material condition in the fourth year of war made indifference tolerable. By then sixteen Latin American nations had broken relations with Germany and four had declared war; with Germany evoking images of militarism and the "superiority of the Krupp factories over the palaces of the Hague," the paper queried, "can a western nation shut its eyes with impunity to the reality and enclose itself in selfish isolation?"

In retrospect, the security threat in Colombia was limited, but German propaganda efforts in Colombia, the U-boat campaign in the Atlantic, and the considerable German economic presence suggested a significant danger in time of war. Germans were among the dominant merchants in the coastal areas; they had banking and shipping interests in the country; some Colombian army officers were German trained, and there had been discussions of concluding an agreement with Germany to send a formal military mission to Colombia. U.S. officials were sufficiently anxious and cautious to send Colombian reports to Berlin for the attention of U.S. ambassador John Leishman, who indicated that the German government was doing everything possible to cultivate its relations with Latin American countries. Most alarming was the completion of a wireless station at Cartagena in the fall of 1913 by the Telefunken company, using German personnel.[67]

Under U.S. pressure, the Colombian government closed the Cartagena wireless station and another on San Andres in 1915, while an American station at Santa Marta remained in full operation, with the sole restriction imposed by the Colombian government that it could not employ citizens of nations at war. Suárez personally preferred that all radio stations be owned by nationals of the hemisphere, but he had no inclination to cancel the German contract in Cartagena. The U.S. minister found Suárez little interested during 1915 in the U.S. concern about the German security threat, although he remained cooperative, and, with the assistance of British Marconi interests, the government subsequently acquired the station.[68]

When the United States broke diplomatic relations with Germany in February 1917, the American chargé stressed that the German and pro-German community was influential in Colombia and that there were well-founded rumors that German submarines were obtaining supplies of gasoline on the Colombian coast. The U.S. minister in Panama also reported that there was strong evidence that German submarine crews were using the island of San Andrés.[69]

In addition to Colombia's strategic location, its possession of platinum increased its wartime significance to the United States. Colombia was the world's second largest producer after Russia, with production controlled almost entirely by the Anglo-American Development Company. The departments of State and Commerce and the War Trade Board all placed considerable importance on the development and control of Colombian production, with the result that U.S. officials encouraged corporate interests to develop the metal. Rumors in 1918 that the Colombian government was considering making platinum production a state monopoly led Lansing to caution that the United States would retaliate against coffee and bananas if there were any restrictions on platinum exports. So sensitive was the U.S. government on the availability of platinum that when shipments declined in mid-1918, the War Industries Board demanded explanation.[70]

During the war, American officials found it difficult to compete with German interests, especially in Antioquia, where the German presence was strong. The Banco Alemán Antioqueño was influential, and its manager was highly successful in convincing local merchants that they had nothing to fear from the U.S. and British blacklists (statutory lists). There were local petitions against what was often seen as unnecessary discrimination against local firms and businessmen by American and British policy. The U.S. Justice Department adopted a hard line, announcing in August that it would not approve any further transactions with the branches of German banks in South America. As a reflection of the level of paranoia reached in Washington, even the Colombian and American branches of the Eder family, which had done so much to develop Colombian agriculture in the Cauca Valley, were placed under scrutiny for their economic dealings with German interests. The U.S. legation also viewed as pro-German one emerging Colombian politician—Enrique Olaya Herrera. Olaya was then director of *El Diario Nacional,* but was later a minister to Washington and Colombian president. Anglo-American threats to place the paper on the British statutory list brought Olaya, or so the American chargé believed, to alter editorial policy and to cancel a printing contract with the German Transocean agency.[71]

Neutral in law, Colombian sentiments certainly inclined toward the Allied powers. Following the armistice in November 1918, an estimated three thousand people gathered in the Plaza Bolívar to hear Ismael Enrique Arciniegas, director of *El Nuevo Tiempo.* A procession then led to the Belgian, British, Italian, French, and American legations, where in spite of heavy rains there were more speeches and praise for the Allies. It was striking that there could be such positive feelings expressed for President Wilson and the United States while the Panama issue was unresolved.[72]

In late 1918, the war in Europe over, Wilson requested the Senate to take action on the Colombian treaty. Wilson was more optimistic about the domestic situation,[73] and there was improvement in Colombia as well with the inauguration in August 1918 of former Foreign Minister Marco Fidel Suárez.[74] The U.S. Trade Commissioner in Bogotá contended that the return of prosperity in Colombia after the war, along with political stability had reduced the intensity of feeling about the canal question. The war years, in his view, had increased the number of contacts between Colombians and Americans and broken down some of the Colombian suspicion, at least in elite circles, of American economic power. Besides, from his perspective the war had already accomplished the transition to American trade and economic dominance, and the treaty was not required to attain that end. At the same time, he conceded that the Colombian business community was anxious to have the indemnity to stimulate economic development, in particular to undertake desperately needed transportation improvements. The new U.S. minister, Hoffman Philip, demurred, contending that completion of the treaty would enhance U.S. prestige and significantly improve commercial prospects.[75]

In the spring of 1921, after seven years of delay, obstruction, and debate, the U.S. Senate ratified the Thomson-Urrutia Treaty in an extra session called by President Wilson with the cooperation of the newly elected Warren G. Harding. One of the most volatile episodes in Colombian-U.S. relations was over, though it cast a lengthy shadow over the future.

4   The New Era

> Colombia requires for its development and progress . . . capital
> to develop its industries and . . . people who will establish . . .
> the technology which made possible the development of higher
> civilizations. (Colombia, Congressional Report)[1]

The conclusion of the long-standing conflict over the
Panama canal route left a bitter legacy, but during the 1920s more immediate matters intruded. Prominent among them were Colombian
economic development, petroleum exploitation, trade expansion, and
American cultural penetration. These were years of economic optimism, appropriately labeled the "Dance of the Millions." U.S. foreign policy toward Colombia in this period included vigorous support
for U.S.-based firms attempting to trade with or invest in the country, efforts to counteract a movement toward economic nationalism,
and support for "progressive pan-Americanism," in which American
"experts" in trade, banking, petroleum development and legislation,
education and health matters, and other areas became increasingly important in shaping the political, social, and economic modernization
of Colombia.[2]

With the ratification of the Thomson-Urrutia Treaty, the U.S. chargé
in Bogotá, Herbert S. Goold, attempted to set the tone of American
policy and Colombian-U.S. relations for the coming years: "It has long
been the desire of these people [U.S.] and their government to give to
the Government and people of Colombia some material evidence of
their very genuine esteem, and it can be said with entire accuracy that
the delay in the ratification of the pact, the delay in this formal manifestation of American goodwill toward the Colombian Nation, has at
no time and in no manner detracted from its sincerity or warmth."[3]
Goold indulged in hyperbole; nonetheless, the ratification of the treaty
marked a watershed. In its aftermath the two nations moved away

COLOMBIA
Economic development

▲	Oil field
△	Gas field
‑‑‑‑‑	Crude oil or petroleum products pipeline
R	Refinery
■	Coal
◆	Emeralds
♣	Gold and/or silver
◇	Platinum
▽	Uranium

CARIBBEAN SEA

PACIFIC OCEAN

PANAMA

VENEZUELA

ECUADOR

PERU

BRAZIL

Golfo de Urabá
Golfo de Panamá
Santa Marta
Riohacha
Barranquilla
Ciénaga
Bananas
Cartagena
El Difícil
Coveñas
Plato
Acandí
Turbo
Bananas
Río Atrato
Río Cauca
Barco Concession
Tibú
Petrólea
Zulia
Cúcuta
Cañon Limón
Río Arauca
Barrancabermeja
Casabe
El Centro
Bucaramanga
Arauca
Coffee
Medellín
Coffee
De Mares Concession
La Dorada
Manizales
Coffee
Muzo
Coffee
Bananas
Cartago
Pereira
Bogotá
Armenia
Río Meta
Río Cauca
Coffee
Guamo
Puerto López
Buenaventura
Cali
Bananas
Río Magdalena
Bananas
Tumaco
Bananas
Orito
Llanos
Río Guaviare
Río Vaupés
Río Caquetá
Río Putamayo
Río Amazon

Kilometres
0   100   200   300   400   500

Miles
0   100   200   300

wm

from the Panama dispute to more productive diplomacy. In 1922 the new American Minister in Bogotá was Samuel Piles, a political appointee with no diplomatic experience but a genial man who was not expected to ruffle Colombian sensibilities.

Colombia's foreign policy in this era was essentially a projection of what Colombian political scientist Juan Tokatlian calls the Suárez Doctrine—a perception that ties with the United States were inevitable and should be constructively pursued, as well as the Wilsonian view that structured legal mechanisms were the most effective means for nations to minimize international conflict.[4] As Tokatlian observes, Colombia and Mexico provide interesting examples in these years of a divergent relationship with and attitude toward the United States, with the concrete manifestations of anti-Americanism more pronounced in Mexico after the revolution, but with the relative stability of Colombian elites contributing to more emphasis on modernization than on nationalism. Nonetheless, much of the debate within Colombian society over the nature and direction of Colombian relations with the United States in this period centered on the degree of control Colombia would be able to exercise over its natural resources and general economic development.

Politically, Colombia and the United States bore remarkable similarity in the decade, with both countries absorbed in the culture of business expansion and progress and temporarily neglecting issues of political reform. Colombian economic nationalism revived toward decade's end, and its organized labor movement showed more vitality than in the United States in the 1920s. Political party conflict also remained vibrant in Colombia during the decade. As in the United States, Colombian intellectual life blossomed, with such young writers and political activists as Germán Arciniegas, Baldomero Sanín Cano, Rafael Maya, Luis López de Mesa, Jorge Eliécer Gaitán, or the brilliant political cartoonist Ricardo Rendón emerging at the time.[5] Colombian writers and intellectuals were important in shaping and reflecting perceptions of such issues as the Panama treaty settlement. Baldomero Sanín Cano, for instance, opposed the treaty, in part at least because of his opposition to excessive United States influence in Colombia.

Later in the decade he wrote in *El Tiempo* that Colombian elites had developed a passionate fascination with the United States: "In the presence of the colossal republic," he lamented, "these people adopt the posture of a small bird before the hypnotic stare of the boa constrictor." Cartoonist Rendón presented Suárez's fall in late 1921 as a casualty of the treaty debate, which was the general view presented in *El Espectador*.[6]

Conservatives continued to dominate national politics until 1930 and the election of Enrique Olaya Herrera. Marco Fidel Suárez stepped down from the presidency in 1921 in the midst of political conflict, and Congress selected Jorge Holguín to replace him for the balance of his term. Routine elections brought to power Conservative Presidents Pedro Nel Ospina (1922–26) and Miguel Abadía Méndez (1926–30). These men were similar in outlook to their counterparts Warren G. Harding and Calvin Coolidge in the United States. Conflicts both between Liberals and Conservatives and within the ranks of the two parties nonetheless continued, with traditional ideological and personality differences exacerbated by the increasing urbanization and gradual industrialization of the country. Those developments brought gradual shifts in the political and economic power structure, in particular the rise of a larger middle sector with industrial interests. Significantly, the first stirring of strong anti-Americanism came from Conservative governments that most encouraged expanded U.S. investment during the 1920s, but the Liberals also pushed politics in a nationalist direction.

Trade and Investment

U.S. trade and investment increased considerably during the decade before declining during the post-1929 depression and a turn toward increased commercial protectionism. During the 1920s, Colombia ranked third or fourth among South American countries (thus excluding the more important Cuban and Mexican trade) in the value of its total trade with the United States, usually third in the value of its imports from the United States, behind Argentina and Brazil, and fourth in exports to the United States. The depression actually increased Colombia's position by 1932 to second in terms of total trade with the United States. World War I and economic growth altered the volume of trade rather than the basic market orientation of Colombia. Before and after the war, the United States was the primary source of Colombian imports, mostly finished manufactured goods, and the main market for Colombian exports of coffee, gold, bananas, and ultimately in the decade, petroleum. In 1919 Colombia relied on the United States for 72.4 percent of its imports, and that remained fairly constant until the depression.[7]

The most critical Colombian trade objective with the United States was secure access for coffee exports, which in 1925 accounted for 18 percent of Colombian gross domestic product and 80 percent of the value of total goods exported; that coffee dependency provided the United States with its main leverage during trade negotiations in the 1930s. Overall, Colombian trade showed considerable expansion through 1928 and then a sharp decline. Colombian exports in 1923 were 54.7 million pesos in value, and imports in that year totaled 65.7 million. By 1928 the respective figures were 162.9 million for exports and 132.9 million for imports; but in 1930 they dropped precipitously to 79.8 million and 69.7 million. Significantly, imports fell off more drastically than exports in 1930, reflecting the reduced capacity of Colombians to purchase imported commodities.[8]

U.S. investors found Colombia attractive in the 1920s. Comparatively rich in unexploited natural resources, especially oil, and with $25 million in indemnity from the United States, Colombia appeared to be entering a new economic era. Private American investors moved into oil development, public utilities, agriculture, mining, and manufacturing and purchased large numbers of Colombian government bonds. By the end of 1930 Americans held almost $172 million in bonds and had channeled another $130 million into direct investments. Ministry of Government registration data for foreign based companies operating in Colombia showed a dramatic increase. New listings for 1920, for instance, included Fidelity Phoenix Fire Insurance of New

York, Hartford Fire Insurance, Sinclair Exploration Ltd.; the following year All America Cables made its first appearance, along with Colombian Proprietary Gold Mines, Ltd., Hexagon Sewing Machine Company, the Motor Union Insurance Company, Ltd., American Coffee Corporation, Marconi Wireless Telegraph Company, Ltd., and the Commercial Union Insurance Company, Ltd. In 1922, with the completion of the Thomson-Urrutia Treaty, there was a flurry of corporate oil activity, with the first listings for Granada Oil Corporation, Leonard Exploration Company, Latin American Petroleum Corporation of Colombia, Mid-Colombia Oil & Development Company, and Transcontinental Oil Company of Colombia, along with Singer Sewing Machine Company.[9]

Much of the diplomacy of the decade involved disputes over American investments and trade and the growing Colombian concern about the perceived threats such investments posed to its sovereignty. There was no Colombian consensus in attitudes toward U.S. foreign investment. Early in the decade, Armando Solano, director of *El Diario Nacional*, lashed out at the "Yankee influence on the coast," criticizing many Colombians for their "grasping" materialism; "we have obliged the foreign negotiator to appraise us lower every day," he charged, "like a horde of beggars and thieves, and then, strutting pompously, we ask for veneration." Solano's critique was revealing of class attitudes as well as the growing American presence. He found the "degenerate aristocracy" especially grasping, although he conceded their greater rhetorical patriotism. The increasing reliance on the English language he found disturbing: "the disdain for persons, such as the minister of finance and myself, who do not speak the language of Roosevelt, is infinite," he lamented. The Liberal Bogotá daily, *El Espectador*, expressed similar concerns later in the decade, suggesting that American capital penetration had consequences distinct from those claimed by "the apostles of the Polar Star," bringing revolutions, coups, and electoral and political manipulation along with "works of progress."[10]

There was occasional violence against Americans and American corporate property in the period, as well as tensions associated with cultural differences between a traditional Colombian society and newly arrived American businessmen and technicians. In early 1921, for instance, an official of the Chocó-Pacific Gold Mining Company complained to the Colombian Foreign Ministry that several assailants (including the municipal judge of the neighboring town of Condoto) had fired on one of the company dredges. The U.S. consul in Santa Marta complained about frequent acts of vandalism against his office and protested to the foreign ministry that the only response of city police had been to point out the dangers of living in New York during the anarchist bombings associated with the Red Scare. U.S. minister Hoffmann Philip informed Colombian authorities that he had received a death threat from Colombian "Communists" protesting the recent death sentence of Sacco and Vanzetti. In a lighter vein, Tropical Oil employees in Barrancabermeja complained in 1922 that a policeman had entered a private home, evidently the only one in town with a piano, to order the occupants not to dance without a public permit.[11]

Generally, however, the consensus in the press, published writings and diplomatic correspondence, suggests that Colombian elites welcomed foreign capital, provided there was diversity of origin to balance the influence of the United States against Britain, Belgium, Germany, and France.[12] Each nation sought to outbid the other. In the course of the decade many American businessmen complained of discrimination by government and private sector interests in favor of European firms. Edward Riley, for instance, a Chicago railway promoter, complained to Secretary of State Frank Kellogg late in the decade that Colombia was anti-American and pro-German, although "realistic" Colombians understood that in the future Colombia would have to accept U.S.-derived development capital, exports, and educational principles. Riley contended that privately Colombians admitted that European civilization had been a failure in Colombia and that only the United States had the needed engineering and construction talent. A more balanced assessment of the Colombian preference for doing business in Europe suggested that this had little if anything to do with anti-Americanism but rather with different methods of doing business. Europeans appeared willing to involve Colombian entrepreneurs and investors in a more direct manner than were American companies. The level of American investment by decade's end does not indicate that the Colombian effort to diversify its sources of foreign investment or trade had been very successful.[13]

The most volatile disputes between Colombian interests and American investment were in the developing oil industry, where Standard Oil of New Jersey and Gulf Oil subsidiaries were the most active; and in agriculture, where the Magdalena Fruit Company, a United Fruit Company subsidiary, was the major economic power on the Caribbean coast and by 1930 the largest single agricultural employer in the country. There were also important developments in Colombian transportation, most significantly railroad construction, but also in commercial aviation, an area that generated substantial diplomatic and commercial tension late in the decade and through the 1930s. New areas of Colombian-American contact during the decade included the health and sanitation work conducted jointly by the Rockefeller Foundation's International Health Board.

The New Era witnessed new political, cultural, and military contacts. For the first time, Colombian army officers attended U.S. Army service schools; the first six officers who went to the United States in 1921 specialized in a wide range of areas, including artillery, engineering, transport, air communications, and air photography. In another development the National League of Women Voters approached Colombia and other Latin American countries to send delegates to a Pan American Conference of Women in early 1922. The U.S. legation in Bogotá the same year distributed a Harvard University pamphlet outlining opportunities available for Latin American students, and the Bureau of Education in the Department of the Interior provided a more general brochure on facilities available for foreign students in American colleges and universities. Such initiatives were indicative of the increased cultural impact of the United States in Colombia and the rest of the hemisphere.[14]

The Oil Industry

The two major petroleum developments and concessions in the 1920s were the DeMares concession in Santander and the Barco concession in North Santander near the Venezuelan border. The Tropical Oil Company, a Standard Oil of New Jersey subsidiary through the International Petroleum Company, operated the DeMares concession under a national government concession from 1919. General Virgilio Barco gained title to the second concession in 1905 and sold it to Henry L. Doherty & Company and the Carib Syndicate during World War I. In 1925 Doherty sold his 75 percent controlling interest in the Colombian Petroleum Company (incorporated in Delaware) to the Mellon interests, the South American Gulf Oil Company.[15] Most of the diplomatic controversy of the interwar years swirled around these two concessions and the issue of control over subsoil mineral resources. The State Department concentrated on ensuring American capital access to oil resources, protecting the concessionary titles of U.S. firms and encouraging Colombian resource and labor laws that did not restrict U.S. companies.

In 1919 under President Suárez the Colombian Congress passed legislation reserving, as had Mexico in the Querétaro constitution two years earlier, subsoil resources to the nation. The Colombian Supreme Court before the end of the year found the legislation unconstitutional; the administration substituted a new statute (Law 120 of December 1919), which enabled surface owners of property privately held prior to October 1873 to hold title to subsoil deposits as well. For property in the national domain or that had become private after 1873, the state reserved title to subsoil resources and identified the exploitation of hydrocarbons as of public utility. An 1888 Colombian law stipulated that foreigners and corporations operating in Colombia were subject to Colombian law. The 1919 initiative represented a general tightening of controls over foreign investment in Colombia, although the U.S. minister did not believe that there was any imminent threat of nationalization of the oil industry. The Colombian press was nonetheless "almost unanimous" (*La Crónica* was one exception) in its condemnation of U.S. attitudes toward oil development. There was a "violent" campaign in some quarters, which the U.S. minister attributed to "outside inspiration," to nationalize. The minister over-reacted to the Colombian situation. *El Nuevo Tiempo* more accurately captured the spirit of the legislation when it contended that acquired rights would be fully protected, that there was no discrimination be-tween nationals and foreigners, but that the country required an up to date law on the acquisition of nonmetallic subsoil deposits. Liberal *El Tiempo*, in the aftermath of the Supreme Court decision, called for oil legislation that clarified Colombia's position, thus making unneces-sary any international agreements on oil development. Seeing the oil issue tied to the approval of the Thomson-Urrutia Panama treaty, the Conservative *El Siglo* editorialized with a wonderful sense of histori-cal irony: "For those who . . . have their eyes on the plate which will bring us those $25 million from the Treaty, there is born anew the hope of eating *buñuelos* [fritters] this Christmas, purchased with our national honor." [16]

Such assurances did not appease a number of U.S. politicians, in-cluding a senator later to become secretary of the interior Albert Fall, who argued (incorrectly) to State Department official Boaz Long that any Colombian restrictions on access to subsoil resources appeared to violate the equality-of-treatment provisions of the 1846 Colombian-American Treaty. In Fall's view, "this difference in the laws and pro-cedures of the Latin American states and the lack of understanding of this existing difference . . . is the cause of more trouble . . . than any other one thing." [17] Secretary of State Robert Lansing, alluding to then "Socialistic" tendencies in Mexico, cabled the U.S. legation to impress upon Colombian authorities the benefit of an agreement guaranteeing U.S. nationals access to Colombian minerals. "It is hoped," he ob-served, "that the enlightened population of Colombia will be prompt to recognize the benefit to their country that will result from such an agreement" but that the "unsettled" nature of property rights in Colombia would discourage needed investment. [18]

Oil company reaction to the revised legislation was comparatively mild. Jersey Standard, Sinclair Consolidated, and Prudential officials thought the law protected private property but that it would not encourage actual investment and development, in part because the Colombian government appeared determined to exercise some government control as well as to maximize revenues. The president of Prudential Oil nonetheless believed the companies would invest in spite of the legislation, an indication of the strong interest in diversification in Latin American oil development in the aftermath of the Mexican Revolution and constitutional changes of 1917. The U.S. foreign trade adviser, William R. Manning, argued that Colombian government royalties were excessive, the areas in which development were permitted too limited, and production level controls by the government too severe.[19]

As oil exploration and development proceeded during the 1920s, Colombian governments addressed the issues of control and revenue. In 1926 the Conservative government of Pedro Nel Ospina revoked the Barco concession title held by South American Gulf Oil, claiming the company had failed to meet its development obligations. A few months later the new Conservative government of Miguel Abadía Méndez unsuccessfully attempted to implement new petroleum legislation specifying the government's rights to confiscate existing concessions. When Congress failed to comply, the administration in January 1928 by decree implemented emergency legislation (Law 84, 17 November 1927).[20]

The Coolidge and Hoover administrations responded strongly to the Colombian initiative, although Secretary of State Henry Stimson refrained from his predecessor's rhetorical hyperbole of Bolshevik threats in Latin America. Both administrations worked closely with the oil industry, with policy premised on a perceived commonality of interest between the state and the private sector. Both administrations were concerned that the Colombian government would grant large concessions to other foreign nationals, especially British, thus challenging the American presence. The United States sought both to placate Colombian sentiment and assist Colombia in drafting oil legislation that would make the investment climate more stable. As part of the process, during 1929 H. Foster Bain, former director of the U.S.

Department of Mines, and J. W. Steel of the U.S. Geological Survey, participated in redrafting Colombian oil legislation. The companies were not entirely pleased with the result. By 1930 they were caught between depression-condition overproduction of oil and the desire to obtain and hold concessions they could develop later when world market conditions improved. The role of American oil specialists in 1929 in redrafting existing legislation provided a breathing space in the public debate until Liberal President Enrique Olaya Herrera took office in 1930 and was able to effect political compromise on the oil issues.[21]

The new legislation that emerged from the Olaya administration was a clear compromise between the earlier Colombian position and that of the companies. It reiterated the concept that the oil industry was of public utility, limited concessions to fifty thousand hectares (except in the Llanos, Putumayo, and Amazon regions, where the limit was set at two hundred thousand hectares), and prohibited the transfer of a concession to a foreign government. Further, Article 6 specified priority in hiring for Colombian labor and equality of pay with foreigners, a long-standing point of resentment and friction and in part a response to the growing militancy of Colombian oil workers in these years. The legislation did open the Llanos to exploitation, reduced royalty payments and placed them on a sliding scale, and suspended export duties on petroleum for the first thirty years of a concession's operation. These provisions did not satisfy a minority of Colombian legislators, who wanted more controls over the hiring of foreign employees and a stronger position on rapid development of concessions by the companies; but the success of the legislation owed a great deal to the determination, moderation, and political acumen of President Olaya.

The administration then turned its attention to the still heatedly debated Barco concession (also referred to as the Catatumbo concession). Gulf Oil officials were anxious to retain the concession because they remained nervous about the security of their Venezuelan holdings, contiguous with the Barco territory on the Colombian side of the border. Given world depression, the company opposed a ten-year limit on the exploration period before production had to begin, and the minimum 6 percent royalty payment the Colombian government sought. By early 1931 the two sides were largely reconciled, owing substantially to the effective work of State Department officials. Jersey Standard's representative in Colombia claimed the new contract was "wonderful . . . the best I have seen come out of Colombia." U.S. financial interests evidently concurred, since a New York banking consortium shortly extended a $4 million credit to the Colombian government.

Press discussion of the contract was lively. During the congressional debate Eduardo Santos's Liberal *El Tiempo* led proapproval forces. Moderate Conservative organs such as Roberto Urdaneta Arbeláez's *El Nuevo Tiempo* opposed the agreement until Urdaneta joined the Olaya cabinet as foreign minister. The Conservative Medellín daily *La Defensa* consistently opposed. The public debate, like that in Congress, followed party lines. The Liberal majority in the House of Representatives facilitated passage; but the narrow Conservative majority in the Senate brought temporary delay. The issue was partly partisan politics; but it also underlined the shifting Colombian perceptions of the world and the place of foreign investment in Colombian society. It was not accidental that Tropical Oil enjoyed slightly better public relations in this period; its local representatives were skilled diplomats and men of culture, with whom Colombians identified. Colombians had more difficulty with Gulf Oil; one official observed that the "difficulty with the Gulf people is that they attempt to treat us like Venezuelans and that simply won't do here."[22]

United Fruit and the Agricultural Sector

Arguably even more volatile than oil in Colombian-U.S. relations during the 1920s was the status of the United Fruit Company's main Colombian operating company, Magdalena Fruit Company and its Santa Marta Railroad.[23] The control of transportation in the banana-producing region was critical to the company's domination in the area. Thus, it is not surprising that much of the controversy surrounding United's operations involved the monopoly held by the Santa Marta Railroad. By 1912 the railroad had ninety of a projected two hundred kilometers of line in operation between Santa Marta and the interior. The original concessions of 1881 and 1886 respectively had specified the rail terminus at El Banco on the Magdalena River. That was confirmed by the Colombian government in 1887, as was the transfer of the company that year to the British-owned Santa Marta Railroad. The department of Magdalena wanted to prevent the company from using the line for essentially private and local movement of crops. However, since a great deal of the territory between the company's main operations and the river was unsuitable for banana cultivation, the company delayed, seeking to have the law altered. United's manager in 1911, Mansell Carr, believed the government's main concern was the prospect of the company gaining total control over the railroad from its British owners, thus consolidating a U.S. monopoly in the area. In reality by 1922 United Fruit was already the majority shareholder.

When the concession expired in 1920, Colombian authorities reviewed the company's record and found that it had failed to fulfill its contractual obligations to build to the river. United Fruit explained that the reason for the delay derived from difficulties with the department of Magdalena over the specific terminus. The company was also convinced that Colombian competitors in the area were behind the agitation. Secretary of State Charles Evans Hughes received assurances from the Colombian minister in Washington that the Colombian government had no intent to nationalize the property, which was the principal U.S. concern.[24]

In the course of the decade company production and export increased significantly. By 1929 Colombia had become the world's third largest exporter of bananas, with exports of ten million bunches in that year, double that of 1915.[25] In spite of the general economic prosperity and expansion of the period, relations between the United Fruit Company subsidiary in the Santa Marta region and various sectors of Colombian society were often strained, with tensions pivoting around the company's policies toward Colombian labor, the impact of company policies on landholders and squatters in the area, as well as company efforts to maintain a monopoly on banana exports from the region in the face of competition from Colombian growers and foreign enterprise.

The Magdalena Fruit Company concentrated on controlling banana exports rather than purchasing growing lands, although by the end of the decade the company held an estimated 30 percent of the banana growing land in the department of Magdalena. It had also become the country's largest single agricultural employer. The balance of the land and production was in the hands of approximately four hundred Colombian growers, but they remained at the mercy of company buyers, prices, and transportation in order to market their product.[26]

One of the first attempts to break that monopoly came from the Cuyamel Fruit Company of Samuel Zemurray in 1927. Zemurray was one of the main United Fruit Company competitors in Central America, and Cuyamel's interests coincided with that of some of the larger Colombian growers anxious to find an alternative marketing company; Cuyamel thus negotiated a contract with the Colombian Banana Cooperative of Ciénaga, directed by Roberto Castañeda. Castañeda's efforts failed, and the following year Zemurray merged his interests with those of United Fruit, leaving the Colombian growers with even fewer marketing alternatives. Another effort by the Colombian Banana Cooperative in 1930 to market their product through a Liverpool firm—at a 25 percent higher price than was available from United Fruit—also fell afoul of United Fruit's monopoly.[27] Arguing that the bananas were already under contract to United Fruit, the company brought suit in England to prevent the fruit from being marketed.[28]

Far more violent was the relationship between labor and the company. Tensions between United Fruit and banana workers in the zone were complex. On the one hand United Fruit maintained excellent health facilities for its regular employees and paid above average wages for agricultural workers, ranging from 75 to 100 percent higher than comparable work elsewhere in Colombia. Such wages indicated both the company's need to attract labor and the level of profits to be made in the export of bananas. High wages and limited options elsewhere in the country attracted an estimated ninety thousand people, almost twenty-five thousand of whom were employed in the banana industry. Since the company hired large numbers of contract laborers paid by piece-work rather than as direct employees, the company argued that it was not legally responsible for the condition of this largely migratory and seasonal labor force.

United Fruit and the Colombian growers sought to increase their own landholdings and to ensure an available labor supply, something both feared they would lose if there was stable, smallhold agriculture in the area.[29] Strictly, this was not a foreign policy issue during the decade, but the pressure on smallholders and squatters was so intense during the period that the landholding situation contributed directly to the labor crises, which did have foreign policy implications. Company policy combined with the emergence of radical organized labor in the region—anarchist groups, the Revolutionary Socialist party, and its affiliated organization, the Syndical Union of Workers—to create a volatile chemistry that boiled over into strike and confrontation in late 1928. Company and local U.S. officials showed an intensely antilabor orientation during the strike, not surprising given the equally antilabor mood of the domestic United States during the 1920s. U.S. and Colombian officials alike portrayed strike leaders as professional agitators, distributing "Soviet literature" to an otherwise satisfied workforce. Strike leaders, especially those from the Revolutionary Socialist party, were radical and from outside the banana zone; but, the magnitude of the strike and its volatility attested to the deep-rooted antagonism to the company. Colombian officials shared this concern about radical labor agitation, but there was equal concern about the arrogance of company officials and the dangers of U.S. intervention. The head of the Department of Labor in the Ministry of Industries and his assistant attributed the strike to several factors: the intransigence of company officials; the desire of local merchants to break into the large sales of United Fruit's commissary operations for its employees; and communist agitation. Significantly, the grievances of the strikers were given little credence by any groups except the opposition Liberal press. Indeed, company and Colombian officials alike viewed the workers as unreliable wastrels.[30]

By early December, with some ten thousand workers on strike, the Conservative government mobilized troops in the area to protect property and lives. The Conservatives were hostile to organized labor, but they were also anxious to avoid any pretext for U.S. military intervention. Such intervention in the Caribbean basin in the late 1920s was unlikely, since the Coolidge administration was anxious to assure Latin America that the Nicaraguan venture was an exception. Consequently, the State Department rejected the request for naval assistance by the U.S. vice-consul in Santa Marta. Colombian forces were deployed to reduce the risk of conflict. That military presence enabled United Fruit to resume partial operations using strikebreakers. Opposition Liberal paper *El Tiempo* in late December criticized American officials for considering intervention and pilloried President Abadía Méndez as a servant of United Fruit, but it nonetheless remained silent on the strike itself save for praise for the moderation exercised by the company![31]

The arrival of government forces rapidly led to confrontation with labor. In an action that inspired a scene in Gabriel García Márquez's, *Cien años de soledad* (One hundred years of solitude), Colombian forces fired on a crowd of strikers and their families in the main square of the town of Ciénaga, southwest of Santa Marta. In the aftermath of this bloody encounter, the strike was effectively broken by Colombian military forces, although sporadic outbreaks of violence continued as a reminder of unresolved tensions in the zone. Foreign investment and economic modernization in the decade thus contributed to internal Colombian political and social tensions at the same time that they added new dimensions to foreign relations.

The political implications of the strike continued through 1929 and the presidential elections of early 1930. A young socialist parliamentarian, Jorge Eliécer Gaitán, pressed for a Congressional enquiry into the government's handling of the strike. Demonstrating those qualities that made him one of the leading figures in the Liberal party before his assassination in April 1948, Gaitán personally investigated the strike, and on the basis of his evidence the House of Representatives Judiciary Committee conducted hearings on the events of the previous December. This action displeased the American minister in Bogotá, Jefferson Caffery, who saw Gaitán and other critics of government policy as political opportunists seeking to exploit anti-Conservative and anti-American hostility.[32]

Gaitán's recommendations had little immediate effect on the situation in the banana zone, although they underlined the need for more sensitivity to the needs of labor and the problems inherent in the monopolistic nature of the United Fruit Company's control over banana export in the area. Gaitán urged government control of irrigation, an export tax on bananas, a revision of United's contracts with Colombian planters to improve prices and relations, the encouragement of Colombian growers, enforcement of existing labor legislation, and regulation of unions. These recommendations remained a dead letter for the moment, and a Senate committee in November 1929 exonerated President Abadía of all wrongdoing in his declaration of martial law and suppression of the strike. Nonetheless, the public furor over the strike helped pave the way for an alliance of a faction of the Conservative party and the Liberals in electing as president the former Colombian minister to the United States, Enrique Olaya Herrera. Olaya's presidency contributed to at least a temporary resolution of many of the outstanding problems then existing between the United States and Colombia, especially over oil regulation.

Aviation Conflict

Tensions in the late 1920s between U.S. and Colombian aviation interests represented a significant combination of commercial and strategic rivalry, an intersection of private and public interest. The situation was especially acute in the case of Colombia, because early commercial aviation development in the country was led by German nationals in the aftermath of World War I. Although U.S. concern intensified in the 1930s with the rise of Nazi Germany, in the previous decade the State Department preferred that commercial aviation in sensitive strategic areas should be in U.S. corporate control. It thus encouraged Pan American Airways expansion in the Western Hemisphere, including its purchase in 1931 of a controlling interest in Sociedad Colombo-Alemana de Transportes Aéreos (SCADTA), the Colombian-German line formed in 1919. Later, in 1940, the State Department pressed Pan American Airways to exercise that controlling interest to purge Germans from the company's operations.[33]

By the mid-1920s, SCADTA was pressing for landing rights in Central America and the Caribbean. This initiative inspired a debate in U.S. policy-making circles over the nature of strategic policy for aviation. In 1925 President Coolidge's secretary of war, Dwight Davis, portrayed SCADTA as a potential threat to U.S. interests in the Caribbean and urged the establishment of a policy in which U.S.-based companies would be supported. In 1927 the Coolidge administration rejected a request for landing rights in Colón, Panama, for a SCADTA subsidiary, most of whose officials were Colombian but whose operations manager was a German national, Herman Kuehl.

The opposition of the U.S. government to SCADTA's request for Panama landing rights raised the level of anti-American sentiment in Colombia. SCADTA officials found support among business interests in Colombia and Panama anxious to enjoy expanded commerce. The Liberal opposition press in Bogotá also presented the issue largely in terms of U.S. restrictions on Colombian economic expansion. Neither *El Tiempo* nor the leftist Liberal paper *El Diario Nacional* accepted the U.S. position that the security of the Panama Canal was at risk; rather they saw the U.S. objections as based on commercial rivalry and the desire to ensure that any U.S. air enterprise in the region should be dominant.[34]

American minister Samuel Piles blamed SCADTA officials for this outburst of anti-Americanism; he saw the agitation as a conscious effort to incite Colombians against the United States in order to gain private commercial advantage. The normally placid minister urged that no assistance be given to SCADTA, which he portrayed as a foreign company and an "absolute menace" to U.S. interests. Piles did favor granting landing rights in Panama to a legitimate Colombian company but persisted in denying such rights to SCADTA. He urged a vigorous campaign to counteract the influence of such foreign interests in Colombia and elsewhere in Latin America.[35]

The State Department formulated its policy on inter-American commercial aviation largely in response to the SCADTA situation. Assistant Secretary Francis White, a major figure in the shaping of American policy toward Latin America during the Coolidge and Hoover presidencies, favored benevolent U.S. intervention. His position on aviation was consistent with that approach. In a basic policy position paper at the end of 1927, White contended that European aviation interests in general and German in particular presented a commercial threat to U.S. interests in Colombia, Brazil, the west coast of Latin America, and Central America. In this instance public officials forged ahead of private sector initiative in linking private commercial development with national interest.[36]

At the Sixth Meeting of American States in Havana the following January, mindful of the strategic importance of the canal, the participants agreed to a series of conventions on commercial aviation. Agreement favored the U.S. effort to limit private and public aviation rights. The conventions permitted two or more states to conclude agreements restricting aviation movement in specified territories for reasons of military or public safety and disqualified from equality of access those aircraft and companies enjoying state support. That restriction clearly applied to SCADTA and Colombia.[37]

The State Department now pressed for a concrete expansion of American commercial aviation in the Caribbean. By July the federal government had granted an airmail contract to Pan American Airways from Key West to the Panama Canal Zone and anticipated service down both coasts of South America. SCADTA was not idle during this initiative, however. It pressed Colombian authorities to block Pan American's access to Colombia and requested permission to establish service to Ecuador, an initiative in which SCADTA had the assistance of the German minister in Quito. SCADTA worked against Pan American in Honduras and in Cuba during 1928 and managed to obtain temporary landing rights in Panama for its hydroplanes near Porto Bello, only twenty miles from the mouth of the canal. This last success proved too much for the U.S. Department of War, which then had all commercial aviation in the Republic of Panama placed under a Joint Aviation Board.[38]

The activities of SCADTA and other non-American airlines in Latin America led the Hoover administration after 1929 to modify the traditional U.S. policy preference to avoid granting special support to one private enterprise over another, on the assumption that such favored support could contribute to monopolistic conditions. Francis White argued that a policy of commercial neutrality could result in U.S. firms losing to foreign competitors; as a result of a cabinet decision in mid-1929 the Hoover administration, somewhat reluctantly, determined to instruct American diplomatic missions in Latin American to give full support to Pan American Airways in their commercial operations in the region.

In the course of the year Pan Am president Juan Trippe developed a small airline to compete with SCADTA in Colombia and also pressed to acquire an interest in SCADTA from Peter Paul von Bauer, an initiative that had full State Department backing as a means of removing a "big thorn" in the development of U.S. commercial policy in Latin America. By the end of 1929 the two companies had signed an operating agrement, but financial control remained elusive for another two years, until SCADTA's financial needs and inability to compete with Pan Am outside Colombia contributed to the sale to Pan Am of a controlling 51 percent interest in the Colombian company.[39] This transfer of financial control had only limited significance until the outbreak of World War II raised new security concerns on the part of the United States.

The International Health Board

There were other significant areas of the American presence that were less volatile but no less important. One was the work of the Rockefeller Foundation International Health Board. In cooperation with Colombian health officials and local doctors and scientists, the board undertook campaigns to eradicate and control yellow fever, malaria, hookworm, and, in general, improve levels of sanitation and health, especially in the Colombian countryside.

President Marco Fidel Suárez in early 1920 formally invited the International Health Board (IHB) to inaugurate a campaign against hookworm. There was widespread optimism in medical and diplomatic circles that such medical endeavors would improve the image of the United States in Colombia with the Panama Treaty still pending. IHB officers in New York even employed their "unofficial" contacts in an effort to have the treaty ratified. The importance Colombian authorities placed on the cooperation and the program was reflected in the presentation of a gold medal and emerald ring to Dr. Louis Schapiro of the IHB when the program was inaugurated in Bogotá. Schapiro reported that Bogotá's elite had turned out at the Municipal Theater for a presentation on the health program by the minister of agriculture. Schapiro wrote optimistically: "As Americans, a greater field presents itself to . . . develop a better feeling between our country and Colombia. They are willing to meet us more than half way and do their part; there remains for us to build on solid ground and to show them . . . that we Americans are not a grasping lot, but . . . are willing to aid constructive efforts to reduce human suffering." Former President Reyes, with more irony than he could have known, indicated that the International Health Board would "repay the injury done" to Colombia by the loss of Panama and that "the name of Rockefeller will live in the Annals of Colombian history."[40]

This government-private sector initiative was extremely timely given the poor health conditions in Colombia in the 1920s. As late as 1929, 42 percent of all deaths in Colombia were of undetermined causes because of the absence of an attending physician. In that same year, an estimated six thousand Colombians died of typhoid, dysentery, and enteritis.[41] Colombian medical practitioners had been actively pursuing solutions to these problems since the nineteenth century. As early as 1888 Dr. Andres Posada Arango of Medellín had called attention to the endemic nature of hookworm in the region, and in 1895, Dr. Jesus del Corral, later minister of agriculture, had been able to identify hookworms in an autopsy. Not until 1911, however, did the Colombian Congress authorize funding a campaign for the departments of Cundinamarca and Tolima. In 1920 Dr. Enrico Enciso was sent to the United States to study on an IHB fellowship. (By 1928 he was director of health in Bogotá.)

In the early campaigns of the 1910s and 1920s IHB and Colombian scientists found considerable resistance and apathy among local populations, and financial stringency added to their difficulties by reducing the number of sanitary inspectors and funds available for the construction of sanitary latrines. Nonetheless, the program treated a substantial number of individuals in the early years, starting modestly with sixteen thousand in 1921 and building substantially to over 570,000 by 1926. Educational efforts, designed to improve awareness of the disease and its prevention, also reached an estimated 1.5 million people in Colombia in 1925 and 1926. By 1928, Dr. George Bevier, then local director reported that most of the larger population concentrations had been treated, especially in the Cauca Valley, and that there was an increased awareness of the need for careful construction of more sanitary facilities. Bevier also anticipated that it would be beneficial were Colombia to increase the number of local health inspectors funded by the departments and municipalities, since a more decentralized system, in his view, was more effective.[42]

There were also private American initiatives to cooperate with the program. For instance, Phanor Eder, of the New York law firm of Hardin, Hess, Eder and Freschi, late in the decade offered to make available as a test site his family's sugar plantations in the Cauca Valley. This plantation, "Manuelita," near Palmira, was considered the largest single sugar plantation in Colombia, with between five and six hundred workers, many of whom lived on the plantation with their families. Authorities did not accept his offer, presumably because the IHB acted only through constituted Colombian health authorities, who likely feared accusations of favoritism toward an "American" enterprise. Nonetheless, the fact that health conditions were poor even on one of the largest and wealthiest plantations was indicative of the extent of the problem. By decade's end, officials believed they had made reasonable progress in raising public awareness on sanitation, hygiene, and health, and prepared the way for a more permanent organization based on universal soil sanitation and general hygiene. Yet, except for the IHB associated hookworm, yaws, and malaria campaigns, the public health system of the country remained rudimentary and unsatisfactory, with public health work concentrated in the port cities. In each department there was only one part-time director of hygiene to administer the needs of, in places, one million people. Only Bogotá had an infant-welfare and antituberculosis program or a training school for professional nurses.[43]

IHB officials were not sanguine about the general degree of commitment to reforms on the part of either local officials or the general population. They perceived that the Colombian population, especially in rural areas, saw laws only as guidelines not requirements. Moreover, the sanitation program experienced difficulty employing conscientious and hard-working personnel. Although the *campesino* was "faithful," he lacked the intelligence required for work in the program. The middle classes and elites varied between honest, active, and intelligent and lazy and "indolent." Hiring personnel for a program such as the sanitation/latrine work was especially difficult because of the view that the work was degrading. In spite of such personnel difficulties and a perception that the population was partially indifferent, officials reported considerable success in their latrine program in Palestina, where 75 percent of the homes had been provided with satisfactory facilities, and contrary to the image of an indifferent populace, it was noted that some people had taken enough interest in their new facilities to install electric lights, hang pictures on the walls, and even grow orchids from the eaves! By 1932 the Palestina project was considered complete and officials moved on to Manizales and Chinchina.[44]

The Colombian government, with IHB support, made considerable progress in improving health research facilities in the 1920s. In 1926, the government purchased a large private laboratory in Bogotá (the Samper-Martinez lab) with three years of seed funding provided by the IHB to pay the salaries of a director and assistant. The lab flourished, producing biological products for human and veterinary work, and handling the blood samples for the IHB-government malaria campaign then under way. In 1928 it was placed under the control of the Ministry of Health.[45]

The IHB experienced considerable opposition from large Colombian landowners, especially in Cundinamarca, but also in Caldas. The opposition seems to have derived from hostility to any external interference between the landowners and their labor force, although one cannot discount possible anti-Americanism. Major landowners in Caldas even had support in their opposition from the departmental director of hygiene, who was an employee of the National Health Service! In regions where there were major labor conflicts, such as Viotá, the IHB made no effort to develop programs.

The Roman Catholic Church hierarchy also proved an obstacle to health reform. Education was a closely guarded preserve of the Church, and the hierarchy clearly looked with suspicion on the "educational" activities of foreign agencies, which were sending brochures on sanitation and disease control to teachers and parish priests throughout the country. IHB officials nonetheless seem to have been very successful in eliciting the support of the Church after initial hesitation, but those who sought broader reforms in the Colombian educational system made little progress. When in 1923 officials attempted to establish a foreign commission to study the educational system, the Vatican made it clear that only a Catholic nation and Catholic commissioners would be accepted, with the result that any inclination to involve the United States gave way to an invitation to Belgium. Colombia had a formal agreement with the Vatican committing the government to "impede the propagation of ideas contrary to Catholic dogma and to the respect and veneration due to the Church in the instruction given in literary and scientific as well as other branches of education." The traditionally European orientation of Colombia was also reflected in the training of Colombian doctors, most of whom went to France, at least for advanced training, although there are records indicating a few U.S.-trained physicians and medical researchers by World War I, and numbers increased in the postwar era as there were improved contacts between Colombian and United States health professions and financial support provided for Colombians to study in the U.S.[46]

The IHB's antimalaria program did not get under way until the late 1920s. As late as 1932 the entire program budget for the country was $8,000, half provided by the Colombian government. In 1929 the Colombian Department of Health employed Harvard pathologist Marshall Hertig to conduct a seven-month survey of anopheline (mosquitoes) to determine the species and varieties found in malarious regions and the degree of natural infection with malaria parasites exhibited by them, as a necessary preliminary step to a control program. Although Hertig unfortunately had to conduct his study during the dry season, he logically concentrated on the Magdalena River towns, principally Puerto Lievano, Puerto Wilches, La Dorada, Barrancabermeja, and El Pedral. Following the study, officials established a control program at Puerto Lievano on the Magdalena River; groups of towns along the river were treated and there were plans to drain swampy areas near habitations, use Paris Green insecticide, and then to extend the work into the Cauca Valley and possibly to Cúcuta near the Venezuelan border. By 1934 they established a model control program in Barrancabermeja, because it had a progressive town council and was close to the oil fields. Researchers found that 27 percent of the general population and 7 percent of the school children in the town had malaria parasites in their blood.[47]

Although this program was not of diplomatic significance, the cooperation of the IHB with Colombian officials in these years in attempting to improve the malaria control conditions in the country was an important area of contact between the two countries. In terms of U.S. self-interest, malaria control was important, as Secretary of State Cordell Hull discovered when he contacted IHB officials after the U.S. vice-consul of the west coast port city of Buenaventura died from malaria.[48]

Yellow fever attracted less attention than either malaria or hookworm from health authorities, although there had been a history of epidemic outbreaks in the country. By the 1920s, however, there were no further outbreaks on the Caribbean or Pacific coasts of Colombia

because of the successful eradication programs in Cuba and Guaya-
quil, Ecuador. More isolated regions, primarily Santander, had outbreaks in 1910, 1918, 1923, and 1929. The IHB sent a commission
into Colombia in 1916 and another in 1923 during the Bucaramanga
outbreak, and control measures were introduced under Rockefeller
Foundation direction. Dr. J. H. Whyte of the foundation indicated in
1923 that "Colombia is considered a world key point and its infection
has centred upon it the anxious scrutiny not only of the nearby Latin
American countries, but equally so . . . our own country."

In 1930 the United Fruit Company in Santa Marta asked the foundation to investigate possible occurrences in the region, but although
there were several confirmed deaths there was no generalized conta-
gion. In the later 1930s the National Health Department placed G. O.
Richardson of the foundation in charge of preventive work in the Santa
Marta area, and the foundation allocated for Colombia $30,000 (from
a total anti–yellow fever budget of $250,000, of which most went to
Brazil). From 1934 to 1940, the foundation allocated $218,000 to yellow
fever work in Colombia as well as the construction of labs in Bogotá
and Villavicencio. The main work by the end of the 1930s included an
intensive study of jungle yellow fever in field and lab, investigation
of animals that might be hosts of yellow fever virus, and the study
of the distribution of the disease. By 1940 officials were carrying out
a large-scale vaccination project in the emerald mining area of Muzo,
where yellow fever had been endemic. Almost the entire population
of the area was vaccinated during the program, although it was believed that the high incidence of yellow fever exposure over the years
had created immunity even for the children. It was also thought likely
that the outbreaks early in the century had been in part the result
of the fact that some three hundred miners had been brought from
high altitudes, where they had experienced no previous exposure and
no immunity. Muzo's comparatively small population was considered
vulnerable to disease, nonetheless, since there was little active agriculture in the area and a high dependency on the traffic passing to
and from the mines for food supplies, and when that traffic was light
as it was by the 1930s, malnutrition became common.[49]

The decade of the new era thus witnessed a substantial increase in commercial, political, and cultural contacts between the United States and Colombia. Although not forgotten, the bitterness over the loss of Panama to the United States gave way to economic development, commercial expansion, and renewed economic nationalism, particularly in the areas of petroleum development, investment, trade, and aviation. The emergence of economic crisis after 1929 in both Colombia and the United States, the short but vicious and costly Colombian war with Peru over Leticia in the early 1930s, and the election of Liberal Presidents Enrique Olaya Herrera in 1930 and Alfonso López Pumarejo in 1934 marked a significant shift in the relations between the two countries. On the one hand Olaya was able to blunt some of the economic nationalism that had emerged in the Abadía Méndez presidency and to move the two nations closer to commercial accord; but the issues that had emerged as possible points of friction between the countries in the late 1920s became more acute once again under Alfonso López after 1934. The shift of the Hoover and then Roosevelt administrations in Washington toward the Good Neighbor policy of noninterventionism in the internal affairs of other American states provided a further basis for accommodation.

5   Depression and Reform

> I do not believe that hostility will ease until . . . American business concerns . . . act towards the Governments and peoples South of the Rio Grande in the same manner as . . . towards people and concerns in the United States. (Jefferson Caffery, 1931)

The economic crisis that came to the world in the early 1930s had significant repercussions on Colombian-U.S. relations. In both countries the unresolved social, political, and economic tensions of the late 1920s and early 1930s in the Hoover and Olaya presidencies spilled over into a period of social and economic reform in the presidencies of Franklin Roosevelt and Alfonso López Pumarejo. Hoover and Olaya brought a measure of stability to an increasingly volatile confrontation over natural resources and initiatives toward improved trade relations. Roosevelt and López, on the other hand, rekindled reform. If Roosevelt brought a New Deal to American society, López brought *la revolución en marcha* (the revolution on the move) to Colombians; both embodied the emergence of the welfare state, labor reforms, and a greater degree of state management of the economy, all trends that paralleled international developments in the depression decade. Both also ran hard up against conservative reaction by 1938, the last year of López's presidency before he was replaced by the more moderate Liberal Eduardo Santos. The depression conditions of the 1930s, the deteriorating international situation in Europe and the Far East, Latin American pressure against U.S. interventionism, and the outbreak of war between Colombia and Peru between 1932 and 1934 conditioned much of the U.S.–Latin American relationship in these years. Clearly there was substantial pressure from Latin America for improved commercial ties, but it was the United States, in particular Roosevelt and Cordell Hull, that linked economic improvement to the achievement of international peace.

135

The Olaya-Hoover Years

The Hoover presidency was more of a holding action in Colombian relations than a new departure, with most of the diplomatic efforts directed toward reducing international conflict and combating economic nationalism. Elsewhere in Latin America, the administration set the groundwork for the Good Neighbor policy, moving away from military interventionism and withdrawing U.S. occupation forces in Central America and the Caribbean. Military intervention was not an issue in Colombia, but the continuing threat of economic nationalism was. Hoover, like his predecessors, sought to curb the development of such nationalism, which threatened American access to investment markets and to strategic raw materials. President Olaya shared Hoover's elusive goal of a stable, international world order and sought to cooperate with the United States to achieve it. Developments in petroleum relations indicated the extent to which Olaya's election in 1930 represented a commitment to a moderate policy toward the United States and a sublimation of the emergent economic nationalism that had increasingly characterized Conservative policy under President Miguel Abadía Méndez. Problems remained, however, in trade, financial relations, and U.S. investment.

Olaya had enjoyed a distinguished public career as journalist-publisher, diplomat, and senator before his inauguration as president in 1930. He had overcome wartime identification by U.S. diplomats as pro-German and anti-American, in time to contribute to the passage through the Colombian Senate of the Panama treaty. He had held a short-lived appointment as minister of Foreign Affairs under President Jorge Holguín before being appointed minister to Washington in the spring of 1922, where he remained until the 1930 presidential campaign. Throughout his term in Washington he worked energetically to establish Colombian-U.S. relations on an amicable and professional basis, clearly sharing Marco Fidel Suárez's view that close relations with the United States were inevitable and better constructive than conflictual. He was not outspoken about U.S. foreign investment and shared with Herbert Hoover the concept that government and international relations should be conducted on a scientific, planned and progressive basis. To critics, he was overly pro-American; to his supporters, among them Hoover and Henry Stimson, men of Olaya's capacity were too rare in Latin American politics. In the course of the presidential campaign he sought to reassure that sector of the Colombian business community which either feared U.S. foreign investment or which had already benefitted from it that he would defend such investment. Clearly, some of his message was directed, as well, at a foreign audience. He cautioned his audience in a major address at the prestigious Bogotá Jockey Club that the American financial community was uncertain of the stability of the Colombian financial market; he contended that American cooperation was "frank and sincere," inspired by "the interest of maintaining close commercial and economic relations."[1]

The policies of the Hoover administration toward Latin America in general and Colombia specifically coincided with Olaya's objective to improve trade and investment conditions, to establish relations on a scientific and institutional basis, and to refrain from intervention in the internal affairs of other nations. Strategic questions played a role for both parties, from the Colombian desire to use U.S. power to offset threatened border disputes with Peru and Venezuela, to the U.S. desire to maintain a pro-American regime in close proximity to the Panama Canal, especially as general international relations deteriorated and hemispheric security and solidarity took on new urgency. As at home, so in foreign policy, the Hoover administration resisted statism in favor of private enterprise in economic development and thus sought to undercut Colombian nationalists who desired the expansion of state controls over the economy.[2]

Trade Policies

Olaya took office only two months after President Hoover signed the controversial protectionist Smoot-Hawley Tariff Act, which brought a chorus of domestic and international criticism. Colombian criticism was more muted than that of many nations because the economy's mainstay, coffee, representing over 70 percent of Colombian export revenues, remained on the duty free list, but there were growing concerns in Colombian circles about the future of Colombian-U.S. trade. In 1930 Colombian imports from U.S. sources were one half the value of 1929; its exports declined but less sharply from 120 million pesos in 1929 to 103 million in 1930, but the following year saw sharper decline in exports to 79 million pesos, then 65 million in 1932 and 46 million in 1933, when the decline began to level off once again.[3]

Olaya took office amidst considerable clamor for protectionist tariff measures, generated mostly by the National Federation of Manufacturers and Producers based in Medellín and Bogotá. By January 1931 he had succumbed to the pressure, implementing an increase on a wide range of foodstuffs, including flour, wheat, refined sugar, and lard, most of which were products exported by the United States. In the case of Cauca Valley sugar production, where substantial amounts of American capital were invested in domestic production, Colombian producers gained from the increased protection against American imports. Under some pressure from Caffery, Olaya attempted to hold the line against excessive tariff measures, but he had to be cautious not to alienate congressional support for other measures, such as the pending settlement of the Gulf Oil concession. As part of the effort to build consensus, the Colombian Congress established a National Economic Council composed of representatives of major agricultural and industrial associations.[4]

In the fall of 1931 Olaya also prohibited the import of a wide range of luxury goods, doubled the duty on a number of agricultural and finished products, and substantially increased that on other goods. Although not directed at the United States particularly, such measures had a negative effect on U.S.-Colombian trade and led to intensified pressures by American interests to liberalize tariff policies. The National Foreign Trade Council in the United States commented specifically on the decline of Colombian imports from the United States in the early depression years. In 1929 the value of American exports to Colombia was 60 percent of the value of its purchases. In 1930,

1931, and 1932, however, the southbound flow of goods declined to 31 percent, 21 percent, and then seventeen percent of the value of American imports from Colombia. Equally disconcerting in 1933 was the decline of the U.S. share of the Colombian market below that of Great Britain for the first time since before World War I. Colombia's shortage of foreign exchange was the main problem.[5]

The deteriorating trade relationship worldwide prompted increasing demand for a new trade agreement. In the Hoover years and at the outset of the Roosevelt administration in 1933, such initiative was along bilateral lines until the 1934 passage of the Reciprocal Trade Agreements Act. Colombian efforts to gain a commercial accord began in the Abadía Méndez administration, and the Colombian-American Chamber of Commerce as well as the National Federation of Coffee Growers in New York worked actively to build support for a new agreement. The creation in 1931 of a Colombian-American Chamber of Commerce in Bogotá to parallel one in New York reflected the desire to improve trade. At the same time Olaya announced that five American finance experts, headed by Princeton economist Edwin Kemmerer, would study possible remedies for the nation's financial difficulties, which had been exacerbated by the costly war with Peru over Leticia.[6]

Franklin Roosevelt's inauguration in early 1933 and his appointment of long-time trade liberalization advocate Cordell Hull as secretary of state gave new impetus to preliminary consideration of a trade agreement. Although Hull was frustrated in 1933 in his desire to have more general trade legislation, the State Department moved ahead with bilateral talks, with Colombia one of the first countries approached. Hull's perception was that trade improvement with Latin America would not only modify the dismal economic picture but also reduce criticism of the United States at the 1933 Montevideo meeting of American states. Olaya's foreign minister, Roberto Urdaneta Arbeláez, was more skeptical about U.S. ambitions in a reciprocity agreement.

Possible trade agreement with Colombia was the subject of considerable discussion in American economic circles. The Department of Commerce sought an agreement that would remove what it considered were discriminatory Colombian duties against American products. A National Foreign Trade Council report, *The Financial and Trade Problems of Colombia in Their Relation to the United States*, prepared in collaboration with the Council on Inter-American Relations, the Colombian-American Chamber of Commerce, and the Committee on Inter-American Commerce, stressed Colombia's overdependence on its four main staples: coffee, oil, platinum, and bananas, the majority of which were exported to the United States. The first task was to alleviate Colombia's foreign-exchange problems.

The bilateral agreement signed in mid-December 1933 was the only bilateral agreement concluded by the United States before the adoption of more comprehensive legislation in the Reciprocal Trade Agreements Act of 1934, and the Colombian-U.S. treaty was thus not ratified by either side. Though abortive, the negotiations themselves and the nature of the lobbying by vested interests on both sides revealed many of the problems that hindered trade between the two countries. On the Colombian side, the main tension developed between traditional agricultural and commercial interests tied to the coffee industry, and the embryonic industrial sector in Medellín and Bogotá, embodied in the National Federation of Industrialists. The latter group argued that the long-term interest of the country lay in economic diversification, not continued reliance on agricultural and raw-materials exports.[7]

This first treaty negotiation paved the way for the conclusion of a subsequent reciprocal trade agreement. Colombian officials were pleased by the U.S. commercial overture. If the Roosevelt administration objective was to alleviate Latin American criticism of U.S. commercial policy at the Montevideo conference in late 1933, then in the Colombian instance they realized their objective. The head of the Colombian delegation to Montevideo, Alfonso López Pumarejo, soon to be Liberal president, presented the main response to Cordell Hull's comments at Montevideo on the need for commercial liberalization. López indicated that he found the U.S. call for trade liberalization a refreshing change in U.S. trade policy toward Latin America but expressed doubt that the economic interests of the major industrial powers were identical to those of Latin American countries.[8] For Colombia, the negotiations over a reciprocal trade agreement during the next few years served to confirm López's reservations.

Colombian Bonds, American Finance

The international financial crisis after 1929 contributed to the Colombian default on most of the government bonds sold abroad in the halcyon days of the 1920s, although the deterioration of enthusiasm in New York circles for the Colombian market preceded the stock market crash and the actual economic decline. The first major warning came in 1928, when the U.S. Department of Commerce issued a special circular on the Colombian economy—the Corliss Circular. The Commerce Department document warned of possible instability in the Colombian financial market, concentrating its criticism on the lack of careful financial policies in the Abadía government and the lack of central direction over the practices of Colombian municipalities and departmental governments. The Corliss Circular reflected concern about the Colombian method of servicing its foreign debt, the level of commitments to unproductive public works projects, and the weakness of government revenues.

Although the reaction in Colombian financial and political circles was mixed, there was general agreement that Colombian finances were sufficiently weak to justify restraint. U.S. officials viewed the Corliss Circular as a service to both countries, because it "prevented the further loss to American citizens of several tens of millions of dollars and a saving to the Colombian Government of a much heavier burden in foreign indebtedness. . . . It was also the influence which made possible the election of Dr. Olaya with all its attendant benefits."[9] Such a view likely exaggerated the impact of the circular itself on foreign investment and certainly failed to understand the domestic Colombian factors that led to Olaya's election.

The Corliss Circular led to reforms in the financial policies of the Abadía administration, to subsequent reforms once Olaya was in office and also to a significant reduction in the flow of U.S. capital to Colombia, with only $2 million in Colombian bonds being publicly offered in the United States in the first half of 1929.[10] The British firm of Lazard Brothers along with the New York Guaranty Trust Company withdrew their bids to become the Colombian fiscal agents, indicative of the lack of confidence in the Colombian situation financial circles.

As president, Olaya focused on the country's financial position, traveling to the United States to meet with American officials and New York bankers. Private and official Washington and New York demonstrated their visible pleasure at Olaya's election victory and their optimism about future prospects. As Olaya disembarked from a United Fruit Company steamer in New York, he was met by representatives of President Hoover, the Departments of War, Navy, and State, and the president of All-America Cables, which was owned by International Telephone and Telegraph. Olaya and the New York financial community quickly came to terms. Seligman & Company agreed to extend the maturity date on short-term bank loans from the Guaranty Trust Company Julius Klein, former head of the Bureau of Foreign and Domestic Commerce and now assistant secretary of Commerce, assisted Kuhn Loeb & Company in negotiating with Olaya, who ultimately succeeded in concluding a contract for a $20 million loan with a consortium of American and British banks. The contract required the Colombian government to maintain a balanced budget, float an internal loan of six million pesos, establish government operations on a "more businesslike basis," and reorganize its system of customs collection.

It was Princeton economist Edwin Kemmerer's mandate to assist Colombia in meeting those terms.[11] His main task in 1930 was improving government revenues and stabilizing the economy. Kemmerer's efforts in the 1920s had already contributed to the establishment of the Bank of the Republic, and the 1930s mission was an extension of the earlier efforts to establish Colombian financial institutions on a stable basis. With a characteristically conservative-progressive approach to economic stabilization, Kemmerer sought to put teeth into Colombia's weakly enforced income tax, to establish an export tax on bananas, to tax the capital value of real property, improve salaries for the central bureaucracy, establish a general customs board, and in general to alleviate the unpredictability of conducting business in Colombia. These initiatives were of mixed success, but their significance lies as much in the reform philosophy that underlay them as in their actual achievements.[12]

The Kemmerer reforms accompanied those in other areas of Colombian administration, including a railroad administration reform measure on which the New York financial community insisted before credits could be extended in 1931. National City Bank of New York and National City Bank of Boston both insisted that the railroad administration be taken out of the hands of government and placed under the direction of professional management. Even Caffery expressed concern about the political implications of Olaya being perceived to be under the direction of Wall Street. Caffery informed the State Department that Olaya's prestige had already suffered and that he was not convinced that Olaya could politically afford to support the Barco concession contract for Gulf Oil with the same vigor or to veto "objectionable articles" in the general tariff bill then before Congress. Caffery contended that U.S. business interests active in Colombia were insensitive to Colombian views.[13]

He cautioned against driving Olaya from office: "It is quite clear that after all . . . Olaya has done for American interests . . . if he turns to Congress with empty hands he cannot retain the presidency." Stimson and assistant chief of the Latin American Division, H. Freeman Matthews, successfully pressed this view on National City Bank officials, who extended a final $4 million credit to the Colombian government, providing at least a brief respite for the beleaguered Olaya administration. Yet Olaya remained under extreme pressure. He was obliged to cancel a proposed trip to the United States in September 1931, and in the course of the next year the country slid toward default on its foreign debt as its international creditors imposed further restrictions. Stimson explained apologetically that it was not "a question of letting him [Olaya] down, but of world conditions over which the Department has no control." Stimson also stressed, in response to the idea that Olaya had come to office with some understanding of U.S. support, that the State Department "at no time . . . either directly or indirectly extend[ed] any sort of promise on a *quid pro quo*." [14]

As Colombian economic fortunes waned, the political and diplomatic context was further clouded in December 1931 by a U.S. Senate investigation of the sale of foreign bonds in the United States during the 1920s. This enquiry—which was initiated by California Progressive Republican Senator Hiram Johnson, a leading Senate isolationist—was premised on the assertion that the State Department had sought advantages for private American companies in Latin America during the 1930s but was inactive in protecting the small American investor from unreliable Latin American government bond sales. In the Colombian case, Johnson specifically argued that the State Department and American bankers had conspired in the spring of 1931 to pressure the Colombian government to settle the Barco oil concession with Gulf Oil in return for financial credits in New York. State Department officials denied the contention in their testimony before the Senate, contending that the settlement of the Barco matter had been generally recognized as important to the general sanctity of contracts, not as a precondition for loans.[15] President Olaya, stung by the suggestion of collaboration with Secretary of the Treasury Andrew Mellon, confirmed State Department testimony.

If the economic situation had been salvageable in mid-1932, the eruption of a two-year war with Peru over the Leticia area on the Amazon frontier cast the die against Colombian solvency. The war was a costly diversion of scarce resources and energy and drove the government toward a moratorium on its foreign debt payments. In late November Olaya signed a private-debts moratorium law; in April 1933 the government announced its intention to suspend payments on the national external debt and the guaranteed bonds of the Agricultural Mortgage Bank, although total default did not come until 1934.[16]

The United States played a minor role in the resolution of the Leticia dispute. The war overlapped the Hoover and Roosevelt administrations, both of which were anxious to maintain stability in the hemisphere and offset Latin American criticism, led largely by Argentina, of U.S. interventionism. In the Leticia conflict the United States endorsed efforts by the League of Nations to achieve a negotiated settlement, even though League involvement in the Western Hemisphere may have seemed to contravene the Monroe Doctrine. Late in the Hoover administration, Stimson warned Peru against military intervention to force its claims against Colombia. The use of force also violated the Stimson-inspired nonrecognition resolution of the American states accepted in August 1932. Stimson was thus enthusiastic in his support for a League of Nations initiative calling on Peru to withdraw from the disputed territory. The Hoover administration even agreed to serve as one of three members on a commission to occupy Leticia until a settlement could be arranged. It was significant that the Roosevelt administration endorsed the decision and participated in the League commission, marking a departure in American policy. This policy decision was less an indication of support for either the League or Colombia than of a desire to steal some of the thunder from Argentina, which continued its attacks on U.S. interventionism. Argentina in mid-1933 approved a resolution condemning "wars of aggression," calling for negotiated settlements of conflicts, and prohibiting "diplomatic or armed" intervention. In October the Argentine foreign minister gained the signatures of six other Latin American states in support of his Anti-War Treaty of Nonaggression and Conciliation. Thus, the Argentines went to the Montevideo conference that December as the seeming leader of American states.[17]

The Leticia conflict with Peru placed an added financial strain on Colombia, but it also occasioned discussion over arms sales and the role of representatives in Colombia of American arms manufacturers. From the perspective of some U.S. senators, arms sales during the Leticia dispute were symbolic of a larger problem of the relationship between arms manufacturers and international wars. In 1934 a special U.S. Senate committee, chaired by isolationist North Dakota Republican Senator Gerald P. Nye, held highly publicized hearings on the munitions industry. Those hearings documented charges that

U.S. military pilots had served as instructors with the Colombian air corps and further pointed to the volume of sale of U.S. weapons to Colombia.

The Senate hearings publicized the role in Colombia of former U.S. military officer James H. Strong, who retired from active service in the United States to become a technical military adviser to the Colombian government during the Peruvian war. Strong allegedly received compensation, contrary to American law, from the munitions industry for acquiring contracts for the industry with the Colombian war ministry. He was dismissed by the Colombian government under that suspicion. During the Senate hearings, the Colombian Foreign Ministry and War Department were anxious that Colombian defense information not be made public in the United States from confidential correspondence. Colombian officials launched a vigorous protest in September 1934 when the committee detailed information of the Colombian harbor defense plan, in particular for Buenaventura on the Pacific coast. Assistant Secretary of State Sumner Welles agreed with the objections of Colombian Minister A. Gonzalez Fernandez, and Cordell Hull formally requested the Nye committee to withhold any information pertaining to Colombian military plans. Any damage had already been committed. Colombia's Senate subsequently passed a resolution calling on the López government to publish the names of those implicated in "secret understandings with the armament sales companies," although there is no evidence that any action was taken.[18]

The Oil Question

Olaya's political fortunes waned with the economic decline in the early 1930s, but his administration did effectively address the long-standing dispute over Gulf Oil's title to the Barco concession in northeastern Colombia. Olaya met with Gulf officials during his trip to the United States as president-elect in 1930 to outline the Colombian desire for rapid development of any oil concessions. His main concern was to counter political criticism that the oil companies preferred to hold Colombian oil in reserve until the international economic picture improved. Gulf Oil took a hard line with the Colombian government throughout the negotiations, apparently in the belief that the U.S. government would intervene on its behalf in the event negotiations proved abortive.[19]

The State Department did not share Gulf's perception of the issue, but it did believe that settlement of the concession and the implementation of oil legislation acceptable to the companies were important conditions for Colombian economic and political stability. To that end the department arranged for Olaya to meet with George Rublee of Covington, Burling, Acheson, Schorb & Rublee, the distinguished Washington law firm, in the hope that he would function as a "buffer" between the oil companies and the Colombian government in the conclusion of new oil legislation. Assistant Secretary Francis White was confident that Rublee as adviser to Olaya would "solve a major difficulty for us, and keep the oil question there from becoming acrimonious and a subject of newspaper discussion throughout this hemisphere."[20] Olaya relied heavily on Rublee for advice on oil matters. He immediately initiated a study of a new petroleum law and reorganized the Ministry of Industries to remove the anti-American group appointed by former Conservative Minister José Antonio Montalvo.

Caffery in particular was struck by the improved political climate. When the right-wing Conservative Silvio Villegas attacked the administration in Congress for its close cooperation with U.S. interests on oil matters, including the Rublee mission, Foreign Minister Eduardo Santos, one of the country's leading moderate Liberals, and Minister of Industries Francisco José Chaux successfully parried the thrust. Caffery was pleased with the direction of Colombian politics, suggesting that "we have a unique opportunity during this Congress for securing a variety of much desired legislation of far-reaching effects on American interests."[21]

The oil legislation and the debate over it marked an important evolution in Colombian-U.S. oil relations. Both governments sought a middle ground between the shoals of nationalism and the economic self-interest of the oil industry. Rublee and Olaya contributed to a more positive attitude not so much toward the companies but toward the capacity of American "experts" to provide an element of neutrality. The British commercial secretary in Bogotá commented perceptively: "Colombians are now beginning to appreciate the difference between the views of representatives of American interests and those of impartial or academic American experts, and . . . to better understand the President's pro-American leanings."[22]

As negotiations over general oil legislation came to a close, the Olaya administration and Rublee turned their energies more specifically to a resolution of the longstanding dispute over title to the Barco oil concession. The State Department was not a party to the final settlement, the Chaux-Folsom contract (named after the minister of Industries and Gulf's representative); but it actively intervened throughout in an effort to smooth the route to agreement. The main points of dispute were required minimum production levels and the amount of royalty the operating company would have to pay on its operations. Folsom appealed to the head office for a compromise, and Francis White lobbied the company to accept Folsom's recommendation. Olaya believed strongly that control over minimum production and limits on the exploration period were critical to public and congressional acceptance of any contract. American officials were convinced of Olaya's sincerity in the matter, that he was making a major concession to the United States to negotiate a contract with Gulf Oil given public hostility to the company. Rublee and Caffery thought that Olaya personally would have preferred to grant the Barco concession to a non-American company, and thus they stressed the need for Gulf to compromise.[23]

Gulf's desire to have a Colombian field contiguous to Venezuela combined with State Department mediation and Olaya's flexibility to produce an agreement. In June 1931 Olaya signed the legislation restoring to Gulf Oil what was believed to be a potentially rich area for oil development. The months of debate indicated how volatile remained not only the contract but ties to the United States, but approval of the Barco concession law at least formally ended one of the most acrimonious disputes in Colombian-U.S. relations since the Panama crisis.[24]

The López Years, 1934–1938

In the waning moments of the Olaya presidency, with Alfonso López the Liberal heir apparent, American diplomatic and business circles were apprehensive about the future. They saw López as anti-American and an unlikely figure to continue the highly cooperative model of his predecessor. López was a vigorous, slight man of intellectual intensity and personal charm. He had risen from the ranks of an artisan class family that was well established in banking and other enterprises by the twentieth century. He was educated in political economy and finance in Colombia, London, and the United States; in 1903 he took charge of his father's business interests in New York, returning to Bogotá the following year to manage family interests. By 1910 López was active in the Republican movement that elected President Restrepo. He participated in founding *El Liberal* and served a term as a Liberal deputy in the department of Tolima assembly before returning to New York to become vice-president of the American Mercantile Bank of Colombia. The bank was an affiliate of the Mercantile Bank of the Americas, formed by J. & W. Seligman & Company, Brown Brothers & Company, and the Guaranty Trust Company of New York, all of which played a significant role in Colombian finance in the 1920s and early 1930s. He remained with the bank until after World War I, when he resigned following a dispute with Seligman, and the bank was sold to the Royal Bank of Canada.[25] During the 1920s López was inactive in politics, although he supported Olaya in 1930 and served briefly as Colombian minister to Great Britain. Prior to his election, López had been outspoken in his criticism of Conservative party financial policies, especially what he viewed as overborrowing in foreign markets and the largely unregulated public works projects of the new era. In 1928 he had warned that the Colombian economy could not continue to generate the funds to service the debts acquired already in the course of that decade. Then, on a persistently rainy November day in 1933, some eight thousand people turned out at the bullring for the Liberal party convention that named López its presidential candidate.

In that capacity he indicated unwillingness to sacrifice the material well-being of Latin American people in the interests of international finance. He spoke against the alleged financial irresponsibility of his predecessors and promised a significant domestic legislative program. In his first major address to Congress following his inauguration, López made clear his view that Colombia's natural resources had been wrongly concessioned largely to foreign interests. American officials were cautious but largely hostile. In contrast to the feting of Olaya as president-elect in New York and Washington, when López traveled to Washington in 1934 to see President Roosevelt, the White House staff observed that it was "too bad the President should be bothered with this visit in the last few days before his departure" on a holiday cruise.[26]

Roosevelt's trip in the summer of 1934 was more than a "holiday cruise," and it had direct relevance to Colombia. Roosevelt in July 1934 visited three Caribbean basin nations as the first president to visit Latin America while in office. One of the three nations he visited was Colombia, where he met in the colonial, walled city of Cartagena with President Olaya in the dying days of his administration. Their exchange of pleasantries had dramatic import. For Colombian-U.S. relations the meeting symbolized the desire of the Roosevelt administration for the continuation of the type of policies with which Olaya had been associated. For the rest of Latin America, it was further evidence that the Roosevelt administration intended to take the region more seriously than had its predecessors. It could also have been interpreted as a caution to Alfonso López as he moved into the presidency.[27]

American officials failed to understand López's liberal ideas, which were not unlike Roosevelt's. He had more interest in social reform and labor than his predecessors, and, like Roosevelt, he directed his energies largely to domestic issues in the mid-1930s. López was a pragmatic liberal, interested not in a Mexican-style restructuring of Colombian political power and a redistribution of economic power but the creation of a more balanced, integrated society in which the fruits of national wealth would be more evenly distributed, with interest-group and class conflict muted. *Acción Liberal,* an influential, left Liberal Bogotá paper, commented shortly before López's inauguration that his ideas were a pale reflection of the Mexican revolution.[28] There was a hint that López was inclined to depart from the premises of the Suárez Doctrine identifying the Colombian future with the United States; yet the *Acción Liberal* observation indicates that there were serious doubts about his radicalism. Although the Communist party during the period of Popular Front supported López, as did the main national federation of labor (the Colombian Confederation of Labor or CTC), the extreme left was unimpressed by the mild reforms and the handling of such major confrontations between foreign capital and Colombian labor as the 1935 and 1938 strikes against Tropical Oil in Barrancabermeja.

López's main concerns were domestic, but his past experience and personal inclinations included international relations, and he was not a narrow nationalist in his perception of Colombia's place in the world. He had served as a Colombian delegate to both the London Economic Conference and to the Montevideo meeting of American States in late 1933. He also appointed former President Olaya as foreign minister when he found he needed Olaya's political influence in the government. López harbored some antagonism toward U.S. enterprises, but it was directed primarily at the United Fruit Company. Conversely, where the oil companies were concerned, he was on excellent terms with H. A. Metzger of Standard Oil, and his only objective was to protect Colombian sovereignty by denying monopolistic concessions in future to foreign enterprise.[29]

In relations with the United States and with American economic interests in Colombia, López inherited several issues from the previous decade. These included United Fruit Company labor relations and landholding problems in Magdalena, oil legislation and foreign investment in the oil industry, and the foreign debt and the efforts of American groups to recoup on their losses. In his treatment of these interests and issues, López manifest less deference to the United States and American models than had Olaya, and he was significantly more supportive of the rights of Colombian labor employed by foreign enterprise than other administrations in the first half of the twentieth century. On the other hand, there was no significant alteration in the basic hegemonic relationship between the two countries during his presidency and considerably less vigor in policy toward U.S. interests than characterized the administration of Lázaro Cárdenas in Mexico at the same time.

The Oil Industry

López made no secret of his dissatisfaction with the general direction of Colombian policy toward foreign oil investment. In his first year in office he took actions that suggested the possibility of a harder line against the companies, introducing new legislation, challenging the tax returns of the Andean National Corporation as well as United Fruit. As president-elect he had appointed a committee to study existing oil legislation. From this group emerged the basis for the oil policy pursued by his administration, and the one significant departure from the past was the emergence of the idea of a state owned and operated oil refinery, a substantially more modest concept than had already emerged in Latin American countries that had established state oil companies for exploration, development, and marketing. Nonetheless, this was four years before Mexico's nationalization of most of its foreign-owned oil industry and the creation of PEMEX. In that sense, López could be viewed as a pioneer.

His administration's oil legislation authorized the establishment of a government-owned refinery to be operated essentially as a public utility. This proposal reflected the persistent belief among moderate reformers in the Liberal party that Tropical Oil's basic monopoly over the marketing of fuel oil, gasoline, and other oil products in Colombia contributed to higher prices for Colombian consumers, and that this could only be altered with direct government intervention in the industry.[30]

The Colombian Senate was ill-disposed to the legislation, advancing arguments provided largely by H. A. Metzger of Standard Oil that such an initiative would reduce the government's revenues from royalties received from Tropical and the Andean National Pipeline at a time of economic uncertainty; in what would have to be viewed as a threat of corporate retaliation, Metzger indicated that in the event the government did build and operate its own refinery, Tropical would increase imports to Colombia from other operations and abandon its own plans for expansion of the Barrancabermeja refinery. Faced with corporate and political opposition in 1934 and Olaya's arrival in the cabinet as foreign minister in early 1935 to assist with the settlement of the Leticia dispute with Peru, the idea of a national refinery was temporarily shelved until after the 1936 congressional elections.[31]

Late in 1935 labor unrest and general social conflict in the oil town of Barrancabermeja, tying up river traffic from there to Cartagena, revived government interest in oil legislation. Critics of Tropical Oil's labor relations came from both Liberal and Conservative parties. In mid-November the House of Representatives sent a committee to the oil region to report on the extent and causes of labor radicalism in the oil industry, although maritime workers on the Magdalena River were also involved. The Communist party was very active among the oil workers, but the dominant element by the mid-1930s was the pro-López Colombian Confederation of Labor, with which the local petroleum workers union was affiliated. The strike itself generated considerable rhetorical anti-Americanism and anti-imperialism.[32]

That committee submitted a highly critical report several weeks later, stressing the inadequate housing of Tropical Oil manual workers outside company property, in contrast to the higher quality company housing. The committee also recommended three pieces of legislation: a government-owned refinery; regulation of labor relations, and government control of medical and health services in industry and agriculture. The committee urged that the companies should no longer be exempt from departmental and municipal taxation, a policy that was believed to have significantly contributed to the poor standard of living of Barrancabermeja workers and their families. The López administration now proposed a modest revision of the 1931 oil law pertaining to refineries, taxes on petroleum reserves on private property, and further limits on exploration periods. Significantly, the government also declared any continuation of the strike illegal and ordered the detention of strike leaders.[33]

Ironically, given the early negative American views of the prospects for foreign enterprise under the López administration, the new oil legislation that emerged from Congress in the course of 1936 was technically superior to the 1931 law and more attractive to many operators and investors, although Tropical Oil officials objected to some of the restrictions. The legislation revealed that neither López nor his minister of Industries, Benito Hernández Bustos, sought to discourage foreign investment. The legislation was drafted without consultation with the companies, however, in a greater show of political independence than had characterized the Olaya years. The British Minister heralded the new law as "striking evidence of the Government's determination to lay real foundations for the development of the petroleum industry by the adoption of far-sighted and stable legislation." The counsel for the Socony-Vacuum Petroleum Company in New York informed State Department official Laurence Duggan that the company was content with the present attitude of the Colombian government toward foreign investment. Gulf Oil shortly announced a pipeline project; Tropical Oil's officials were determined not to challenge the Colombian government's hectarage limitations for fear of public reaction. Passage of the new law stimulated investment in the industry, in what a Tropical Oil official later called the "second epoch of exploration in the country."[34]

A companion piece of legislation conformed to López's reform views on the need to protect and enhance the power of Colombian labor. Law 149 specified that "no industrial, agricultural, commercial or any other enterprise" with a monthly payroll in excess of one thousand pesos could hire more than 20 percent foreign employees (meaning essentially technical and supervisory/managerial employees) or 10 percent foreign labor (meaning essentially unskilled, manual labor).

The law also controlled the amount of payroll that could be allocated to each of those groups, although there were qualifications allowing the employment of foreign technicians not available in Colombia.[35]

Such labor reforms were overdue and rather limited in scope. By the end of the 1930s Tropical Oil had a substantial labor force: more than thirty-four hundred Colombians and two hundred North Americans on the DeMares concession alone, compared with approximately five thousand Colombians who were employed in a much older industry—the manufacture of cigars and cigarettes. Given the high concentration of labor in the oil industry and problems associated with the disparities between the more skilled foreign employees and the largely unskilled Colombian workers in the 1930s, it was not surprising that the industry should have been one of the most volatile from the 1920s on and the source of militant organized labor groups until recent years.[36]

In early 1938 another major labor crisis emerged among Tropical's workers, who had similar demands: improved wages; an eight hour day; better health facilities and services, including the construction of a hospital; at least one month's notice to be given by the company for eviction from company housing; and prohibition against company reprisals for worker involvement in union activity. Following a month of abortive negotiations, in April the union struck. Led by a liberal Barranca doctor, nationalist, and labor activist, Gustavo Buenahora, and CTC delegate Diego Luis Córdoba, on April 12 several hundred workers defied a mayoralty order against public demonstrations; as they rallied in the main plaza, police and troops fired on the crowd, killing three men. The attack effectively ended the strike.[37]

Under the López administration Colombia presented no challenge to the presence of U.S. and other foreign oil companies in the country; at the same time that the López government attempted to establish clearer parameters for the operation of those firms in the national interest, the administration provided a more stable political environment for foreign investment. Thus, at the time that a furor erupted in Mexico in 1938 over the nationalization of foreign oil companies, the Colombian minister of industries, César A. Pedraza, could in all conscience issue an official reassurance through the pages of *El Tiempo* that foreign oil contracts in Colombian were secure. The Suárez Doctrine appeared intact even during the most reformist years.[38] By the late 1930s U.S. foreign policy had attained its objectives in Colombian oil development, although Colombia's choices more than U.S. policy had made this possible. Such choices derived essentially from the class and political dynamic of Colombian society itself.

United Fruit

López policies toward the United Fruit Company did not differ significantly from those in other areas of U.S. investment, although he was personally antagonistic to the company. Personal views aside, his efforts to draw organized labor into the ranks of the Liberal party inevitably made for tension between his government and national and foreign banana interests in Magdalena. In the fall of 1934 López sent his minister of war, Marco A. Auli, to negotiate a settlement between workers and planters. He negotiated an increase in the minimum wage from 80 centavos to 1.20 pesos with representatives of the Magdalena Banana Cooperative. Continued employer opposition to increasing wages and improving working conditions under the economic restraint of the decade, however, combined with labor agitation to produce an uneasy peace. The manager of the Magdalena Fruit Company reasoned that strike leaders had achieved additional prestige from a wage increase, and he warned President López that unless the Colombian government adopted a less conciliatory attitude toward labor and brought stability to the industry, the company would discontinue its operations in Colombia. López reminded Bennett that popular dissent was a sign of a healthy political society, and he perceptively added that it was virtually impossible for a foreign corporate interest with such influence and visibility not to be the target of some public hostility.[39]

A congressional enquiry into these problems, however, concurred with the United Fruit rather than the Lopez interpretation of the sources of labor unrest in the area. The majority report of the commission praised the medical services made available by United Fruit to its employees and criticized the independent planters for poor working conditions on their operations. Both minority and majority reports balanced their criticism of the ineffectiveness of the departmental government in law enforcement with their hostility toward the radicalism of local labor. The majority report clearly favored foreign investment in principle and portrayed labor agitation as a threat to the stability of the industry. Even the minority report lauded the United Fruit Company for its irrigation development in the area and flood control on the Aracataca River. The report also identified several unresolved problems for which the company was blamed. One was the company's opposition to the establishment of independent Colombian banana-producing operations; another was the ubiquitous complaint of United's abuse of its economic and political power in the region. Six years after the bloody 1928 strike, the author of the minority report noted that there had been no significant modification in the company's use of contract laborers for whom the company denied social welfare responsibility.[40]

An additional issue that shaped labor relations was land invasion of largely uncultivated lands by *colonos* or squatters. As Catherine LeGrand has carefully documented, between 1929 and 1934, with the decline in market demand for bananas, United significantly reduced its acreage by some seventy-five thousand hectares. An estimated ten thousand hectares were occupied by *colonos*. The company's response was ambivalent. On one hand, company officials did not wish to relinquish claim to the land when the economy improved; on the other hand, *colonos* operating these lands were preferable to groups of potentially troublesome unemployed workers in Santa Marta or the loss of that labor to other parts of the country. The company thus insisted that the *colonos* sign tenancy documents recognizing company title. If they failed to do so, the company took eviction action or leased land to larger Colombian growers in return for an agreement that the growers deal with the *colonos*. The company does not seem to have recovered the lands lost during the depression years. This land issue remained a major cause of labor agitation in that period.[41]

No legislation devolved from the congressional reports until 1936, when the Colombian Congress implemented two bills that had application to the industry: Law 149 restricted the portion of payrolls that could be allocated to nonnationals; and other legislation placing a two-year limit on contracts for the sale and export of bananas and authorizing the establishment of national government inspection of bananas. To encourage national producers in competition with United, the legislation also provided that the Magdalena Banana Cooperative could accept twenty-year, 8 percent interest mortgages from landowners. The two-year limit was later modified, but United officials argued with the State Department that these were unwarranted and discriminatory initiatives. Both Sumner Welles and Laurence Duggan, as senior department officials, nonetheless rejected entreaties from the company for diplomatic support, responding that the dispute was one of a domestic Colombian nature. The department maintained that position through 1936 and 1937, even when confronted by requests from the American minister in Bogotá for permission to use his good offices on the company's behalf. Duggan's and Welles's response were a clear indication of the shift in approach that had taken place within the department with the election of Roosevelt and the appointment of Cordell Hull as secretary of state.[42]

Magdalena Fruit officials in Colombia sought to undercut the spirit of the legislation and to control prices by concluding five-year supply contracts with Colombian growers before the law came into effect, although the company did attempt to offset criticism by enabling Colombian planters with long-term contracts to share in international price increases. López was sufficiently irritated by the company's transparent defiance of its efforts, that in 1937 the minister of industries and labor submitted a bill to the Senate requesting extensive government control over the banana industry in production and marketing. The legislation also provided for possible expropriation of property on grounds of public utility and social interest, harking back to the debate over land policy after World War I and to the principles embedded in the Mexican constitution.[43]

The legislation was ultimately declared unconstitutional by the Supreme Court in 1939,[44] but it reflected the depth of disaffection with the United Fruit Company. Hostility ranged across the political spectrum and was embodied in the conclusions of congressional committees as well as the editorials of the Communist party weekly *Tierra*. Indicative of those tensions, national police arrested United manager George Bennett on charges of bribery of a public official and theft of a public document, although the charges were subsequently dismissed. The intensity of the domestic political turmoil over relations with United were also evident in the Senate's decision to censure former Olaya cabinet member, Pedro María Carreño, for allegedly receiving legal fees from United during the time he was in the cabinet. That action did not occur until Santos was in the presidential palace; in the interim, the López adminstration made no overtures to smooth over the problems. United Fruit in turn indicated that it would not take steps to control the spread of Sigatoka disease (leaf blight), which was threatening the banana plants or to increase the prices paid to Colombian planters.[45] The stalemate continued.

The Reciprocal Trade Agreement

The place of United Fruit was one of the more fractious issues in Colombian-U.S. relations in the López presidency. Of more fundamental importance to the binational relationship but no less controversial, however, was the negotiation of a reciprocal trade agreement under the provisions of the 1934 Reciprocal Trade Agreements Act. Only a few weeks after López's inauguration as president, the State Department instructed the American chargé in Bogotá to open the question of a renegotiated commercial agreement with Colombia based on the previous bilateral agreement. Although there was optimism in Washington and Bogotá that the new agreement would be rapidly concluded, negotiations and debate over ratification took almost two years and revealed the same areas of disagreement over trade directions, the issue of economic diversification, and the U.S. fear of competition from European and Asian commercial interests that had been present in the first treaty discussions.[46]

U.S. exporters were optimistic during talks with Colombia, Brazil, Haiti, and Cuba. The *New York Times* reported that American firms were engaged in an extensive advertising campaign in anticipation of expanded trade opportunities; yet cotton textile manufacturers in the United States complained that neither the recently concluded agreement with Cuba nor those pending with Colombia and other Latin American countries had improved their competitive positions against European and Asian exports. Throughout the discussions, there was a running feud between the State Department, especially Cordell Hull, and the presidential foreign trade adviser, George Peek, who sought to use the trade agreement as a weapon to bring Colombia into line on foreign-exchange controls and its defaulted foreign bonds. There was scepticism of a different order in the Department of Commerce. Henry Chalmers of the tariff division, for instance, contended that the main weaknesses in the Colombian treaty were continued Colombian reliance on coffee exports, which did not improve its capacity to purchase U.S. goods, and the failure of the United States to make adequate concessions on a wider range of imports from Colombia, which in turn might have led Colombia to move away from protectionism of its agricultural sector.[47]

Following public hearings in Washington on the agreement, several new provisions emerged in the revised version of the treaty, not all well received in Bogotá. The American chargé now reported a significant change in mood in the López administration and difficulty in gaining access to the president. The situation improved slightly in 1935 with the addition of Olaya to the cabinet and with the appointment of López's brother Miguel as minister to Washington. With their assistance, by July the agreement had been signed. Assistant Secretary of State Sumner Welles gave much of the credit for the final agreement to the efforts of Miguel López.

The main Colombian dissent against the agreement came from industrial groups, including the dominant Federation of Industrialists and the National Association of Colombian Industry. Geographically, opposition was based in Medellín, the most industrialized sector of the country and a Conservative party stronghold. *El País*, a Conservative party paper in Medellín, contended the agreement would destroy small Colombian industries and make the nation no more than a "subsidiary of the United States." The leading Medellín Conservative paper, *El Colombiano,* carried similar articles. Prominent Conservative Silvio Villegas strongly supported the position of Medellín industrialists. Antioqueño labor also protested against the agreement; a petition submitted to Congress in early November was signed by some seven hundred textile workers, though it received little attention in Bogotá. On the other hand, regional antagonism to wheat growers and flour milling interests on the Bogotá sabana led some agricultural interests to support the agreement, arguing that only less-expensive imports from the United States could break the sabana monopoly. In the press, there was favorable support from the leading Bogotá Liberal dailies, *El Espectador* and *El Tiempo,* and *El Heraldo Industrial* of Cali spoke in favor of the accord.

The Liberal majority in Congress meant that victory for the agreement was inevitable as long as it had the support of the López administration. Even some of those who supported the agreement, such as Boyacá Senator Hector Vargas, did so feeling that the agreement was an imperfect one. He eloquently suggested that he was voting for the treaty in spite of the fact that its provisions gave important concessions to the United States with little more in return than assurance of the status quo for Colombian exports. He claimed he took this stand in an effort to demonstrate to the United States "our sincere desire to cooperate . . . toward the re-establishment of the balance and rhythm of our commercial interchange." The trade patterns of the next few years confirmed his assessment.

The U.S. Bureau of Foreign and Domestic Commerce viewed improved U.S. trade results as deriving directly from the agreement. There was also an improvement of the U.S. position relative to its European and Asian competitors. In the important area of textiles, in 1935 the United States ranked third behind Britain, which overwhelmingly dominated Colombian imports with 55 percent, and Japan with 12 percent of the Colombian market. By the end of 1937, the first full year of the agreement, the U.S. share had risen to 20 percent and had significantly surpassed that of Japan. This result conformed to the effort to create a more homogeneous hemispheric approach to commercial relations and to break down protectionist barriers. Seen in that context, the Colombian agreement was a step in the right direction. U.S. chargé in Bogotá, William Dawson, commented in late 1937, "It appears that the Colombian Government's commercial policy is definitely tending to approach the basic purposes and objectives of the trade agreements program of the United States."

The 1930s thus represented an important decade of transition in Colombian-U.S. relations, away from the venomous conflicts of the Panama Canal era and the contradictions of the 1920s with an emphasis on unbridled economic growth superimposed on a traditional, agricultural society struggling to find its national identity in a period of rapid modernization. Despite persistent conflicts, there was a growing sense among Colombian leaders that they could maintain close relations with the United States without losing their ability to exercise some leadership in the hemisphere and engage in domestic reform. The commercial negotiations and the consequences of the Reciprocal Trade Agreement nonetheless suggested how difficult it would be to reorder the Colombian economy away from its traditional path as long as the main international market forces tended to reinforce a reliance on the traditional agricultural sector.

By 1938, the imminence of war in Europe, the desire for hemispheric security, and confidence that Eduardo Santos, like Olaya earlier in the decade, would be a voice of moderation in protecting U.S. interests in Colombia prompted the United States to raise the status of its legation in Bogotá to embassy level. Spruille Braden, significantly an individual with major investment interests in Chile, became the first U.S. ambassador. In recommending the enhanced status to President Roosevelt, Cordell Hull stressed improved relations with Colombia, the substantial level of U.S. investments, prospects for increased investments, and the important moderating role of Colombia within the inter-American system.[48]

6 War, Diplomacy, and Hemispheric Integration

> We have learned that our ocean-girt hemisphere is not immune from severe attack—that we cannot measure our safety in terms of miles on any map. (Franklin D. Roosevelt, 9 December 1941)

The outbreak of war in Europe in the fall of 1939 and U.S. entry following the Japanese attack on Pearl Harbor in December 1941 had a paradoxical impact on Colombian-U.S. relations. Above all, the wartime experience emphasized the economic and strategic interdependence of nations in the Western Hemisphere. In the Colombian instance, U.S. preparedness from 1939 and actual mobilization after 1941 required close economic, political, and strategic cooperation between the two nations. On the other hand, the war generated debate within Colombian political circles, not simply between Liberals and Conservatives but also within the Conservative party, over the appropriate stance to be adopted toward both the Axis nations and the Allies. Ultimately Colombia broke diplomatic relations with the Axis powers, participated in hemispheric defense operations (especially coastal antisubmarine patrols); unlike Brazil it did not offer to commit military forces overseas. Wartime conditions, especially U.S. demands for strategic raw materials, tended to undermine Colombian economic nationalism and even economic independence. Culturally the war years seem to have marked a transition to a greater degree of Americanization, with some Colombian intellectuals more aware than in the past of literary and intellectual currents in the United States.

World War II facilitated the achievement of several longstanding U.S. foreign policy objectives in Colombia. The two most dramatic examples were the de-Germanization of Colombian commercial and military aviation and the deflection of nationalistic petroleum legislation, both legacies of the 1920s and early 1930s. Those developments in aviation and oil, however, were only part of a much broader range of cooperation.

The Roosevelt administration was fortunate to have Eduardo Santos in the Colombian presidency during the preparedness campaign and the first year of war. Santos's election in 1938 as the candidate of moderate Liberalism marked the end of López era reforms, and from the U.S. perspective promised to usher in a period of pro-American cooperation. Bogotá-born and a lawyer by profession, Santos had served previously as foreign minister and in Europe as a Colombian diplomat. He was a long-time director of the prestigious Liberal *El Tiempo*, a position he had used to support Olaya and criticize López. By the time he took office in 1938, any lingering doubts among American officials of his desire to cooperate with the United States had disappeared.[1]

Santos moved promptly once in office to replace a private British naval mission, which had been in Colombia since 1935, with an official U.S. naval mission, and he followed the naval initiative with a request for assistance in aviation. Before the end of the year both agreements were in place. These growing military links with the United States happened to coincide with Colombian-German tensions in late 1938, when Colombian authorities recalled their minister-designate from Berlin in protest over his treatment for taking photographs of anti-Semitic actions.

More formal ties to the United States did not pass without remark from Colombian critics, especially on the Conservative right, where there was a decided inclination toward European traditions and sincere empathy with Nazi Germany and Fascist Italy. The Bogotá Conservative daily, *El Siglo,* published a lead article by prominent Conservative Guillermo Camacho Montoya critical of the military, indeed any, ties with the United States. Camacho's analysis verged on racism in his critique of the cultural poverty of "Sax-Americans," who had achieved distinction only in such relatively insignificant technological advances such as "toilets" and "paved roads," while the Germans and Italians, fresh from their achievements in the Spanish Civil War, had more to offer Colombia culturally and militarily. Camacho was seemingly untroubled by the contradiction between his preference for ties with "Catholic" nations and his inclination toward Prussian military prowess.

Camacho's views did not represent either majority Colombian opinion in late 1938 or even the prevailing views in official Conservative ranks, although major leaders in the party such as Laureano Gómez would also break their lances against Santos's pro-U.S. policies in the course of the war. Nonetheless, Gómez and *El Siglo* from 1939 to 1941 were more isolationist than they were pro-German; indeed they strongly criticized Nazi Germany in this period. As a prominent senator. Gómez was also in a better position to influence government policy. Unlike Camacho, Gómez saw the world struggle as one between Christianity and secular materialism, not between communism and Catholicism. Gómez's early criticism of Santos and the United States was premised less on anti-Americanism than on his basic concern that the 1939 Panama conference declaration establishing a zone of neutrality for several hundred miles around the hemisphere south of Canada would draw Latin America inevitably into the war.[2] Nor was Gómez appeased by the arguments of Foreign Minister Luis López de Mesa that the Colombian government was not committed by any of the Panama agreements to take military measures in the event there was a belligerent naval action in Colombian waters. He was equally critical the following year of the idea of mutual assistance against extracontinental aggressors in the Act of Havana. To Gómez, it was the United States not the rest of the Americas that was threatened by external aggression, and he did not wish to see Colombia drawn into the maelstrom. His arguments in this regard were not unlike the isolationist attacks in the United States on Roosevelt's neutrality policy. Also like his U.S. counterparts, Gómez was critical of what he considered were executive actions bypassing Congress.[3]

The Conservative party criticism of Santos's foreign policy was not, in essence, fundamentally anti-American, although there was a strong strand of such views in the Conservative press in 1940 and 1941. Yet, American Ambassador Spruille Braden was as much concerned about the comparative silence of those Conservatives who were pro-

American but hesitated to tangle with Laureano Gómez, as he was with the critics themselves.[4] As much as there were cultural affinities to Europe and Conservative preferences for the order and hierarchy that seemed embodied in European corporatism, there were also by World War II strong business associations between Colombian Conservatives and U.S. capital in agriculture and industry. Medellín, as the most industrialized city in the country, was after all also a Conservative stronghold. Conservatives, as pragmatists, accepted the Suárez Doctrine of the inevitability of ties with the United States and the desire to make those relations as productive as possible.[5] Consequently, Conservatives voted during the Santos administration in support of his foreign policy decisions, and Santos received almost as much opposition from the leftist-Liberal Alfonso López forces as he did from the Conservative party. Tensions and contradictions there were in Colombian thought and politics, but on the whole the drift toward the United States in Colombian politics and policy was unmistakable by this time.

The U.S. military missions began their work early in 1939, and within a short time Colombian pilots, naval officers, artillery and infantry specialists, and technicians were traveling to the United States for more formal training. This development marked the beginning of what would continue on a larger scale into the cold war years and suggests the importance of World War II in providing the momentum for cold war hemispheric integration in military matters.

German military success in Europe, especially the defeat of France in June 1940, contributed to additional strengthening of the Colombian-U.S. military relationship as the German threat to hemispheric security seemed to intensify. In September 1940 the United States committed itself, as part of general hemispheric defense planning, to a series of defensive measures with Colombia, including liaison between military staff, exchange of security intelligence information, measures for coastal patrols, joint training of personnel, and continued lending of technical advisers. The U.S. government was committed to defend Colombia, as it was other Western Hemisphere nations, in the event it was attacked by a nonhemispheric power. Immediately following Pearl Harbor, the foreign ministers of the American republics met at Rio de Janeiro and agreed on a program of hemispheric cooperation to meet the Axis threat. The program, which was adhered to in varying degrees by all of the republics before the end of the war, included potential breaking of diplomatic relations with the Axis, the suspension of commercial relations, joint military efforts, and increased production of strategic raw materials.

Colombia was the first South American nation to act on these premises after the Japanese attack at Pearl Harbor and the U.S. declaration of war. Colombia broke diplomatic relations with Japan one day after Pearl Harbor and with Germany and Italy on 18 December. On 7 December President Santos urgently cabled the Colombian ambassador in Washington requesting information on U.S. government actions and the state of public opinion toward a new world war. The following day, Colombia released a declaration indicating that it would be faithful to the resolution of hemispheric solidarity adopted at the Havana and Lima conferences of American states; it simultaneously broke diplomatic relations with Japan and announced that it would take all necessary steps to assist in the protection of the Panama Canal.[6] Later in December the Colombian ambassador informed Cordell Hull that in conformity with the principles of hemispheric solidarity, the Colombian government had determined not to treat as belligerents either the United States or other American republics then at war.[7] Before the end of January 1942, the Santos administration took executive action to tighten control of potential sabotage and espionage by placing restrictions on private foreign clubs and the movement of foreign nationals; the Transocean news agency was closed down and several employees arrested; and the government suspended the naturalization of naturalized citizens suspected of taking part in activities that threatened national security.[8]

Colombian authorities had already in early 1941 arrested several Germans engaged in propaganda activities.[9] In March 1942 Colombia concluded with the United States a Lend-Lease agreement that had been under discussion for over a year and which provided that the United States could supply up to $16.2 million in defense materiel to Colombia at half the real cost and with no payment of interest.[10] In June and July, following the sinking by a German submarine of the Colombian schooner *Resolute* in the Caribbean and the machine-gunning of crew members set adrift in a lifeboat, the Santos administration froze the assets of Axis nationals in Colombia. American officials pressed the government to go further, to freeze the assets of all foreign nationals with economic ties to the Axis countries, believing that the use of the Proclaimed List (a blacklist against firms trading with the enemy) was not in itself sufficient to restrain trade. Colombian officials preferred to establish national controls over Axis firms in Colombia in order to reduce the negative impact on the Colombian economy of British and American blacklists. There were inevitable tensions over the Blacklist, both as to its contents and to its administration. American officials were prepared to discuss the list with a Colombian consultative committee, but the State Department stressed that it was not prepared to have the Colombian government engage in prior screening; control had to remain in Washington, and American officials continued to insist that nationality was not the main criterion for inclusion on the list, but rather direct or indirect ties to Axis interests. An illustration of what was acceptable was the change of the *Banco Alemán Antioqueño* to the *Banco Commercial Antioqueño*, which was taken off the Proclaimed List when it clearly severed ties with Proclaimed List nationals.[11]

In May 1942 the two countries signed a new military agreement extending for four years the U.S. Army and air corps missions in Colombia. This initiative was important for American security on the Caribbean and Pacific coasts close to the Panama Canal (an issue on which even Conservative leaders Laureano Gómez and José de la Vega were in agreement); it was also hoped to ensure that Colombia was weaned away from rightist European military influences. As late as the end of 1941 Colombia employed a former Franco general and two pro-Vichy French officers who had remained in Colombia after the fall of France in 1940. American Ambassador Spruille Braden, never shy to speak his mind, stressed to the Colombian chief of staff that he hoped the latter would see "that any foreigners to be taken on in the future were of the proper democratic mind." [12]

Santos administration cooperation with the United States was not without criticism from within Colombian political circles, although with the exception of the Laureano Gómez faction of the Conservative party there was little strident anti-Americanism. Debate stemmed as much from internal political issues, in particular the early 1942 presidential elections, and from concern about excessive use of presidential discretionary powers, as from actual opposition to the United States. President Santos had granted secret permission to the U.S. military to use Colombian territory for its forces, especially antisubmarine warfare activities. All sides recognized that the main value of Colombia to the United States in the war was its proximity to the Panama Canal and the need to keep the country free of Axis penetration that would threaten the canal. Conservatives worried that this might draw Colombia into the war itself, although there was less opposition to the basic premise of helping to defend the canal. When, in mid-1942, President Santos met with the Colombian Senate Foreign Relations Committee to discuss joint Colombian-U.S. military cooperation, including convoying ships in the Caribbean, two of the leading old line Conservatives, Gómez and José de la Vega, declined to attend.[13] Although there was a general concern about the maintenance of Colombian sovereignty, Gómez was relatively isolated in his anti-Americanism. As historian David Bushnell has indicated, moderate Conservatives, led by Roberto Urdaneta Arbelaez, publicly supported the Santos administration's foreign policy, while Gómez's *El Siglo* castigated him as the instrument of American business interests in Colombia. That Gomez's ideological orientation was as sincere as it was opportunistic was reflected in his participation in early 1944 in the formation of the Legion Condor, a falangist organization with some one thousand members. The organization was entirely upper-middle class, with the four members of the directorate socially prominent Conservatives, one of them, Borrero Olano, the director of the Cali newspaper, *Diario del Pacifico*. State Department officials, as much as they may have been antagonistic to the views of Gómez and *El Siglo*, were determined not to be seen to interfere. The American Republics Division officials indicated that there should certainly be no attempt made to "strangle" *El Siglo*, either by withdrawing American advertising or by placing it on the Proclaimed List. In part the rationale was that Gómez himself tended to go off on political tangents but that many of his backers included important pro-American elements who should not be alienated.[14]

Under these circumstances, relations with the United States became a minor issue in the May 1942 presidential elections, which pitted former Liberal president Alfonso López against Carlos Arango Vélez, the candidate of dissident right wing Liberals and the Conservatives. During the campaign, U.S. officials were relatively sanguine about the significance of the election for U.S. policy. They anticipated a slight plurality for López, but in any event were confident that no possible victor would swing Colombia away from its present foreign policy orientation. Nor did they anticipate that the Colombian military would interfere in the election. The campaign itself further confirmed what U.S. observers had argued earlier about the orientation of the Conservatives, that there were prominent individuals in the party prepared to support U.S. links. In fact, Arango Vélez had been a stronger proponent of hemispheric solidarity than had López. The former's ability to capture Gómez's support suggests that neither consistency nor foreign policy was the key to understanding Gómez's political preferences. Near the end of the campaign Arango Vélez indicated that he favored increasing Colombia's contribution to the war effort, placing the nation on a military footing, and intensifying controls over fifth column activities; such views were discomfiting to his party.[15]

In July, following Lopez's comfortable victory in the election, he traveled as president-elect to the United States on an official visit amidst rumors that Colombia was considering a declaration of war against the Axis. His reception in 1942 was far more enthusiastic than in 1938. State Department Assistant Secretary Philip Bonsal told Sumner Welles on the eve of López's arrival that relations with Colombia had "never been better," with the Colombian economy enjoying growth resulting from greater diversification. The visit, which included an official White House dinner and meetings with Pan American Union and State Department officials, provided a visible occasion to demonstrate adherence to the principles of hemispheric solidarity. López used the opportunity to advance his ideas on a Pan American League of Nations, which were in a sense realized in the creation of the Organization of American States following the war. López and the Liberal government consistently stressed the desire during the war, in particular at the Chapultepec meetings in 1945, to have the inter-American system strengthened.[16]

Among the subjects the State Department prepared for discussion with López during his 1942 visit were oil concessions, the banana industry, and the American military use of Colombian territory. Both the oil companies and U.S. officials were concerned that the companies could not meet the drilling requirements on their concessions because of the shortage of steel and of drilling equipment during the war. Thus, they wanted to have the Colombian government suspend the requirements for the war period in order to avoid any forfeitures of concessions, and on this point they were successful. The already tense situation in the banana industry created by ongoing labor problems and the continuation of Sigatoka disease in the plants had been exacerbated by the wartime shortage of shipping facilities. The Magdalena Fruit Company was anxious to withdraw from the region. To buffer the economic impact of such a withdrawal, the Export-Import bank was prepared to extend a substantial credit to assist with the economic rehabilitation of Magdalena. By the fall of the year the company had made arrangements for a gradual withdrawal from the country— with a staggered discharge of dock workers, agricultural laborers, and others—and for the investment of funds in agricultural machinery, seed, animal breeding, and irrigation to provide alternative employment. In the other area of concern—U.S. military access to Colombian territory—López was committed to the Santos cooperation; but he stressed the importance of congressional approval in order to avoid subsequent political embarrassment for his administration and for the United States. He was also concerned about the implications of the U.S. intelligence gathering operations in the country. Ambassador

Arthur Bliss Lane urged that there be sharing of that information with Colombian authorities to protect the Colombian government from domestic political criticism.[17] López's official visit to Washington was clearly a success diplomatically and politically, and it contributed to agreement on the outstanding issues, but it did not generate any new and tangible Colombian contributions to the war effort.

The Liberal governments of Eduardo Santos and Alfonso López at least rhetorically shared the views of the Roosevelt administration on the significance of the struggle against the Axis powers. Before leaving office in 1942, Santos publicly linked a victory of the United Nations with the survival of Colombia. Two years later, during the Normandy landings of Allied forces to commence the opening of a second front, President López stressed the official Colombian interpretation of the issues involved in the war when he congratulated President Roosevelt for the successful operation; López portrayed the American effort as one on behalf of the "liberation of the oppressed peoples," and his message was liberally sprinkled with references to the defense of civilization and the service to humanity in freeing "enslaved" nations.[18]

There was little significant alteration in the Colombian political orientation on the war question from 1942 to 1945. The López administration extended nonbelligerency status to Brazil when the latter declared war on Germany in August 1942. In late 1943 the Colombian government declared a state of belligerency against Germany.[19] It declined to recognize the Vichy France government, and continued to pursue anti-Axis domestic policies, ultimately interning a number of German and Japanese nationals in early 1944. The Colombian government continued to seize the properties of Axis nationals into early 1945.[20] In 1943 the Colombian Congress enacted an economic defense plan, which, among other provisions, allowed the control of prices of drugs, general merchandise, and foodstuffs; it further authorized the issue of government bonds to enable the government to purchase telephone, transportation, electric power, and other public utility companies in the national interest. The income and the cash balances of those foreign firms that were placed under government control had to be invested in Colombian government bonds. By early 1945 American officials were reasonably pleased with Colombian progress in this area; a number of German interests had been bought out by Colombians and the Colombian government, including Empresa Hanseatica and Industria Quimica Colombiana. In general, however, the large German drug and chemical companies, including Bayer, Schering, and Instituto Behring, successfully resisted private purchase. American officials sought unsuccessfully to have them expropriated.[21]

What opposition there was to this policy orientation came from the Conservative party, although factions of the army also turned against López in 1944. In the debate over declaring a state of belligerency, for instance, thirteen Conservatives voted against the measure. Outside Congress, some groups sought more direct action against the Axis. The Colombian Confederation of Labor, for example, which was Liberal-dominated, urged a declaration of war. Following the sinking of the *Resolute* in 1942, some city councils called for a declaration of war. That was not to be.[22]

The Campaign Against the German Presence

In addition to the use of the blacklist and the sustained efforts to restrict smuggling of products to the Axis, the United States brought considerable and ultimately successful pressure to bear on Colombian authorities to purge German nationals from Colombian aviation, something that Washington had sought since the 1920s. The war provided what seemed to be an appropriate occasion to bring the objective to a conclusion.

Concern about the presence of German nationals in SCADTA intensified in 1938 when the State Department learned that SCADTA president Peter von Bauer was under pressure from Berlin to regain the controlling stock interest held in the company by Pan American Airways. State Department officials urged Pan Am president Juan Trippe to counter that initiative by assuming more active control over SCADTA. The transition to the Eduardo Santos administration in 1938 facilitated Colombian cooperation, since Santos had no opposition either to the greater degree of American control or to the purging of German personnel as long as the move did not occasion a public debate. Ambassador Spruille Braden commented in late 1939 that Santos wanted to be presented with a "fait accomplis."[23] Braden was a critical actor in the drama. He was determined to remove what appeared to be a very real potential threat to U.S. interests in Colombia and to the Panama Canal. SCADTA still dominated aviation in the country; its pilots were the only Colombian aviators with experience in combat—during the Leticia conflict; it had a large collection of aerial photographs; it flew close to the Panama Canal; its staff was largely German, some of whom were Luftwaffe reservists. Others were simply skilled German aviators and technicians who had emigrated after World War I.

Clearly, even if the pressure was American, the initiative had to come from the Colombian government. The Santos administration then employed 1938 legislation requiring 51 percent Colombian ownership of national aviation companies to justify the creation of Avianca (Aerovias Nacionales de Colombia), absorbing both SCADTA and a much smaller Colombian private line, SACO. Since U.S. officials opposed any approach that would allow non-American control in what appeared to be wartime conditions, American and Colombian officials reached a compromise solution in 1940 that enabled Pan Am to retain financial control, reserve 20 percent of the stock for Colombian nationals, and provide the Colombian government with an option to acquire 40 percent of the stock. To Chief of Staff George Marshall Colombian cooperation in these initiatives was a "source of deep gratification."[24]

The purging of German personnel that accompanied the corporate transition was, in the mood of the time, an inevitable precaution. As much as there is incontrovertible evidence that many of the SCADTA pilots had Nazi connections, the purging of Germans and Austrians in SCADTA has to be understood as part of a larger anti-German antagonism that emerged in Colombia during the war and which even affected school programs. Such anti-German sentiment was never as strong in Colombia, however, as it was in the United States during either World War I or II. SCADTA officials also attempted to distance themselves from Nazi policies and connections. As early as 1938 von Bauer had assured Braden that as an Austrian his views were not those of Germany's and that he himself would dismiss any Nazi sympathizers among his staff.[25] His admission that there were such sympathizers, however, simply increased the U.S. determination to take no further chances with the organization. By September 1939 the Colombian government had ordered Colombian military copilots on all SCADTA flights, and by late 1939 or early 1940 all German pilots, ground crew, and managerial staff, including von Bauer, had lost their positions to Colombian or American personnel designated by Pan Am.[26] Even those German aviators who attempted to branch out on their own by establishing competing firms were rapidly brought into check.[27]

The main objective may have been achieved, but the general issue persisted into the postwar years, when the question of relicensing former SCADTA pilots and other personnel arose. As late as 1946, a U.S. career ambassador, John C. Wiley indicated to President Ospina: "My personal conviction is that it is highly desirable . . . for the Colombian Government to find ways and means to divorce enemy races within Colombia from any association with Colombian aviation." Wiley attached a list of problem individuals, including a former SCADTA mechanic and radio operator whose house had been raided by the police, uncovering a number of films of Colombian harbors; a second example was that of a former SCADTA airport manager, August Jost, who was believed to have been a rabid Nazi and active member of the Gestapo. Former SCADTA official Hans Hoffman visited the ambassador with his attorney to protest the American pressure to prevent him from playing an active role in Colombian aviation. He objected that the question of civil aviation development in Colombia was a strictly Colombian matter. Hoffman was an especially awkward case because he had been decorated by the Colombian government, was wealthy and socially prominent, and his wife a close friend of President Ospina's wife. Nonetheless, the Colombian government yielded to U.S. insistence, and Hoffman was even blocked from becoming manager of a private flying club.[28] The Colombian government initially granted temporary licenses to other former SCADTA pilots but, under American pressure, did not renew them.[29]

Economic Cooperation

The war in general increased U.S. economic assistance for Colombia. The Export-Import Bank, for instance, extended three major loans to Colombia during the war: $20 million in 1941 for highway construction; $10 million in 1943 to assist agriculture; and $3.4 million in 1944 for the construction of a hydroelectric plant.[30] The value of coffee exports also soared, from 116 million pesos in 1940 to over 154 million in 1942. Overall trade with the United States also increased. Colombian imports from the United States rose from a value of 81 million pesos in 1938 to 131.4 million pesos in 1941, although there was no significant change in the volume of imports until 1942, when U.S. entry into the war resulted in a diversion of U.S. goods. The result was a dramatic decline in Colombian imports from the United States in that year to slightly more than 83 million kilos, with a value of only 62 million pesos. That situation changed as the war progressed. By 1945 the United States sold more than 190 million pesos in goods to Colombia. Exports to the United States followed a slightly different pattern, with a dramatic increase in both the volume and value: from 94 million pesos in 1938 to 134 million pesos in 1941.[31]

The main Colombian economic concern at the outbreak of war between the United States and the Axis powers was the implication of U.S. price controls for Colombian coffee exports. Colombian authorities throughout the war supported the basic U.S. quest for trade liberalization, which Colombian diplomats viewed as a logical continuation of Cordell Hull's prewar position. Nonetheless, Colombians by instinct and necessity feared the loss of their coffee markets. Only a few days after the U.S. declaration of war, the Colombian ambassador in Washington called a meeting of the Inter-American Coffee Board to study the situation created by the U.S. Office of Price Controls

(OPA), which the day before the meeting had pegged the maximum price of coffee at prices prevailing in New York on 8 December. He viewed the situation as extremely serious, not only for coffee but for all products produced in Latin America, if the United States controlled prices on the main products it imported while the producing countries had to pay increased costs on imported goods. In the case of coffee the OPA agreed before the end of the month to raise the prices of all types and to adjust future prices to take into consideration increased costs of transportation and insurance, thus passing on increased costs to U.S. consumers.[32] Colombian-U.S. cooperation in the area of strategic and critical raw materials control and development was an especially important area of wartime relations and part of the larger hemispheric program of raw materials control. American investments in the country were substantial before and during the war, representing in 1943 over 71 percent of total foreign investment, compared with the relatively insignificant second-place British investment of 13 percent. The overwhelming majority ($122.9 million) was portfolio, and of direct investment, most remained in mining and oil ($75 million) and trams and utilities ($25.8 million).[33] U.S. officials sought not only to develop Colombian resources for the war effort and to attempt to alleviate economic dislocation occasioned by the war, but also to ensure that those materials did not reach Axis hands. In 1940 the Export-Import Bank granted a $10 million credit to the Bank of the Republic to provide necessary dollar exchange for purchases in the United States. (That amount was repaid in 1943.) There were additional credits extended in 1941 and 1943 for public works, agricultural development, and railroad and electrical power projects.[34]

The result was the creation of a program to stimulate production of certain critical materials and of a preclusive buying program to restrict the free-market sale of materials outside the hemisphere. Colombia was not as significant a producer of essential materials as Venezuela with its oil, Bolivia with tin, or Chile with copper. Colombian coal deposits were among the world's largest, although this was not considered either a strategic commodity or one in short supply in the United States. It was an important producer of oil; cinchona bark, from which quinine was extracted; divi-divi, used for tanning and dyeing leather; and various wood products, including balsa. It was considered to have potential for natural rubber, mica, quartz, and copper production. Most significantly, since before World War I the country had been one of the three main world producers of platinum, which was essential for the production of electrical contacts, including parts in aircraft.[35]

Since Germany was dependent on imported platinum, the U.S. government developed programs to purchase the entire Colombian output and to counteract smuggling of platinum to Axis agents. U.S. concern about Axis intentions in Colombia were well founded; as early as 1937 and 1938, Germany had greatly increased its purchases of Colombian platinum, reaching a level almost equal to U.S. imports of the commodity from Colombia. Once the war was under way there was overwhelming evidence of smuggling of Colombian platinum through Ecuador and Brazil to Chile and Argentina. The United States enjoyed a considerable advantage in the fact that the main producer of Colombian platinum was an American-owned firm, the South American Gold and Platinum Company.[36]

Early in the war, U.S. planners selected Colombia for a pilot project study of the feasibility of a program to develop natural resources for wartime military-industrial use. It was recognized that Colombian local and national politics might prove an impediment. Under the Liberal governments of Alfonso López and Eduardo Santos, Colombia sought to attain self-sufficiency in wheat and cotton, two major export products of the United States in normal economic times. U.S. officials were also displeased with what they perceived to be continued indiscriminate Colombian government funding of unproductive public works projects, fluctuating attitudes toward foreign investment, overdependence on coffee exports, and a negative attitude to even a modest level of immigration. Although the U.S. record on wartime refugees may not have been admirable, an element of anti-Semitism may also have played a role in the Colombian position. In spite of U.S. concerns about the level of Colombian commitment to wartime goals, War Production Board officials concluded that it was worthwhile for the United States to support a development program in Colombia, involving American financial and technical assistance, to increase the production of strategic raw materials.[37]

Early in 1943, the two countries concluded a formal agreement on the allocation of raw materials. Colombia agreed to make available to the United States "all basic or strategic materials necessary for the defense of the hemisphere found on public property" or produced by private individuals. To maintain the semblance of Colombian sovereignty, the agreement stipulated that "the exploitation and production of such items will be affected in accordance with the laws governing such matters." Under the agreement Colombia contracted to provide exclusive export of such materials to the United States. Colombia reserved the right to fix prices and to retain essential supplies required for its own use. Any facilities that were constructed under the program were to revert to the Colombian government at the end of the war. American interests involved in the development program were granted exemption from import duties on goods required to develop Colombian raw materials.[38]

During 1943, in addition to developing the raw-materials program, the two governments concentrated on control of platinum smuggling. Of the world's major producers only Colombia was not at war with Germany. Since the German airforce and mechanized army depended heavily on imported platinum, and since even small amounts of the metal were of high value, smuggling to Axis agents was both attractive and difficult to police. The Colombian prefect of the Office of Exchange Controls decreed that platinum producers in the Chocó and Atrato regions had to sell their produce directly to the Bank of the Republic offices in that area, thus hoping to reduce thefts from producers' agents traveling to distant branches of the bank. Reflective of the importance that the international community placed on the commodity, enforcement of the decree was to be under the jurisdiction of the National Police, the Office of Exchange Control, and the British and American embassies.[39]

Late that year a former British intelligence officer and an employee of the Chocó Pacific Company, working under the supervision of the

U.S. representative in Bogotá of the Board of Economic Warfare, assumed direct charge of selling platinum produced in the towns of the region. This measure, combined with the earlier decree requiring sale of platinum directly to the Bank of the Republic, increased fines, and threats of deportation for foreign nationals contributed to improved control; but the evidence suggests that smuggling continued on a high level. During 1943 American officials estimated that there was an increased diversion of a thousand ounces of platinum per month over the level of 1942, and 30 percent of real production was being smuggled to the Axis. Officials in the field reported that lots of twenty to forty pounds were readily available on the black market; the U.S. legal attaché indicated that some one hundred pounds appeared monthly on the contraband markets of Cali, Cartagena, and Barranquilla for sale and export. In mid-1944 officials in Lima arrested a Colombian and his two accomplices with 104 pounds of platinum in their possession. Officials traced this individual's first smuggled shipment to Rio de Janeiro in 1943, a second to Buenos Aires, and a third to Peru. During early 1944 FBI, U.S. Army and Navy, and U.S. Commercial Company officials experimented with entrapment techniques to try to undercut the smuggling. Contraband control purchases of platinum by American and Colombian agents were conducted until September 1944 when the military situation in Europe was deemed sufficiently under control to discontinue them. U.S. and Colombian officials believed that the German-born population was a security risk and acted accordingly. Under Secretary of State Edward Stettinius, for instance, urged that the names of known, prominent smugglers be put on the Proclaimed List as a way of restraining others. Equally important in understanding the problem, however, was the nature of platinum mining and the local populations in the producing regions in the isolated and unhealthy Chocó and Atrato regions in the Northwest. Very small-scale miners had used platinum for many years as a form of barter with small-town merchants. In the Chocó alone, it was estimated that there were fifteen to twenty thousand natives, most descended from black slaves imported into the area in the colonial period, engaged in platinum collection and trading in the six towns of the area. Those miners who were employed by the main company, the Chocó Pacific Company, were easily supervised and in any event received cash wages. Some of the small-scale miners and merchants had in the past been licensed to sell platinum, and when they did so they often sold a portion to the Bank of the Republic and a portion to *contrabandistas*. The common practice of barter, the dependence of the local population on the activity, a long tradition of common knowledge smuggling across the Panama border, and traditional local hostility to the isolated national government in Bogotá all frustrated efforts to bring a swift or even successful resolution of the smuggling.[40]

By early 1944, American officials were reasonably pleased with the progress made in their general program of developing Colombian raw materials directly and by contract with U.S. agencies. By that stage the Foreign Economic Administration (FEA) and U.S. Commercial Company had seventy-two key personnel in Colombia alone. The programs for the production of barbasco, quartz, mica, balsa, cinchona bark, various fibres, scrap metal, and platinum were well developed. FEA agents believed that Colombian government cooperation had improved the relations between American officials and local producers. Colombia was now providing 13 percent of U.S. platinum requirements, 9 percent of rotenone, and 5 percent of balsa. It was the main supplier of cinchona bark.

By this time, the U.S. Rubber Reserve Company also had concluded a contract with the Colombian government for the purchase of the entire Colombian production of rubber, except for an amount to meet domestic requirements. As part of the preclusive buying approach, the export of manufactured rubber from Colombia was restricted to U.S. destinations. Examples of the levels of production and of export to the United States that were being realized in these and other commodities included (for the month of February alone) 118 tons of albarco, 30 tons of coffee, and 16 tons of fique fibres, with prospects for another 100 tons per month, almost 600 tons of cinchona, and over 420 tons of hides. With respect to balsa, much of the best wood was isolated, and Colombian dealers lacked the technical or financial means to exploit those resources. Consequently, U.S. botanists and foresters were employed. They also constructed transportation routes in the jungles to move the wood from collection points to the nearest railroad or river port. Such operations had short-term value; but it was also anticipated that transportation development would benefit the postwar Colombian economy. In addition, the Nestlé company oversaw the construction of a new concentrated coffee plant in Cali, to produce for export, and of a new powdered milk plant to produce for the domestic market. Both plants were constructed with steel imported from the United States, and hence their completion depended on U.S. allocation of a critical wartime commodity.[41]

A number of complications clouded this otherwise promising picture of expanded natural resource development. One was profiteering. As much as Colombian and American officials attempted to restrain price increases, high demand and scarcity encouraged merchants to avoid government controls and exploit profit potentials. The second, a far more serious problem, was the dislocation in the Colombian economy that resulted from the U.S. wartime controls over exports of critical materials, especially such semifinished goods as steel, which were required in the Colombian construction industry.

At the foreign ministers meeting in Rio in January 1942, the Roosevelt administration pledged to provide the other American republics with civilian goods and materials on a basis of equality with U.S. citizens and to attempt to supply the "minimum needs required for public health and safety in order to maintain the essential economies of the other American Republics." FEA officials appear to have interpreted the agreement narrowly, concentrating their efforts on providing Colombia with the equipment and supplies needed to produce "petroleum and a number of strategic and critical materials needed in the war effort."[42] After April 1942 all applications in the United States for export licences were considered only on the basis of essential need in the foreign country and the availability of shipping space. In the case of Colombia, the restrictions of U.S. exports had serious potential impact. In normal times, Colombia imported a wide range of goods, including, for instance, substantial quantities of rayon yarn and real silk in connection with its textile industry, steel products, ascorbic

acid, cranes and other machinery, fluorspar, graphite, lead, and thia-
mine chloride. How severe restraints were is reflected in the fact that
for 1942 the Board of Economic Warfare allocated to Colombia only
forty-three thousand pounds of rayon per quarter, when during the
previous four years actual use had been in excess of 143,000 *kilograms*
per quarter.[43]

U.S. export controls had a definite impact on the Colombian construction industry and exacerbated the urban unemployment problem, leading Colombian and American officials to fear social and
political unrest. The situation was most acute in and near Bogotá,
where the construction industry was concentrated. In an effort to
alleviate the plight of urban labor, the Colombian government and
the U.S. Export-Import bank in 1942 funded a program of low-cost
housing construction and road building in various parts of the country. Colombia's superintendent of imports, Antonio Pradilla, a former
governor of Cundinamarca, indicated to the U.S. embassy in mid-
1942 that employment in the construction industry could not easily
be shifted to other sectors because of the absence in Colombia of a
strong industrial base, in particular of war-related defense industries.
Pradilla estimated that more than 120,000 inhabitants of Bogotá alone
earned their livelihood directly or indirectly from construction and
that some 27 percent of the materials necessary for the industry to
function were imported from the United States.[44]

The general wartime concern over raw materials and natural resource security logically also affected the situation in the oil industry,
where the American companies and State Department officials had for
over a decade been attempting to modify existing Colombian legislation to improve the investment environment. The election in 1938 of
Eduardo Santos contributed to the willingness of the Colombian executive to revise the legislation, as did the friendship between James
Terry Duce of the Petroleum Administration for War and President
López after 1942. A willingness to negotiate was one thing; achieving results was another matter. Efforts to gain a modification of the
hectarage limitations on oil concessions, for instance, proved elusive,
and when very modest reform legislation did result in 1941, following

persistent efforts by Spruille Braden and the first Colombian minister of mines and petroleum, Juan Pablo Manotas, Congress proved recalcitrant.[45] The political will to achieve real reform in this area was weak. For one thing, the companies were a convenient whipping boy for politicians in both parties; for another, there were wartime shipping problems and difficulties obtaining steel for pipeline and refinery construction that appeared to lend credence to the long-held Colombian view that the companies were procrastinating in achieving a high level of production. Even the success of the Colombian Petroleum Company in 1939 in achieving commercial levels of production and completing a pipeline to the Caribbean coast in 1939 did not dispel that view. Some of the criticism was well deserved: the failure to make a more concerted effort to train Colombians for higher level positions; poor relations with labor, whether organized or unorganized; an admission to Ambassador Braden by Tropical Oil officials that they had been dishonest in reporting their employees' salaries for income tax purposes. *El Siglo* in 1940 even charged that Colombian Petroleum Company employees had been shooting Motilón Indians on its Barco concession.[46] What received little public credit and attention were the modern medical and housing facilities that Tropical Oil, the most enlightened of the companies, had constructed at Barrancabermeja.

A softening of the official Colombian position on foreign investment in the oil industry did not go so far as to reverse the commitment that the Tropical Oil Company's De Mares concession should revert to the state at the end of its lease after the war. At that time the government also formed a state oil company, ECOPETROL, to which the property was transferred in the early 1950s after several years of acrimonious labor conflict and charges that the company was letting the property deteriorate because of the impending transfer. The Barrancabermeja refinery did not come under ECOPETROL control until 1961. In the interim the company rented the refinery from the government. There was also a corporate reorganization in 1950 with the old Canadian-based Tropical Oil Company dismantled and replaced by the International Petroleum Company of Colombia, a subsidiary of the International Petroleum Company of Peru and, more importantly, Standard Oil of New Jersey.[47]

Cultural, Educational, and Propaganda Initiatives

The war and immediate postwar years occasioned the most significant efforts by the United States to take social and cultural diplomacy seriously. Efforts in this area ranged from the work of the U.S. Children's Bureau under Katherine Lenroot to cooperate with the Colombian government in improving social services for delinquent and abandoned children to the establishment of cultural centers. The work of the Children's Bureau was an area in which Ambassador Lane and Nelson Rockefeller were especially interested, although following the completion of a report on the subject by Elizabeth Clarke of the bureau, the Colombian government took few steps to alleviate the problem.

By far the most significant and enduring innovation was the establishment of binational centers under the jurisdiction of Nelson Rockefeller and the Office of the Coordinator of Inter-American Affairs, at first only in Bogotá and later in most of the main cities of the country.[48] Established in 1940, the Centro Colombo-Americano in Bogotá was at the time one of the largest cultural centers operated abroad by the U.S. government. It rapidly became one of the most active. Its main function was to increase awareness and understanding of American institutions through the teaching of English and American civilization and presentation of and general cultural programs that included music concerts and art exhibits. That the center met a perceived need in Colombian society was reflected in the attendance statistics at various functions by the end of the war, when over 1,200 students were registered in English language instruction and another 1,700 attended monthly concerts, films, and lectures. The initiative was believed sufficiently successful to justify opening an additional center, the Academía Interamericana in Medellín.[49]

By 1947, U.S. informational and education activities in Colombia involved a staff of three Americans and seventeen Colombians. The binational centers employed two American directors and a modest staff of English instructors, some of them American, but the majority Colombian. The cultural affairs officer, Jacob Center, represented the high quality of diplomatic personnel who were being assigned to the country, a gentle step toward dispelling the image of Latin American postings as undesirable. Center held a doctorate from Harvard, had studied in Paris, and taught at Harvard and the U.S. Naval Academy at Annapolis before being posted to Bogotá.[50] After the war, cold war issues increased the incentive to maintain an information and educational program, with the result that these activities were transferred to the jurisdiction of the newly created United States Information Agency.

Colombian and American cultural leaders found that they could mutually benefit from the other's expertise during the war. A case in point was the effort to share information on colonial restoration projects. In 1944 the director of the Casa Colonial, which was the Colombian National Museum of colonial art and history, housed in a restored Spanish colonial home, visited the United States as the guest of the State Department to inspect U.S. archives, libraries, and museums, and in particular such colonial restorations as Williamsburg.[51]

World War II had an enduring impact on Colombia and Colombian-U.S. relations. Politically and militarily the two nations cooperated fully in hemisphere defense, even though Colombia remained aloof from actual participation in the war. The development of cooperation between the two nations during the war consolidated the prewar movement to closer relations fostered by Suárez and Olaya, and the wartime debate in Colombia over relations with the United States never reached the level of acrimony that had characterized relations in the aftermath of the Panama crisis earlier in the century. The Colombian debate over the war did indicate the continuation of differing perceptions of the Colombian role in the world, the desirable route to modernization, the extent to which Colombians sought to tie their future to that of the "Polar Star." The ties—culturally, politically, and

economically—to Europe were still very strong. Economic links to the
United States were now overwhelming, but the cultural and political ties to Europe continued to have deep resonance. World War II
shook some of the confidence of those Colombians who continued
to look to Europe as the superior model. In specific areas such as
natural resource control and development, the war demonstrated the
highly interdependent nature of the Western Hemisphere economies
and the vulnerability of export economies such as Colombia's to drastic alterations in international markets. On a political and diplomatic
level there was a striking degree of cooperation between Colombian
and U.S. officials in developing an administrative structure that would
facilitate wartime cooperation, not only in raw materials allocation but
across the spectrum of interaction. On balance the Liberal administrations of Eduardo Santos and Alfonso López pursued realistic policies,
which respected the high degree of dependence on external markets
and reflected the traditional intellectual, political, and economic ties
to Europe and the reality of U.S. hegemony.

7 Cold War and Containment, 1945–1960

> An uncertain economic situation and a prolonged and almost hopeless state of underdevelopment are creating disillusionment, confusion and discouragement among the people of Latin America." (Alberto Lleras Camargo, 1958)[1]

Our understanding of Colombian developments during the cold war has suffered from a concentration on Cuba and Guatemala in the 1950s, Cuba and the Dominican Republic in the 1960s, and El Salvador and Nicaragua in the past decade. The political crisis in Colombia predated those in Cuba and Guatemala, and the reaction of the United States to that crisis and the perceived threat of communism was characteristic of the main contours of U.S. policy in the pre-Castro years. The military security program and the containment of communism in Colombian politics and organized labor both reveal the consistent efforts of the United States to bring Colombia within the larger framework of cold war defense and to foster those moderate anticommunist (and anti-Peronist) elements in the political mainstream. The evidence also indicates a factor that is often overlooked, that the cold war issues were generally of more significance to the United States than they were to mainstream Colombian politics, although there were differences between Conservatives and Liberals. Indeed, even in Colombian-U.S. bilateral relations it is arguable that the Colombian persecution of Protestants and of American Protestant missionaries ranked with cold war issues as important topics of diplomacy in the 1950s.

From the end of World War II to the early 1960s, Colombia was an important part of U.S.–Latin American policy. It was the virtual social and political revolution in Bogotá, touched off during the 1948

founding meeting of the Organization of American States, that provided concrete evidence, at least in the eyes of President Truman and
Secretary of State George Marshall, of the vitality of hemispheric communism and the need to ensure security against its spread. The crisis
of 1948 in Colombia ushered in more than a decade of political strife,
bloodshed, and dictatorship that marked a dramatic shift in traditional political practice; little of this crisis was related to communist
activity, but from the perspective of the United States such instability
threatened the capacity of the United States to achieve its objectives
in the nation and region. With some irony, it was at the Bogotá Conference that the Organization of American States was established as
the first institutional embodiment of regional security organizations
established by the United States in its construction of the cold war
edifice. In the 1950s Colombia was the only Latin American nation to
commit troops, albeit a token battalion and warship, to the Korean
War. By the late 1950s and early 1960s it was two Colombian Liberal
presidents, Alberto Lleras Camargo and Carlos Lleras Restrepo, who
earned a substantial share of the credit for whatever reforms there
may have been in inter-American relations during the Kennedy and
Johnson years. Even before but especially after 1960 Colombia was
targeted as the "showpiece" of U.S. aid programs, as the United States
sought to compensate for the "loss" of Cuba. Colombia remained on-
side in the cold war; but then there had been no real danger of a
different result.

The Bogotá Conference and Its Aftermath

The United States approached the Bogotá meetings in 1948 in the
hope that it could divert criticism in Latin America that the United
States was neglecting the Western Hemisphere in favor of other areas
of the world, manifested primarily in the form of the Marshall Plan
for Europe. There had been, for instance, considerable criticism in
Colombia of George Marshall's 19 September 1947 speech in Rio de
Janeiro calling for hemispheric security. Colombia was also one of the

Latin American leaders in pressing for economic reforms and assistance. They made little progress at Bogotá in 1948, more at Caracas in 1954.

The U.S. delegation was a powerful one. Headed by Secretary of State George Marshall, it included Averell Harriman, secretary of commerce; John Snyder, secretary of the treasury; Norman Armour, assistant secretary of state for political affairs; William Martin, Jr., chairman of the Export-Import Bank; and a number of ambassadors and senior State Department officials, including William Beaulac, then ambassador to Colombia. Secretary of Defense James Forrestal believed the conference was of major importance to the U.S. armed services because of the proposed creation of an Inter-American Defense Council. The U.S. military had also taken a substantial role in working out the fundamentals of the proposed Organic Pact of the Inter-American System (the Organization of American States) and was vitally interested in the proposed agreement for Inter-American economic cooperation; it was anticipated this approach would "lay a foundation" for bilateral agreements that would permit the United States to acquire and conserve materials needed for mutual security. Forrestal thus insisted on the inclusion of technical specialists in petroleum because of its importance to the United States and to several of the Latin American countries, and he was supported by the National Security Resources Board.[2]

There was debate in the United States over the degree of government involvement in Latin American economic development. State Department officials in the Truman and Eisenhower administrations preferred government encouragement of private sector involvement rather than foreign aid. Seymour Rubin of the Department of State, for instance, found the proposed project of Basic Agreement on Inter-American Economic Cooperation too one sided in favor of Latin America. Even the reiteration of the longstanding U.S. emphasis on equality of access to raw material, scientific and technical advances, and producer goods, Rubin thought, would be of little real value, given the evident refusal earlier of the Latin American states at the Havana meetings to concede that the United States should have such guaranteed access. Rubin added that the United States would be making a substantial commitment to technical assistance and cooperation under the proposed pact, although it was already doing so under the United Nations Economic Committee on Latin America and the International Trade Organization. The National Foreign Trade Council and the Council for Inter-American Co-operation, in a lengthy joint statement, were even more pointed than Rubin in their comments on the excessive role intended for the state rather than the private sector. They contended that the main objective of the policy on economic co-operation should be to strengthen economic development and to resist communist influences; this required the reduction of trade barriers, creation of a "proper climate" for the international flow of capital, and general strengthening of the private enterprise system. The National Foreign Trade Council believed that the current project would submerge these goals in state regulations and controls and minimize the rights of private capital at the expense of the obligations of private investors, thus generally reducing the incentives for private capital investment. John Laylin of the law firm Covington, Burling, Rublee, Acheson and Shorb—which represented a number of U.S. firms, including American Smelting and Refining, International Telephone and Telegraph, Kennecott Copper, Pan American Airways, and Standard Oil of New Jersey—informed the secretary of state that the proposed basic economic agreement would seriously weaken the position of private enterprise in Latin America and discourage further investment; Laylin expressed the view that bilateral agreements would be preferable to a multilateral one, which would tend to reduce the area of agreement to the lowest common denominator.[3]

In his opening address to the conference George Marshall reiterated those views, stressing that the burden of world leadership had fallen on the United States since World War II and that the United States required the support and cooperation of other nations in economic development. Marshall contended that the United States could respond positively to the economic proposals of the other American nations, but he had little concrete to offer. The Colombian hosts pressed U.S. delegates from the outside on economic questions. President Mariano

Ospina Pérez told the delegates that although international security was important, given the "economic inter-dependence of peoples," the conference should address economic needs. Colombian delegates cleverly turned to U.S. political symbols and the ideas of U.S. political leaders to advance their arguments. For instance, Carlos Lozano y Lozano, president of the Colombian delegation, appealed to Wilsonian ideas of equality; economic objectives of the Atlantic Charter; and the memory of Washington, Jefferson, Bolívar, and San Martín. Concretely, Lozano y Lozano stressed that Latin America needed more private investment, assistance with its major balance of payments problems, increased production, and expanded trade. Praising the work of the Marshall Plan in Europe, he called for a similar project in Latin America.[4]

While the delegates debated, the political symbol of reform liberalism in Colombia, Jorge Eliécer Gaitán, was assassinated as he and several associates left their offices for lunch. Within hours, Gaitán's death triggered the mobilization of opposition political groups as well as what was generally considered an uncontrolled mob. Like most politicized mobs, however, this one had its logical targets, symbols of authority, of perceived oppression, and power: the mob lynched the suspected killer of Gaitán, Juan Roa Sierra, and dragged his remains before the presidential palace. There the body remained for two days, save for his hands which the police removed for the convenience of later identification. The conference rooms themselves were attacked and sacked, driving delegates into the sanctuary of suburban north Bogotá. Religious institutions, from schools to convents and churches, viewed as symbols of vested authority, especially of the Conservative elite, were attacked. Conveniently located stores and homes were looted, especially liquor stores and businesses belonging to Jews. Among the buildings damaged by fire and explosives were the Foreign Office, the Ministries of Justice, Communications and Interior, the building which housed *El Siglo;* the palace of the papal nuncio. The Bogotá police by most accounts went over to the rioters; indeed the Fifth Police Precinct, held by some five hundred members of the force, was the last important center of the revolt to capitulate to regular armed forces brought in from other parts of the country. By the time the carnage was over and rage satiated, parts of the central business district were reduced to rubble; authorities estimated that five hundred were dead in Bogotá. During the next decade, as the nation virtually collapsed into prolonged civil, class, and economic strife, an estimated two hundred thousand people lost their lives.[5] On the twentieth anniversary of the assassination, this author stood among several thousand others on the corner of Avenida Jiminez and Septima where the tragedy had begun, listening to a series of orators, who mounted a makeshift podium to vent their spleen. The villains were predictable: the Colombian oligarchy; the Conservative party; American capitalists; the United States. It was as though time had stood still in the intervening years.

George Marshall had little doubt who had caused the rioting. Although he had been no supporter of Gaitán, to whom the Department of State referred as a "demagogic Liberal party leader with an immense following," he was certain, as he informed a special meeting of the delegation chiefs to the conference, that "this situation must not be judged on a local basis, however tragic the immediate results to the Colombian people. . . . It is the same definite pattern as occurrences which provoked strikes in France and Italy. . . . In actions we take here regarding the present situation, we must keep clearly in mind the fact that this is a world affair—not merely Colombian or Latin American." Averell Harriman indicated that "international communism" aided by local elements in Colombia had capitalized on Gaitán's death to wreck havoc. When President Truman was preparing his memoirs years later he commented on the Bogotá crisis: "They had a tremendous riot there stirred up by the communists." Colombian officials were especially struck by the extent to which U.S. commentators saw the riots as the work of international communists.[6]

This concern with communist conspiracy was not limited to U.S. officials. The Colombian investigating magistrate obtained from the U.S. Embassy reports prepared in the months before the conference by the CIA. These documents alleged that Gaitán had received substantial funding from the Soviet embassy in Bogotá through an intermediary who was a professor at the national university. Nonetheless, the CIA reports drew a distinction between the communist activities and the assassination of Gaitán, which they concluded was an act of personal revenge by Roa Sierra. In subsequent years, as Colombian authorities continued the investigation, Colombian Commander S.S. Piedrahita, sensitive to allegations of Colombian official complicity in the murder, contended to the director of the CIA that neither the Conservative nor the Liberal parties had motive to have Gaitán murdered. Indeed, the Conservative party found it convenient that Gaitán's politics divided the Liberals and weakened them at the polls. The CIA emphasized to Piedrahita that at no time had the agency obtained information that communists were planning to disrupt the Bogotá Conference; nor did it have information implicating in the assassination foreign individuals or Colombians with foreign support. Significantly, Colombian officials, in conducting their own investigation, were sensitive to McCarthyism in the United States and loathe to make any statements that would lend support to McCarthy in his charges that the State Department harbored communists.[7]

In the United States, some were skeptical of Marshall's assessment of the causes of the rioting. Walter Lippmann pilloried the Truman administration's assumption that "all discontent is Communist inspired." Duncan Ackman in *PM* (the Washington tabloid) faulted the "fanatical" right wing in Colombia, suggesting that the United States was partly to blame for its support of Laureano Gómez for conference president. *Newsweek, Time, The Nation,* and *New Republic* all stressed the role of Colombian Liberals in the Bogotá outbreak, for taking advantage of the popular sentiment for Gaitán and calling for vengeance over the Liberal radio stations, but they conceded that the communists capitalized on the situation. The dichotomy of views in the American media was reflected in the contrast between *The Nation's* assertion that only congressmen in a state of acute hysteria could credit the communist conspiracy thesis and *Life* magazine's basic thesis in its seven pages of coverage that the riots provided ample evidence of the communist capacity to capitalize on crises.[8]

A decade later, with the Red Scare behind them, senior State Department officials no longer held to the communist conspiracy explanation of the *Bogotazo,* but they could not reject entirely the idea of communist opportunism. Assistant Secretary of State Roy Rubottom wrote in May 1958 that although the majority of the rioters were Gaitán's loyalists from among the lower classes, the communist element had taken full advantage of the chaos. A communist-controlled labor congress meeting in Cali in December 1947 approved holding demonstrations during the conference in an effort to disrupt the proceedings, to draw attention to the high cost of living and the general plight of the working class, and to protest against American imperialism and U.S. support for the Colombian Conservative party.

The communists hoped to bring about a general strike and the downfall of the Conservative party government of Mariano Ospina Pérez. Yet, Gaitán himself had issued a public appeal for the masses of the Liberal party to resist any outbreaks against the conference. Rubottom concluded: "It has been generally held since the events of April 1948, that the charge of Communist organization and direction of the rioting was over-emphasized. Both President Ospina and General Marshall made statements attributing the catastrophe to Communism. . . . There is no question that Gaitán's demagogic attacks on the Liberal oligarchy, the Administration, the vested interests, the National Association of Industrialists, and his frequent threats to resort to force to attain his ends were as sufficient to foster the mob violence and class hatred displayed as any assertions the Communists ever made, and they influenced a great many more people."[9]

William Sanders, who in 1948 was in Bogotá as an adviser in the American delegation, expressed the view that Gaitán's death was the result of the work of a "lunatic" fringe of the Conservative party. The historical evidence is very strong that for months prior to the conference political violence, especially in rural areas between Liberals and Conservatives, had been constant, with Liberals largely the victims of both general Conservative attacks as well as more organized violence under the auspices of the political police organized by the Ospina administration. In February 1948 there was a mass demonstration of some one hundred thousand in Bogotá to protest the violence in the countryside that was driving people out of their homes and creating a disastrous economic and social climate in the nation. Ospina exacerbated the situation by declining to appoint Gaitán to the Colombian delegation to the conference and pressing the reactionary Laureano Gomez for conference president. The general strife in the countryside combined with the fraudulent denial to Liberals of their rightful victory in the congressional elections of March 1947, created a volatile situation on the eve of the conference. Gaitán's death was simply the spark that detonated the powder keg.[10] Regardless of the accuracy of claims of communist involvement, Colombia broke diplomatic relations with the Soviet Union shortly after the conference, only four years after the López administration established them.[11]

In the subsequent decade the United States sought to stabilize what appeared at times to be the virtual collapse of the Colombian political system. In 1948 and 1949, two National Union Conservative governments failed. The inauguration in 1950 of Laureano Gómez as president served to exacerbate the already catastrophic relations between Conservatives and Liberals. In the fall of 1952 a major crisis drove many Liberals, including Carlos Lleras Restrepo and Alfonso López, to seek political asylum outside the country. Liberals were purged not only from military and senior police positions but also from diplomatic posts, and the government favored the Conservative Union of Colombian Labor (UTC). The army and the Church at this stage appeared to favor a coup led by former President Ospina Pérez, but the Ospinistas themselves favored a government by military junta. In October General Gustavo Rojas Pinilla, former chief of staff and former vice-director of the Inter-American Defense Board in Washington, educated in engineering at Tri-State College in Indiana, returned to Bogotá. Perhaps reluctantly, he emerged as head of a junta government and by the following June had acquired dictatorial powers, the first regime of that nature since that of Rafael Reyes in the early twentieth century.

Economic issues complicated the political crisis during the cold war years. By 1949 foreign investment in Colombia was in decline, largely as a result of political uncertainty, but also in response to Colombian government controls over exports, foreign exchange remissions, raw materials quotas, and the establishment of a state oil company, ECOPETROL, to operate the former Tropical Oil concession at Barrancabermeja. The U.S. Department of Commerce concluded that improvements in the agricultural and livestock industries and even in oil production had been offset by the withdrawal of American oil interests and the reduction of exports by those remaining. The United States also declined in importance as a market for Colombian exports as European recovery and Canadian development increased the capacity to buy in other areas. The United States nonetheless remained the most important Colombian trading partner in this period, taking over 90 percent of Colombian coffee, 100 percent of its gold, 100 percent of its platinum, and 81 percent of its bananas in 1949.[12]

In spite of the Colombian political crisis in the early 1950s, U.S. private investors channeled $271 million in new investments into the country between 1950 and 1954. In keeping with U.S. government preference in the Truman and Eisenhower presidencies, two-thirds of all U.S. investment in Latin America in those years came from private sources. U.S. direct investments in Colombia increased from $193 million in 1950 to $260 million in 1954 and $289 million in 1956. For the last year, petroleum investments amounted to $103 million, manufacturing $70 million, and public utilities $40 million. Earnings from those investments in that year were $22 million (compared with $51 million in Cuba). Even United Fruit, which had largely withdrawn from the country earlier, expanded in the 1950s through its two subsidiaries, the Sevilla Fruit Company and the Magdalena Fruit Company. The largest privately owned hydroelectric company in the country, the Colombian Electric Company, was a subsidiary of the American and Foreign Power Company. Leading manufacturing interests included: B. F. Goodrich, U.S. Rubber, Standard Brands Inc., and W. R. Grace & Company. U.S. firms employed over forty-four thousand people in Colombia, forty-three thousand of whom were Colombian nationals.[13]

The 1950 International Bank for Reconstruction and Development (IBRD) mission headed by economist Lauchlin Currie was evidence of both optimism and the need for economic reform in Colombia. It also indicated some fundamental differences in attitudes toward development policies between Colombians and the United States In his IBRD report, "Basis for a Development Program for Colombia," Currie was bullish on the potential for Colombian development, commenting, as so many of his predecessors had in the previous century, on the rich natural resources and the twelve-month growing season. He did not, however, endorse the idea of completing the Paz de Rio steel mill project that was dear to Colombian developmentalists, who saw such industrial diversification as a means to achieve modernization. Currie and U.S. embassy officials thought otherwise, fearing that Colombia would engage in the development of steel production behind high protectionist barriers. The Paz del Rio project was still an issue when Secretary of State John Foster Dulles met in Bogotá with Colombian officials in mid-1956.[14]

National Security

The Department of State Office of Intelligence Research worried amid the early 1950s political crisis that "because of strategic, political and economic considerations, Colombia's radical departure from customary practices is of vital concern to the United States."[15] Such economic and political instability was precisely the type of fertile seedbed for communism that the United States sought to sterilize. The CIA contended that the influence of communists in Latin America, Colombia included, was far greater than numbers would indicate because the traditional social order was breaking down. Even in countries such as Colombia, where the means existed to provide a more equitable distribution of wealth and political power, traditional conservative elites had no intention of reforming. "This repressive tendency hinders even moderate change and so renders more likely the eventual outbreak of revolutionary violence. In Colombia there is already widespread guerrilla resistance to the regime."[16] During the next decade, through military assistance, economic aid, and political support for those moderate elements in the political mainstream and in the labor movement, policymakers worked to counteract the debilitating effects of both civil war and military rule.

The aftermath of the Bogotá crisis in 1948 brought changes in both the United States and Colombia. Harry Truman that fall moved into his second term with his own electoral mandate and Dean Acheson became secretary of state. Although a cold warrior, Acheson was clearly more sensitive to third world issues than Marshall had been, and he proceeded at least to give the impression that he was turning the United States away from its policy of neglect in Latin America. Both administration officials and Latin American diplomats received Acheson's major speech on 19 September 1950 as confirmation of the new direction of policy, and his rhetoric was accompanied by increased economic and military aid programs, as well as more State Department activity in Latin America. By the fall of 1950, Assistant Secretary Edward Miller had visited eight Latin American countries and was intending to complete the tour before the end of the calendar year. Although the statement applied to the Eisenhower administration a decade later, it was equally applicable to the Truman administration's objectives in the military aid program for Colombia: to continue Colombia's cooperation in hemisphere defense, to preserve and strengthen its democratic institutions, to support free enterprise and encourage foreign capital investment, and to achieve balanced social and economic development.[17]

In part from expedience and in part from a fundamental acceptance of cold war assumptions, Colombia was the only country in 1950 to commit troops to fight as part of the United Nations force in Korea, designating one battalion and a frigate, the *Almirante Padilla*, to serve overseas. Foreign Minister Evaristo Sourdis, speaking for the outgoing Ospina administration in June 1950, indicated that the "Colombian Government has once more ratified its unrestricted adherence to the international policy as practised by the United States." In the same period the Colombian ambassador to the United States addressed his fellow Latin American diplomats on the subject: "The United Nations Without the Soviet Union," in which he contended that anything the United Nations had achieved had been without Soviet involvement.

To the ambassador the threat of the Soviet Union to the Western Hemisphere was immediate. The records of the Comisión Asesora in the Colombian Foreign Ministry for this period underline the degree of Colombian anxiety about communism. It is striking how much of the record pertains to efforts to keep track of communist activities in Colombia and other countries in the hemisphere. The Colombian minister in Panama, for instance, interpreted the attempt on Truman's life by a Puerto Rican nationalist as communist-inspired and part of a larger plot to kill the conservative presidents of Panama, the Dominican Republic, Colombia, and Peru.[18]

Ideologically committed as they were to the basic premises of the cold war, Colombians expected a payoff for their contribution. Conservative Colombian governments in the 1950s persistently sought financial support from the United States in return for loyalty. The *Revista* of the Bank of the Republic noted as early as July 1950 that the war in Korea was expected to affect the economies of the Western Hemisphere, given the interdependence between Latin America and the United States. The Colombian ambassador to the United Nations, Roberto Urdaneta Arbelaez, pressed for the United States to support International Bank for Reconstruction and Development funding for Colombia in order to implement some of the reform recommendations of the Currie mission. Given the cost of maintaining the Colombian battalion overseas and the continued deterioration of Colombian political life, it was not surprising that the government should have sought tangible rewards for the show of solidarity with the United States. By late 1952, Colombia was threatening to withdraw the battalion, with what the United States thought would be disastrous morale consequences among the United Nations forces and the Latin American nations. Washington officials recognized that financial considerations were the major factor keeping other Latin American countries from making a commitment and believed that Colombian withdrawal would be fatal. Colombian officials requested reimbursement for the costs of maintaining overseas the battalion that had already been trained and equipped at U.S expense. When he moved in to the presidency, Urdaneta did provide assurances that the troops would not be withdrawn.[19]

Far more comprehensive was the establishment of the Mutual Security program during the Truman and Eisenhower years. Military aid was only one dimension of overall U.S. hemispheric strategy during these years, although the cultural and economic aid programs received less attention and funding. By 1950 the military aid program was the core of hemispheric security and a sharp reminder of the cold war objectives of U.S. regional programs. In May 1950 Truman approved National Security Council Document 56/2 (NSC 56/2), "United States Policy Toward Inter-American Military Collaboration."[20] Although there was some concern reflected in this document about the use of U.S.-supplied weapons against internal political foes rather than in the global struggle against communism, the outbreak of the Korean War diverted attention from the ethics of military aid programs.

Colombia was one of the three major beneficiaries of U.S. military aid in Latin America. By 1950 the United States had assigned Army, Navy, and Air Force attachés and missions to Colombia, and under the military equipment and sale program it had sold over $6 million in equipment, including two reconditioned frigates. Under the 1952 Military Assistance Agreement with the Colombian government, the United States was committed to assist in developing and maintaining the Colombian military for defense of the hemisphere, specifically to equip one anti-aircraft battalion and one infantry battalion; to provide two destroyers, and one fighter squadron. The language of the agreement was unambiguous as to the intended enemy. The opening statement proclaimed that "the security of Colombia and the United States of America, together with that of the other countries of the western hemisphere, is threatened by the imperialistic designs of the USSR."[21]

Colombia's main assignment was to defend its coastal approaches because of proximity to the Panama Canal, and there was sustained support to develop that capability during the decade. Total U.S. expenditure for Latin America during the period 1950–57 was $156 million; of that Colombia received $18.3 million and Brazil $52.13 million, with Chile in second place. For fiscal year 1958, the appropriation sought by the State Department for Colombia was only $1.8 million, insignificant when one considers that the total appropriation for the year was $2.4 billion. By the end of 1958 Colombia had also received sightly less than $9 million in economic aid, essentially the Public Law 480 assistance (surplus U.S. agricultural produce). The total non-military development assistance for Latin America in fiscal year 1957 amounted to $60.8 million. Mutual Defense Assistance Program aid, entirely military, accounted for $35.5 million. In the case of Colombia, the United States allocated some $300,000 to special projects designed to strengthen the capability to combat active communist subversion.

On a broader diplomatic front, Colombian officials played an important role during the early 1950s in attempting to bring solidarity to the Latin American position on military cooperation with the United States Colombian Foreign Minister Gonzalo Restrepo Jaramillo was president of the Political and Military Committee at the Fourth Meeting of Foreign Ministers in 1951. He and the Colombian representative on that committee, Eduardo Zuleta Angel, were given much of the credit by U.S. officials for the success of the committee's discussions. The Colombian minister of war believed that if Colombia had a direct role to play in hemispheric defense, its strategic position on the Caribbean and Pacific required a strong air force. U.S. Ambassador Beaulac urged that advantage be taken of the Colombian willingness to assist.[22]

The Truman and Eisenhower administrations were confronted with the predictable problem that weapons and other war materiel provided for hemispheric defense could also be employed against domestic political foes; there was also concern that equipment supplied was not effectively deployed. From the perspective of a series of Colombian governments during this period of political strife, maintaining peace in the hemisphere included internal peace and stability. The State Department demurred; defense meant defense against "extra-continental aggression." Nonetheless, Dean Acheson informed the U.S. embassy in Bogotá that the U.S. intention was not to segregate those Colombian units equipped with U.S. arms from the remainder of Colombian forces, and they were thus available for the "legitimate tasks of an armed force."[23] José María Bernal, Colombian Minister of War, and Cipriano Restrepo Jaramillo, ambassador to the United States, stressed to state department officials in a meeting in June 1952 that internal security was of paramount importance to the Colombian government, of higher priority than its participation in the Korean War or hemisphere defense. They contended that only military action could contain the guerrilla movement, which they claimed was inspired by a small but forceful communist minority. Although the guerrillas were in general poorly equipped, those near the Venezuelan border were able to obtain machine guns and other weapons through Venezuelan and Panamanian suppliers. Moreover, they had support in Venezuela of left-wing sympathizers.[24]

Bernal continued to press the request for military supplies. Thomas Mann, of the office of the deputy assistant secretary of state for inter-American affairs, indicated that the equipment requested was consistent with what had previously been discussed with the Pentagon and the embassy, but he felt strongly that it should be refused because it was clear the equipment would be used to maintain internal order, which under current political circumstances meant suppression of the legitimate political opposition. He recognized that it would be difficult to deny the request without risking Colombian withdrawal from Korea and hence suggested a modified package minimizing the "anti-personnel" weapons that would be used against domestic opposition. Mann suggested that to placate the Colombian government the United States give some assurances on reimbursement for the expenses of the Colombian Korean battalion and a higher degree of support for the Mutual Security Assistance Program, including the transfer of some training airplanes and naval equipment. There was no unanimity on the issue among U.S. policymakers; on the one hand the chief of the U.S. military mission sent to Bogotá to negotiate with the Colombian government felt that there should be an increase in the amount allocated to the air force; on the other, the Pentagon would not authorize the inclusion of the eleven hundred pound napalm bombs Colombia requested, on the grounds that they would be used against the Liberal opposition, and they also refused in 1952 and 1953 to authorize an export licence to enable Colombia to purchase the napalm through a commercial supplier in the United States.

The United States sought to separate U.S. strategic policy in the hemisphere from Colombian domestic problems. The Military Assistance Advisory Group (MAAG) in Bogotá, for instance, recommended in 1952 that it be separated from the existing U.S. military missions in Colombia, because the latter were under contract with the Colombian government to perform specific duties. Clearly, it would be difficult for it to police the use of war materiel supplied under the Mutual Defense Assistance Program. The State Department thought this especially important in Colombia, where the internal disorder was of such a nature as to require both "good judgment and firmness" in dealing with the possibility that Colombia might want to divert the equipment to its "insistent internal needs." [25]

The military coup in mid-1953 by Gustavo Rojas Pinilla and the dictatorial regime that he inaugurated brought other difficulties for the United States, but in terms of the Mutual Security program there were perceived advantages to the military regime. As early as July the department anticipated that in the aftermath of the Rojas coup the bilateral military program would be implemented more rapidly. It was noted that internal fighting already appeared to have been reduced, and Colombian air force personnel were being reassigned to the Mutual Defense units; the fighter squadron was expected to be operational in two months and all air force training concentrated at the Cali air base. The light bomber squadron would not be organized until there was sufficient equipment, but an estimated 75 percent of the material needed for the anti-aircraft squadron, formed in January 1953 by presidential decree, was in place and three hundred recruits were being trained. Beyond these commitments, the United States was reluctant to expand its military obligations in Colombia during the next several years. The Joint Chiefs of Staff in September 1955 indicated that they could not justify funding additional Colombian units for the Western Hemisphere because of the need to balance "the strategic military considerations bearing on the Colombian request against strategic military considerations of a global nature."[26]

In addition to moving ahead with the Mutual Security program, the Rojas administration took steps to improve its internal intelligence system. In October 1953 José Maria Chaves, then counsellor of the Colombian embassy, requested the services of three U.S. experts to establish the machinery for an intelligence and counterintelligence operation, and he requested consent to discuss their plans with J. Edgar Hoover and Allen Dulles. Less than one month later the government, by decree, formed a new intelligence service. The new organization, like the U.S. CIA, was responsible directly to the president; it was intended that it should import more modern intelligence methods from the FBI. Its intent was clear, to provide the regime with more centralized security control in domestic political matters, but from a U.S. perspective it could also improve hemispheric security.[27]

Eisenhower administration officials were able to work with the Rojas military regime—occasionally more easily than with the chaotic and repressive Conservative governments that preceded Rojas—but their consistent preference was a return to democratic government. During the Rojas period, there was more official U.S. attention to Colombia than there had been earlier. This was indicative of the greater attention to Latin America under Eisenhower than under Truman rather than of preference for the political system Rojas represented. From 1953 to 1958 a series of prominent U.S. officials visited Bogotá: in 1953 Milton Eisenhower, Assistant Secretary of State John Cabot; Assistant Secretary of the Treasury John Overly; Assistant Secretary of Commerce Samuel Anderson. In 1955 officials from State and the Export-Import Bank and the secretary of agriculture made official visits. In 1956 John Foster Dulles arrived to discuss military relations, Colombian exchange problems, coffee prices, U.S. aid to the Paz del Rio steel mill, and press censorship under the Rojas government. The Nixon trip followed the fall of Rojas in 1957.[28]

The Eisenhower administration responded to the collapse of the Rojas dictatorship in May 1957 with general optimism. It was pleased that there appeared to have been at least a temporary compromise

among Liberals and Conservatives, largely through the skillful negotiations of Alberto Lleras Camargo. Still, it fretted about the apparent
increase in guerrilla activities in several areas of the country. There
were other obstacles to a peaceful transition to democracy. Former
Conservative President Laureano Gómez returned from exile in October 1957 to add his obstructionist tactics to the political stabilization
efforts. Nor was the economy in sound condition. With prices for coffee low on international markets, it was difficult to service the old
external debt, let alone current commercial ones. The Export-Import
Bank continued to allocate funds for the liquidation of commercial
debts, as well as for highway construction, agricultural development,
transportation improvements, hydro-electric development, port improvement, and hotel construction.

Among American officials, there were mixed emotions about the
swing of the Colombian public mood away from militarism. Ambassador John Cabot worried that the new antimilitarism that accompanied
the reaction against the Rojas dictatorship and the decade-long violence in the country would undermine support for hemispheric security programs; yet he argued in August 1958 that the main U.S. concern
should be to keep the democratic government in place and to emphasize economic and social rehabilitation rather than the "military field."
"If we wish Colombia to undertake further military programs . . . in
our interest . . ." he argued, "we must also pay for them—if only as a
means of protecting Colombia from overwhelming economic burdens
at this time." Cabot thought the effort worthwhile in continuing to
train Colombian military officers in the United States. "This training,"
he observed, ". . . increases their friendliness for the United States
and imbues them with the idea of democratic, non-partisan service
which has . . . often been lacking in Latin American armed services."[29]

In spite of the weak economic situation, Cabot was sufficiently optimistic about the political environment that he recommended Colombia
be made a "showcase" for American aid and economic cooperation.
Colombia had a good record, he argued, of treating U.S. capital fairly,
and he anticipated that Alberto Lleras Camargo, due to be inaugurated
in August 1958, would be especially pro-U.S. He was concerned that

Colombians could do more to make effective use of PL 480 assistance, however, which made available U.S. agricultural surpluses for foreign use. In part this reticence derived from Colombian desire to protect their large agricultural interests rather than ensuring their "people are adequately fed." As Cabot noted, the long term answer to Colombian requirements was increased domestic production, rather than import substitution through the PL 480 program. The generally deplorable economic condition of the country gave Cabot and other officials little hope that the Mutual Security program was viable. Cabot observed in early 1959 that without improved economic conditions there would be no amelioration of social and political conflict, and without such stability, he cautioned Secretary of State Christian Herter, "discussion of the country's ability and willingness to carry out its defense obligations is pointless. . . . Colombia is incapable of maintaining internal order, much less undertaking regional defense obligations." Although he anticipated that in 1959 there might be some increase in assistance from the Export-Import Bank and the International Bank for Reconstruction and Development under the circumstances, he stressed that the military-aid program should contribute if possible to improving the economic conditions in the country by, for instance, reducing military repair costs and providing employment opportunities for more Colombian labor.[30]

Colombian Labor, Communism, and the Cold War

Although the military assistance program was from the U.S. perspective clearly targeted at hemispheric defense, both Colombian and American officials were also anxious to contain any potential domestic insurgent communist movement during these years. There was no significant guerrilla movement until after the Cuban Revolution, in spite of Conservative efforts to label as communists those dissident Liberals who took up arms for survival as well as protest during the 1950s. To the credit of American officials, after initial hysteria and hyperbole at the time of the *Bogotazo* in 1948, they were relatively rational in distinguishing between general political opposition to the Conservatives and to the Rojas regime, and on the other hand, a communist labor and political sector. By late in the decade Ambassador Cabot was optimistic that the Communist "situation" was under control. During the decade, however, he advocated an expansion of both U.S. and Colombian efforts—through the United States Information Agency, for instance—to "fight fire with fire."

U.S. anticommunist efforts in Colombia during the 1950s were sporadic in nature, but U.S. officials concentrated on the Colombian labor movement and worked closely with U.S. labor officials. Colombian communism after World War II was disorganized and posed little threat to hemispheric security or traditional elite control in Colombian politics or labor, but there were still persistent efforts to purge the labor movement of communist elements on the left and Peronist influences on the right. The party was divided into three factions by 1947: the official party under Gilberto Vieira; the workers party of Augusto Durán; and some petroleum workers unions led by Diego Montaña Cuellar. The party was briefly outlawed from 1956 to 1957 and recognized in December 1957 on the assumption that it was easier to monitor its activities if it was public. The total party membership was only five thousand at its peak in the decade; it gained no political offices, and under the bipartisan, national front plan after 1958 it was ineligible to run candidates for office. Further, for many years after 1948 Colombia had no diplomatic relations with either the USSR or with other Soviet bloc nations, although Colombia and Czechoslovakia exchanged consular officers.

The Colombian labor movement at the time was sharply divided between the Liberal CTC (Colombian Confederation of Labor), which in the late 1940s had communist members, and the Conservative UTC (Union of Colombian Workers). Conservative labor was concentrated in the Medellín area, which was the most industrialized. Liberal strength in organized labor was concentrated among the railway workers, although they gained adherents from among newly organized sectors, such as state employees, including Avianca Airline workers. The communist movement experienced some success in organizing in the oil industry, where FEDEPETROL was the dominant group in the Standard Oil Barrancabermeja De Mares concession and refinery operations, which reverted to the state in the late 1940s. Communist and socialist support was also strong in the Viotá agricultural region of Cundinimarca near Bogotá.

In the course of the decade, U.S. officials and American trade union leaders sought to reinforce the Liberal labor groups in Colombia as the most effective bulwark against communism. Throughout the period the United States preferred the political center to the right or left within mainstream Colombian politics and the labor movement, although such efforts were not systematic until the establishment in 1962 of the American Institute for Free Labor Development, the first president of which was George Meany. Even in the interim, however, the State Department and U.S. labor officials worked with Colombian counterparts to achieve common goals.

In the oil industry the U.S. embassy played a direct role in labor negotiations after the war; the evidence suggests that objectives went considerably beyond containing Communist influence to restricting organized labor power itself. In efforts to create a new labor code in 1948, for instance, representatives of the oil companies met with the Colombian minister of mines and petroleum, the minister of labor, and embassy officials. The embassy sought to exclude any provision for compulsory arbitration from the new code of labor as well as to transfer the authority to declare the legality of a strike from local labor judges to the superior labor tribunals in the department capitals.[31] Embassy officials were pleased in 1948 when the Socony-Vaccum Company was able to negotiate a new contract with its workers without the intervention of Diego Montaña Cuellar and FEDEPETROL. In labor negotiations that year with Tropical Oil, the company strongly opposed increased power for labor-management committees in the area of personnel selection. Tropical and the other companies opposed labor demands for employment guarantees and for worker control of the job evaluation and promotion scale. As in early decades the Colombian government turned to U.S. oil industry expertise for advice on the labor situation, on this occasion to Max Thornburg, former

State Department oil adviser and Standard Oil of California executive. He reported directly to President Ospina that Colombian labor legislation went beyond the companies' ability to pay and interfered with the management of the industry.[32]

State Department officials encouraged such prominent Liberals as Carlos Lleras Restrepo to use their influence to purge communists from the labor movement. U.S. officials introduced him to AFL and CIO leaders and to Department of Labor officials in Washington. U.S. labor leaders were willing to invite the CTC to attend a contemplated Western Hemisphere labor congress hosted by the International Congress of Free Trade Unions (ICFTU) but only on the condition that the CTC join the ICFTU and withdraw from the more radical Latin American Confederation of Labor (CTAL). The AFL proved more difficult, as Serafino Romualdi informed Lleras that the AFL was unwilling to involve the CTC unless all communist elements were removed. That pressure appears to have had the desired result, since *El Tiempo* shortly announced the break with the CTAL and affiliation with the ICFTU. By late 1950 U.S. Ambassador Willard Beaulac was pressing Washington to invite Colombian labor leaders to the United States on grounds that the communist elements had withdrawn from the CTC.[33]

This initial success ran into heavier opposition by 1952, not only from a new offensive by Colombian communists but also from evident Peronist influences. The guerrilla and communist groups appeared to be emerging as more united. In August 1952 a national assembly of guerrillas met in Viotá, attended by such leading Colombian communists as Pedro José Abella and Victor Julio Merchán. U.S. officials were drawn to Gustavo Rojas Pinilla in part because of his public position that he was anxious to mount a more effective offensive against this "Communist" element and the guerrilla movement, although they remained sceptical about the degree of Colombian government commitment and capacity to deal effectively with the insurgency.[34]

There was also U.S. concern about Peronist agitation in Colombia during the Rojas years, although that concern may have been misguided, as a later Colombian foreign minister insisted to me. Certainly Argentine and pro-Argentine groups distributed considerable amounts of Peronist, anti-American propaganda in this period, including efforts to show the deficiencies of American aid programs. In addition to pamphlets and flyers, radio Santa Fé carried a program called *Noticias Argentinas*, featuring the sultry female voice of "Gloria." The embassy also expressed concern that the afternoon daily, *Diario Gráfico*, owned by Laureano Gómez's family, had begun to carry pro-Argentine items. In addition, there was at least circumstantial evidence linking CTC officials with pro-Peronist Colombians; for instance, the Friends of Argentina organization was formed at the home of Hernando Rodriguez Morales, who was secretary of the CTC and president of the CTC-affiliated Federation of Workers of Cundinamarca. The American Consul in Barranquilla suggested that Peronists were attempting to "capture" the Colombian labor movement and to that end the Argentine government had sent five delegates from the Argentine General Confederation of Labor to work with the Argentine embassy in Bogotá and Colombian labor groups. Subsequently these groups were influential in establishing a Peronist Colombian labor federation, the CNT, which it was believed had a number of affiliates in the Barranquilla region, primarily among brewery, electrical, tobacco, and shipbuilding workers. Colombian labor leaders were sufficiently concerned about these activities to discuss the situation with U.S. embassy officials. This evident growth in Peronist influence alarmed Colombian liberal labor leaders and American officials alike because it coincided with an assault by the Colombian government, especially after Rojas Pinilla came to power in mid-1953, and the Roman Catholic Church on the liberal CTC. Consequently, U.S. government and American labor representatives continued to press the two major Colombian labor federations to cope with communist and Peronist influences. One of the more concrete demonstrations of that concern was a meeting of a CIO representative with Colombian leaders in early 1953 at which the CIO offered funding to assist in the task.[35]

Rojas Pinilla did not move openly toward Peronism until early 1956 when he launched his Third Force movement, billed as an alliance of the military and labor, with crossed rifle and shovel the symbol.

The initiative was abortive, in any event, and Perón was no longer a factor in Argentina, with the result that the Colombian CNT collapsed, suggesting that its support was highly ephemeral. Nonetheless, between 1953 and 1956 the threat of Peronism on the right and communism on the left seemed real enough to American officials concerned with Colombia. Maintaining the CTC as part of the "free" trade union movement in the Americas was critical from the U.S. perspective. It was a domino that must not fall, and the threat from the Rojas government and the Roman Catholic Church to the free trade union movement put undue pressure on that bulwark.[36]

The Eisenhower administration compromised its efforts to gain support among Colombian liberals with its involvement in the Guatemalan coup of 1954 that brought down the reformist government of Jacobo Arbénz. Only the Colombian Conservative press portrayed the fall of Arbénz as a cold war issue. The leading Conservative daily of Medellín, *El Colombiano*, editorialized that the main danger to American democracy was indifference to the threat of communism. *El Día* and *La Republica* in Bogotá also stressed the threat of communist infiltration in Guatemala, not only as a danger to American democracy but as a threat to all Christian culture. The Liberal reaction was more complex. Although the prominent Liberal intellectual Germán Arciniegas conceded that communism may have made inroads into Guatemala, the responsibility for the appeal of communism in the nation was the imperialism of the United Fruit Company, and the U.S. government was an accessory to the company's role. *El Espectador* criticized a suggestion in the *New York Times* that it was only academic whether or not the United States had actually invaded Guatemala. To the Liberal paper, the United States had "incited to rebellion" and engaged in invasion jointly with Honduras, Nicaragua, and Guatemalan rebels.[37]

For Colombia, the Guatemalan crisis was a sideshow, having little impact on Colombian domestic or foreign policy. The ultimate collapse of the Rojas dictatorship had little to do with cold war issues, although the tangential linkage of violence in the countryside and the labor movement with communism contributed to both domestic discontent with his government and American preference to see him replaced by a more democratic and representative government.

His government came to an ignominious end in 1957 as other factions of the military, Liberals, and Conservatives reached the conclusion that stability could not be realized under his mandate. Although there is absolutely no evidence that the United States contributed to his demise, the fall of Rojas was deemed sufficiently important to serve as the subject of a report to the National Security Council by CIA Director Allen Dulles in May 1957, under the heading "Significant World Developments Affecting US Security." President Eisenhower wrote to the president of the transitional military junta expressing approval of the "steady progress" being made toward the reestablishment of constitutional government. Following uneasy negotiations between Liberal Alberto Lleras Camargo and the grand old man of Colombian Conservatism, Laureano Gómez, then in exile in Spain, the two parties agreed to the establishment of a National Front government, which would remain in force until the 1970s.[38]

Ironically, the crises and repression of the Rojas years, which had been initially hailed as a promise of stable government, weakened basic Colombian political and economic institutions, including the liberal labor movement, and created more fertile soil for the Communist party. American embassy officials detected a concerted Communist effort in late 1957 to organize unions and penetrate and control existing unions. The embassy reported a striking increase in Communist propaganda during the year, with three new periodicals appearing on a regular basis, wider distribution of broadsheets, and the formation of a Communist front organization, the Institute of International Cooperation.

Actual Communist party membership and voting strength, on the other hand, appears to have remained relatively constant, although there was a major strike against a Bogotá steel fabrication plant, in which Sears Roebuck had a financial interest. The embassy claimed that the strike was guided by Communist labor organizers affiliated with the Cundinamarca Federation of Labor. Under U.S. pressure the CTC was induced to withdraw its support for the strikers, and the lengthy strike collapsed. Early the next year there was a major general strike against the American-owned Frontino Gold Company, which considered the strikers "semi-Communist." This strike was sufficiently volatile that American and British dependents were evacuated, and the Colombian Minister of Labor sent in troops and police to keep peace and to prevent damage to the mines. The same company was the scene the following year of a two-month strike supported by the Communist party, which presented the clash as a struggle against American imperialism. In the oil industry in 1958 Diego Montaña Cuellar and the oil workers unions that he represented continued to be active against both foreign companies, such as Shell in that year, and against ECOPETROL, which now operated the Tropical Oil concession and refinery. American officials concluded that only a major effort on the part of the UTC and company officials kept the workers of the Texas Oil Company from shifting union allegiances. Anti-Communist oil workers were assisted directly by U.S. oil workers, who provided a subsidy to the UTC and supported the publication of anti-Communist literature.[39]

The ruling transitional junta between Rojas and the National Front, with U.S. endorsement, escalated its attack on pro-Communist groups in an effort to strengthen the free trade union movement. In February 1958 the Junta issued a decree that was viewed by an ICFTU-ORIT (the regional organization of independent workers) mission as the most significant labor measure in a decade to strengthen free labor; among other features it provided for the automatic check off by managements of organized plants in cooperation with national and departmental labor federations, and stipulated that nonunion workers wishing to enjoy the benefits of a collective agreement already in force had to pay to the union local one-half of the normal union dues, with deduction at source. During this period George Meany appealed to the State Department to try to meet Colombian government financial needs to forestall economic crisis; the State Department also assisted with the operation of a training program in the United States for Latin American labor leaders, including Colombians. The ICFTU-ORIT assigned David Sternback, formerly of the AFL-CIO international affairs department, to try to reconcile UTC-CTC differences in an effort to strengthen the overall noncommunist labor movement in Colombia. Sternback was frustrated in his attempt during 1958; he found the CTC leadership severely weakened by the military regime, lacking initiative, and out of touch with the rank and file during a period that the Communist party was making a concerted effort to build a worker-campesino alliance. A number of unions in Cali and Medellín claiming CTC affiliation were heavily communist influenced, in his view. Although he was able to bring the UTC and CTC leadership to the negotiating table, to play midwife to the creation of the Cundinamarca Organization of Syndical Unity, and to have the UTC and CTC establish a national coordinating committee that began publication of a labor periodical *Unidad* (financed in part by the United States Information Service and ICFTU-ORIT), by September 1958 Sternback found antiunionist sentiment so strong that he asked to be recalled. The AFL-CIO subsequently sent Latin American labor expert Serafino Romualdi, who would later serve as first executive director of the American Institute for Free Labor Development, to encourage a broader labor front. He learned from President Lleras Camargo that the latter's objective was frustrated in part by strong resistance within his own party to any cooperation with labor elements that had supported the Rojas dictatorship, as much as he shared the concern about increased communist activity. Nonetheless, an overwhelming majority of the CTC's executive committee remained noncommunist, and as much as State Department officials at decade's end worried that none of their or U.S. labor's programs had been very effective, there seemed to be no clear danger of major communist influence in Colombia. The firmly anticommunist orientation of the Colombian Confederation of Labor was reflected in several cartoons published in its *Revista* in 1959, indicating, in the opinion of the U.S. labor attaché, a clear public break with communism. The April issue carried a cartoon depicting a man in dark suit marked with the hammer and sickle banging his head ineffectually against a stone wall bearing the insignia "ORIT—Pan-Paz-Libertad."[40]

The Eisenhower administration was relieved by the inauguration in mid-1958 of Alberto Lleras Camargo as president. Although not un-critical of the United States, Lleras was committed to positive relations, to free enterprise, hemispheric solidarity, and anticommunism. He was also one of the Latin American leaders, like Juscelino Kubitschek of Brazil, who pressed the Eisenhower administration in the late 1950s toward a greater commitment to economic and social development. Lleras wrote Eisenhower in late 1958 expressing his strong concern that an "uncertain economic situation and a prolonged and almost hopeless state of underdevelopment are creating disillusionment, con-fusion, and discouragement among the people of Latin America, with the inevitable consequence of political instability and grave social un-rest which are constantly militating against the effectiveness of the democratic system."

Lleras enjoyed considerable credibility in American and Latin Amer-ican political and diplomatic circles. An editor of the prestigious *El Tiempo* from 1930, he founded and then directed *El Liberal* from 1938 to 1942, as well as the weekly magazine *Semana* in 1946. He had served as interim president of Colombia in 1945 and 1946, completing the term of Alfonso López; as director of the Pan American Union; and as sec-retary general of its successor, the Organization of American States. Earlier he had been Colombian ambassador to the United States and in 1945 had made what American officials considered an important con-tribution as a Colombian delegate to the San Francisco United Nations meetings.[41]

President Eisenhower and American officials encouraged the new Colombian president during Lleras's official visit to Washington (sig-nificantly, accompanied by, among others, the presidents of the two major Colombian labor federations). The administration wished to demonstrate to all of Latin America that the United States heartily approved the effort to restore a democratic government in Colombia. American officials were also anxious to bolster Lleras's domestic politi-cal situation, since he was under fire from the left-wing Liberals led by Alfonso López Michelsen and the Laureanista faction of the Conser-vative party, including Belisario Betancur and Diego Tovar. The U.S.

embassy cautioned that López Michelsen was pressing for recognition of the Communist party once again as well as renewed diplomatic relations with the Soviet bloc.

There was thus a very public display of American hospitality for Lleras. In addition to the state dinner at the White House and private conversations with Eisenhower, Lleras was feted in New York by UN Secretary General Dag Hammerskjold and by Nelson Rockefeller and the business community at New York's Knickerbocker Club. He addressed a joint session of Congress on inter-American affairs and received an honorary degree from Johns Hopkins University, where Milton Eisenhower was president. In Miami, he unveiled a statue of Santander and visited an exhibition of Colombian art at the University's Lowe Gallery.[42]

If the intention of the visit on both sides was to produce immediate and tangible results, there was cause for only limited celebration. Lleras supported Eisenhower through the U-2 spy plane crisis and against Khrushchev's hard line on the Paris Summit. He also maintained an anti-Castro stance on the Cuban Revolution, although he insisted that the Cuban issue should be handled through the OAS, not unilaterally by the United States. Lleras's main concern with Cuba went beyond U.S. cold war interests; he feared the spread of guerrilla warfare into Venezuela and Colombia. As early as August 1959, Colombian Foreign Minister Julio César Turbay Ayala chaired the session at the Santiago foreign ministers meeting that issued a declaration confirming the commitment of the OAS to democratic forms of government, free elections, the rule of law, human rights, and freedom of expression. Lleras also supported more initiatives toward disarmament and recognition of Communist China in the United Nations. He informed the U.S. ambassador that he thought it "unacceptable" that 600 million people should be unrepresented.[43]

Nonetheless, Lleras's first priority was not foreign policy but economic development and stability, and he pressed for more U.S. economic and military assistance. He experienced some success in the late stages of the Eisenhower administration. In terms of military support, an American antiguerrilla specialist team in 1959 recommended that the Colombian government receive assistance for its antiguerrilla campaign, although the American preference was that Colombia purchase the equipment, since the Morse Amendment to the Mutual Security Act forbade military aid for internal security use. At the same time, U.S. officials viewed the Colombian situation as sufficiently critical that if Colombia could not afford to purchase the equipment, the United States should provide it. The White House was essentially supportive of Lleras's effort to shift Colombian military training away from conventional tactics toward antiguerrilla methods.

On the economic side, the White House and State Department fully supported Colombian efforts under Lleras to cope with the massive debts accrued during the Rojas dictatorship and with the serious social and economic development problems that confronted the country at the end of the 1950s. Shortly before traveling to Washington, Lleras unveiled his "platform of economic development and social welfare," involving agrarian reform, improved education, and economic modernization. It was estimated that reform would require additional foreign investment of $80 million annually and $100 million in foreign loans. In keeping with the belief that the turn of events in Cuba required urgent action, in August 1960 the U.S. Congress authorized appropriations of $500 million to establish a special inter-American social development fund. The following month, representatives of the American republics signed the Act of Bogotá, which among other provisions included a commitment to make a vigorous attack on economic underdevelopment and the sources of political unrest.[44]

The Eisenhower administration marked no sharp break ideologically with either its predecessor or its successor insofar as U.S.–Latin American policy was concerned, although it is easy to identify differences of emphasis, of style, rhetoric, and tactics. American policymakers, working in cooperation with the private sector, sought to reinforce indigenous anticommunist elements in Colombia in order to maintain hemispheric solidarity against a perceived Soviet bloc threat and to bolster a free trade union movement that would pose neither a security threat nor a challenge to free enterprise and foreign investment. In the Colombian instance, in contrast to the policy that was pursued in Guatemala, the United States was more successful in maintaining support for a vital center, with definitive inclination toward the political center, against either military rule or a more reactionary, outdated conservatism on the right and communism on the left, although one should not underestimate what was basically a "quest for spoils" rather than fundamental ideological differences between the Liberal and Conservative parties.

Yet, it is difficult to assess how critical U.S. actions and efforts actually were in influencing the direction of Colombian politics during the first decade and a half of the cold war. Colombia was a traditional, Catholic, primarily agricultural society, which had experienced a substantial degree of modernization and industrialization, and the emergence of a more liberal, business-oriented middle class that was superimposed upon rather than fully integrated into that traditional society. The civil war of the 1950s had little if anything to do with either indigenous or international communism but rather with the continuation of a century-long struggle between a liberal and a conservative political philosophy, based as they were on differing attitudes toward the Church, economic change, and the desirable degree of political pluralism in the society. The United States and American investment was on the whole clearly associated with the liberal orientation, as much as it may have convenienced some U.S. interests to maintain a more traditional society. American interests consistently supported the liberal center, the position held for instance by Lleras Camargo or Lleras Restrepo, rather than the more populistic or socialistic ideals of either Jorge Eliécer Gaitán before 1948 or Alfonso López Michelsen by 1960. The American contribution, while impossible to measure statistically, thus reinforced rather than directed Colombian domestic and foreign policies. Colombia needed little additional encouragement to move into the anti-Soviet and later the anti-Castro camp. If the United States had a vested interest in free enterprise, anti-Communism, a free labor movement, and political pluralism, Colombians had an equally strong vested interest in ensuring that this was the direction of Colombian politics. One errs in attributing too much influence to the United States in the achievement of those goals.

8 Decades of Optimism and Crisis, 1960–1990

> Rodó, the great Uruguayan creator of 'Ariel,' traced the course of the spirit of our race and set the destination of our development in the cultivation of that immortal spirit, in contrast to Anglo-Saxon pragmatism. (Belisario Betancur, Brussels, 1983)

Colombian history since 1960 has witnessed a continued emphasis on economic progress, a search for means to alleviate crushing social problems associated with rural-urban migration, emigration, political crises occasioned by guerrilla movements, and the massive shift in power occasioned by the rise of the drug industry. As in the pre-1960s, Colombian views of relations with the United States and the rest of the world have varied from pro-Americanism to resentment of U.S. power. Throughout, Colombians have sensed the intimate relationship between the internal political and economic crises and international relations in the debate over extradition of major drug traffickers in the 1980s, alternative routes to economic modernization, the role of the military in politics, or the conflict between guerrillas and para-military "death squads."

Resolution of these issues has been elusive because even in elite political circles Colombians have lacked a real societal consensus on fundamental issues. Relations with the United States have remained a persistent fact as Colombians debate these questions. Despite the intrusive presence of the United States, there have been efforts—as there were in the 1920s and 1930s—to achieve trade and investment diversification, to pursue a Central American policy distinct from that charted by the United States, and to resolve the drug crisis without U.S. intervention. In final analysis, the United States has retained its hegemony, partly because such problems cannot be resolved uni-laterally.[1]

The Alliance for Progress

The cold war and the international repercussions of the Cuban Revolution in 1959 shaped Colombian-U.S relations in the 1960s on the international stage. That context even informed the Colombian debate on economic development and political stability. The revived U.S. interest in Latin America in the 1960s was relatively short-lived, however, as the deepening crisis in Vietnam absorbed the time, ener-gies, and resources of the Johnson and Nixon administrations. Even Vietnam did not reduce U.S. involvement in Latin America to the policy of neglect that had characterized the first decade of the cold war, although the basic assumptions of the cold war, redefined by the Kennedy and Johnson administrations to focus on the Third World, remained at the core of U.S. policy.

Cold war considerations—the Cuban Revolution, Vietnam, and the Nixon-Kissinger movement toward détente with the Soviet Union and China—provided a degree of thematic unity and continuity in U.S. policy from 1960 to 1975. The last of U.S. ground forces were with-drawn from Saigon in 1975, and the United States moved toward recognition of China. On the Colombian side, the election of left-Liberal President Alfonso López Michelsen in 1974 brought to an end the first sixteen years of the National Front. For both nations, then, the mid-1970s seemed to represent a watershed, a departure from the preoccupations of the previous two decades.

The dominant Colombian political figures in the 1960s were Alberto Lleras Camargo (1958–62) and Carlos Lleras Restrepo (1966–70), both Liberals and both inclined to cooperate with the United States in hemi-sphere affairs in the interest of economic development. Lleras Res-trepo pursued a more independent and critical path than either Lleras Camargo or his immediate Conservative predecessor, Guillermo Leon Valencia (1962–66), who served an undistinguished term between the

COSTA
RICA

C A R I B B E A N   S E A

CANAL ZONE

Colón

*Panama seceded
in 1903*

Barranquilla

ATLÁNTICO

Santa Marta

Riohacha

Cartagena

Ciénaga

GUAJIRA

Panamá

Golfo de Urabá

Golfo
de Panamá

*PACIFIC
OCEAN*

SUCRE

CÓRDOBA

CÉSAR

MAGDALENA

BOLÍVAR

Petrólea

ANTIOQUIA

NORTE
DE SANTANDER

Barrancabermeja

Cúcuta

Quibdó

Medellín

El Centro

VENEZUELA

SANTANDER

Bucaramanga

RISARALDA

CALDAS

Pereira

Manizales

Arauca

QUINDIO

Tunja

ARAUCA

Buenaventura

Armenia

CUNDINAMARCA

BOYACÁ

VALLE
DEL CAUCA

Ibagué

Girardot

BOGOTÁ

CASANARE

Tumaco

Cali

TOLIMA

CAUCA

Neiva

Villavicencio

NARIÑO

Pôpayán

SPECIAL
DISTRICT

Puerto López

Pasto

HUILA

M E T A

V I C H A D A

Orito

N

PUTUMAYO

GUAVIARE

E C U A D O R

CAQUETÁ

GUAINÍA

VAUPÉS

*Territory lost
to Ecuador
from 1880 to 1942*

A M A Z O N A S

P   E   R   U

Rio Napo

*Territory lost
to Brazil
in 1904 and 1905*

Leticia

The Republic of

COLOMBIA

B   R   A   Z   I   L

Political divisions

Source – Instituto Geográfico "Agustín Codazzi", Colombia, 1989

Kilometres

0   100   200   300   400   500

0   100   200   300

Miles

wm

two Liberals. All were absorbed by the fundamental problem of attempting to reconcile economic development with social justice and political democracy. The National Front governments of the 1960s and early 1970s in Colombia sought economic development and social justice, including expanded educational opportunities; but they did so within a highly controlled political system, which forbade the participation of all political parties save the Liberals and Conservatives. Such a system of controlled democracy was perhaps necessary for the maintenance of some degree of peace, given the historic conflicts between the two parties; it was also likely necessary to have such political stability in order to make progress on the economic front. Colombians, however, paid a high price in the long term for placing more value on stability and the appearance of order than on the resolution of fundamental problems of distribution of power—economic, social, and political. The basic irony of these results lies in the fact that Colombian and U.S. governments in the 1960s and 1970s sought some degree of reform in order to forestall real revolution.

The Kennedy administration seized the reform initiative in response to the Latin American challenge to promote economic growth and forestall social revolution. The Eisenhower administration had already established the agenda, responding to Latin American pressures in general and to the Cuban Revolution specifically. By the time Kennedy came to office the long-desired Inter-American Bank was a reality, Congress had agreed to the establishment of a social development trust fund, and the Act of Bogotá in 1960 had signaled a commitment to economic development in the Americas. Although these initiatives gained Kennedy's support as presidential candidate and president-elect, they clearly predated his inauguration.[2]

On the eve of Kennedy's election, the twin themes of the Cuban Revolution and economic development were paramount in hemispheric affairs. At the Bogotá Conference, Colombian officials were emphatic that they intended to press the United States for reforms. They wanted the repayment of loans in local currencies not in U.S. dollars; improved terms of trade with the United States; and price supports for basic commodity exports, such as coffee, where Colombia and other major producers had been pressing for years to gain U.S. support on an international agreement.

For a nation such as Colombia, which in 1961 produced 13 percent of world coffee exports, this issue was of vital concern. Between 1950 and 1959 coffee exports generated over 77 percent of all exports proceeds and 69 percent of all foreign exchange earnings on goods and services.[3] President Lleras Camargo, in the charged atmosphere of the conference, reiterated the half-threat, half warning of his visit to the United States earlier that year: "Latin America is on the edge of an economic and social crisis without precedent in its history."

As Lleras called for a new Marshall Plan for Latin America, several hundred demonstrators in the Plaza Bolívar outside the meeting chanted "Cuba sí, Yankees no." Lleras predicted that a "revolution against poverty" was coming to the Third World. The issues to be confronted were basic not only to the Americas but to the "free civilization of the West." Lleras's main objective was to achieve a level of industrialization that would leave Latin America free from the effects of the drastic price fluctuations that plagued Latin American exports to the developed world. Only in this way could there be social and political peace in Latin America.[4]

Colombian delegates were active in the debates over commodity export controls and the Cuban issue, in the former instance collaborating with U.S. delegates to draft a resolution calling for consultation; the International Coffee Agreement was signed in New York two years later.[5] Many hailed the final Act of Bogotá as a blueprint for action on agrarian reform, housing, health, and education.[6] The mood was one of optimism; the atmosphere was electric for many Latin Americans and Americans alike, who believed that long-sought changes now had official support.

The Lleras Camargo administration, prior to the lauching of the Alliance for Progress, moved ahead slowly and cautiously on several reform fronts, with U.S. assistance, particularly in agrarian and educational reform.[7] Thus, when Kennedy made his dramatic announcement at the White House on 13 March 1961, that his government was prepared to support a massive aid program for Latin America under

the Alliance for Progress label, Colombian leaders responded favorably. Luis Enrique Bello, chief of the diplomatic division of the Colombian Foreign Ministry, identified a Kennedy address in February 1961
on Latin American relations as "new testimony to his unquestioned
commitment to this hemisphere."[8]

The alliance was a multipronged development initiative, but, like
the Eisenhower aid programs, the focus remained on the promotion
of private sector foreign and domestic investment over the long term,
especially the fostering of Latin American initiatives. The U.S. pledge
of $10 billion in public aid over the coming decade dwarfed the Eisen-
hower commitment of $500 million in assistance, and matching funds
were expected to come from the private sector.[9]

Cultural Diplomacy and Popular Culture

During the Kennedy years there was renewed emphasis on cultural
diplomacy and a rethinking of the role of the United States Information Agency. The administration redefined the mission of the agency
to embody concepts that had been put into practice earlier in the
overseas radio work of Edward R. Murrow. The agency continued its
counterpropaganda role, emphasizing in its programs and literature
aspects of U.S. life and culture that would facilitate a better understanding of U.S. foreign policies. The Kennedy team more explicitly
defined the mission to link foreign policy and culture, to influence
foreign attitudes as a means of shaping the foreign policies of other
peoples. The reverse side of the approach required that the president and other foreign policy decision makers be sensitive to and
apprised of the implications for foreign public opinion of specific U.S.
foreign policy initiatives. Consistent with Alliance for Progress goals,
the United States Information Agency was to emphasize the themes of
self-help, mutual responsibility, and the need for cooperative action,
and throughout the decade the agency's targets for information distribution and contacts were labor leaders, university and some secondary school students, and "communicators" (that is, writers, journal-

ists, and broadcasters), especially those who were young enough to be among the opinion shapers of their nations in the coming generation.[10]

Cultural programs, whether of the USIA variety or such initiatives as the Fulbright program, played a significant role in the Kennedy program in Colombia and elsewhere in Latin America, although in budget terms Latin America ranked a consistent third behind Asia and the Near East. Within Latin America, Colombia, important as it may have been as a showpiece for U.S. aid, received considerably less USIA assistance than several other nations in the region. In 1968, for instance, Colombia was one of seven countries that received more than $300,000 in budget allocation, but this placed it behind Brazil, Argentina, Chile, Mexico, and Venezuela. Between 1949 and 1986, in the area of educational exchanges, which have since the late 1940s enriched contacts between U.S. and Latin American academics and students, 1,140 Colombians received grants for university study in the United States. Another ninety-one received support for advanced research; there were 321 grants for teaching or educational seminars, forty-eight university lecturers, and seventeen Hubert Humphrey Scholars. Six hundred and eighty-six U.S. citizens received support for university study, advanced research, or teaching in Colombia during the same period. Almost 50 percent of those awards were for U.S. university lecturers to teach in Colombia.[11]

Not all cultural contacts, and perhaps not even the most important, have been those envisaged by Kennedy and his predecessors in cultural diplomacy.[12] In a more general sense it may be impossible to measure the influence of U.S. culture on Colombia, either elite or mass culture. Such cultural influences have also flowed in both directions. Colombian immigrants, tourists, and students in the United States have brought their own influences to bear, along with the impact that Colombian imports into the United States—coffee, cocaine, bananas, oil, textiles, gold, platinum, and flowers, among others—have on American perceptions and lifestyles. Who can measure the physical, psychological, and economic impact in the past twenty years of the illegal drug traffic?

Colombian immigration to the United States in the past thirty years has furthered direct contacts between the peoples of two nations and contributed to U.S. perceptions of Colombian society, politics, and culture. The Colombian-born segment of the U.S. population is less striking than that of the dominant Hispanic groups—Cuban, Mexican, and Puerto Rican—but it has been professional and middle class and, like the Cuban, comparatively prosperous. In 1960 fewer than three thousand Colombians migrated to the United States. Five years later the number had substantially increased to almost eleven thousand, compared with twelve thousand from Central America. Over the decade from 1961 to 1969, more than sixty-five thousand Colombians sought to make their homes in the United States. Between 1971 and 1980 almost seventy-eight thousand Colombians followed their predecessors. Between 1981 and 1986 another sixty-three thousand made the transition. It is evident that this migration preceded the drug wars and was occasioned by more deeply rooted perceptions in Colombia about economic and political opportunities in the United States. With rates of unemployment comparatively high, including in some of the technical and professional areas, it was not surprising that emigration was an option. Among medical graduates, for instance, in the early 1970s 11 percent left the country, although some returned as employment became available. As with other Hispanic immigrants, Colombians have clustered in previous Hispanic enclaves, including Miami and New York. In 1987, for instance, of almost 12,000 Colombian immigrants, 3,700 chose New York, 2,300 Florida, and 1,900 New Jersey, while only 850 went to California and fewer than 400 to Illinois.[13]

The superficial evidence of the U.S. cultural penetration of Colombia is strong and highly visible, ranging from technology, fast-food restaurants, and mass-circulation magazines (*Time, Newsweek,* and *Playboy* and other soft-pornographic magazines) to the more recent advent of satellite-carried television in upper-middle class Colombian homes and hotels. That influence is evident as well in advertising features in the Colombian print media, in the comic books that Colombian children read, in clothing styles, films, and music preferences of young Colombians.

One should be careful not to exaggerate either the degree or the impact of such "culture." There is a good deal more to culture than hemlines and rock music, and in the case of Colombia a very rich national and international cultural heritage has served to ensure that American popular influences are as superficial as they are omnipresent. In addition to the deeply embedded European legacy of more than four hundred years, every Colombian region has its own folkloric traditions; there are remarkable contrasts between Caribbean and Pacific coasts and the highlands, between black and Indian and white, between campesinos and small town residents and the sophisticated upper-middle classes of the cosmopolitan cities.

In the broader sweep of Colombian cultural development, in literature the influences were decidedly European—Spanish and French— as in the model of Chateaubriand for the famous Colombian romantic novel *Maria* by Jorge Isaacs (1867) or in the academic work of Colombia's two most influential philologists, Miguel Antonio Caro and Rufino José Cuervo, founders of the Insitituto Caro y Cuervo in the early twentieth century. True, as early as the mid-nineteenth century, the highly influential Colombian poet Rafael Pombo lived in the United States and was a friend of Henry Longfellow. By the late nineteenth century, one might trace the influence of Edgar Allen Poe on the French symbolists, including Baudelaire and Mallarmé, and in turn on such Colombian writers as the poet Miguel Angel Osorio or in the symbolist and psychological dimensions of Tomás Carrasquilla's novels (*En la diestra de Dios padre*, 1897). Yet, one looks in vain for the leading U.S. literary figures of the nineteenth century: Emerson, Whitman, Thoreau, Melville. Classics were the norm in literature, music, and architecture among the Colombian elite.

Even in the 1980s, although American performers made their appearances, the Colombian Symphony (established 1936), the Bogotá Symphony, or the Bach Choir featured European composers. When they featured Colombian composers, such as Guillermo Uribe-Holguín, the emphasis was on indigenous themes. Uribe-Holguín, for instance, in his many compositions incorporated pre-Columbian themes and rhythms, drawing on the inspiration of the Chibchas in the symphony "Of the Earth" and in his opera "Furatena," named for the Chibcha goddess of emeralds. Even in more "popular" music, American rock is balanced in influence by Afro-Caribbean infusions on the coast, in the rhythms of the fandangos, *porros*, and *mapalés*, or the *cumbia*, which is indigenous to Cartagena, or the *bambuco*, which derived from the Indian highlands. In architecture, the models for Colombian architectural schools have been Scandinavian, German, Brazilian, Italian, and French. In town planning, the leading inspiration was the Frenchman Le Corbusier, who was also highly influential in Canada.[14]

The U.S. influence in Colombian literature became stronger in the post-1945 years. The most influential Colombian writer of this century, Gabriel García Márquez, beginning with the publication of *La hojarasca* (Leafstorm) in 1955, acknowledged the influence of William Faulkner. Similarities have been noted between Faulkner and García Márquez's use—in a 1952 short story ("Someone Has Been Disarranging These Roses"), in *La hojarasca,* in *Cien años de soledad* (One hundred years of solitude), and in *El otoño del patriarca* (The autumn of the patriarch)— of multiple perspectives and narrators, the ambiguity in temporal patterns, the technique of using several stories that provide a unified tale, the regional contexts of their novels (Macondo for García Márquez, Yoknapatawpha County in Faulkner), and the genealogical techniques (five generations of the Buendías in *Cien años*).[15] In an interview in the early 1970s, García Márquez acknowledged Faulkner as his early mentor. He also depicted his 1961 bus trip with his wife and young son from New York to Mexico as "homage to Faulkner." In addition to Faulkner's influence on García Márquez, one cannot escape the presence of the United Fruit Company in *Cien años de soledad,* any more than could the residents of the Santa Marta banana zone.

García Márquez has become one of the most widely read authors of his generation with a wide audience in the United States. A less-prominent example of a Colombian intellectual influenced by United States cultural and social history is the Costeño doctor and writer of negritude, Manuel Zapata Olivella. Zapata's passionate convictions (and those of his sister and brother) in developing the culture and history of black Colombians derived in part from the inspiration of such black American writers as Langston Hughes, Claude Mackay, Richard Wright, and later James Baldwin. Significantly, his introduction to that literature came from French translations. His memoir of his travels through the United States from Mexico after World War II, *He Visto la Noche* (I have seen the night) had reached a third edition by 1980. It is a perspective—often moving, frequently perceptive, and unique— by a black Colombian of black America. Significantly his sister Delia is the founder of the major Colombian folkloric dance group, and his brother a prominent novelist.[16]

Among more academic Colombian writers, only a few have obtained a following in the United States. The most prominent to have done so is Germán Arciniegas, a president of the Colombian Academy of History, whose sweeping historical essays on Latin America and the Caribbean have since the 1940s been translated and widely read in North America because they so effectively bridged the popular and academic genres. These are only suggestive ideas of what needs to be a more systematic analysis of transcultural exchanges. Ultimately the intellectual history of the Americas will build on the pioneering work in the field of literature by E. Anderson Imbert.

In purely popular culture areas, developments in sports reflect the same pattern of symbiosis between North American and traditional Latin American patterns. Soccer, cycling, and the bullfight in Colombia remain the national pastimes, although baseball and basketball have gained some popularity, especially on the coast and in part because of satellite television broadcasts from the United States. That influence has also been bidirectional; the Colombian media noted with some pride in 1968 that Harvard's soccer goalie was a Colombian economics student.

In other areas of entertainment, there is no doubt that U.S. films (combined with Argentinian and Mexican) dominate the market and popular consciousness. A Colombian film is a rare event in the mass market. A typical evening's fare in Bogotá in the late 1960s offered films with Julie Christie, Kirk Douglas, Jack Nicholson, Alan Ladd, Ann Bancroft, Dustin Hoffman, Adam West, and Shelley Winters.

Yet, in the same week that these American feature films were screening, Feder Grofé, foreign author and director, was discussing his film, *Orgullusos, malditos y muertos* (The proud, the damned and the dead) which had been made in Villa de Leiva using four Colombian actors and Colombian technicians. Comic strips in the leading urban newspapers in these years featured Dick Tracy (who also graced the front cover of *Semana* in 1990), Peanuts, Batman, the Flintstones, Mutt and Jeff, Jiggs and Maggie, James Bond, and an indigenous Colombian strip Copetín on Bogotá street children. Again, it is this dynamic interplay between indigenous and foreign influences in the Colombian environment that has contributed to modern Colombian culture.

Implementing the Alliance for Progress

This broader cultural context is important for an understanding of the manner in which Colombians responded to the U.S. foreign policies in the post-1961 years. The Lleras Camargo administration strongly endorsed the anti-Communist and developmentalist premises of the alliance. Foreign Minister Julio Cesár Turbay Ayala informed a Bogotá press conference in July 1961 that the inter-American system depended on "peace, security and well-being," that the system was not only legal and political but also economic and social. The basic task was to ensure "the right of people to participate in the advantages of civilization and to experience all the advantages of social progress with liberty."[17] In economic policy, as Juan de Onís and Jerome Levinson noted some years ago, Lleras Camargo and other leading Colombian Liberals who emerged from *la revolución en marcha* of López Pumarejo in the 1930s were essentially fellow travelers of the philosophy of the New Deal, and they thus felt very comfortable with and supportive of Kennedy's New Frontier.[18]

Colombia, invoking the 1947 Rio Treaty of Mutual Assistance, took much of the initiative in calling the 1961 Punta del Este meeting of inter-American states to consider the threat to continental peace posed by Cuba. Colombia sent a bipartisan delegation of Liberals and Conservatives to Punta del Este. That delegation stressed that the existence of a "Marxist-Leninist" government in the hemisphere was incompatible with the inter-American system. In December, Colombia broke diplomatic relations with Cuba for violation of human rights by the Castro government and its export of revolution. This action reflected a shared concern with the United States over perceived communist subversion. The major difference between the Colombian and the U.S. position on Cuba was the stress that Turbay and Lleras Camargo placed on the importance of acting through the Organization of American States rather than U.S. unilateral action." [19]

Lleras Camargo was one of the most vigorous advocates of an effective and active OAS as the instrument of the inter-American system. He rejected the notion that the system derived from the Monroe Doctrine, although he clearly supported hemispheric solidarity against external threat. In his view the successive use of force by the United States to achieve its foreign policy goals in Latin America demonstrated the dangerous possibility of the emergence of a "new imperialism." The function of the inter-American system was to prevent such intervention and enforce international law.

It was thus fitting that Colombia was the first Latin American nation to draft an Economic Development Plan under the alliance. Colombia also supported an array of transitional institutions for social and economic reforms that had been initiated previously, including a low-cost housing institute; a National Planning Board; a National Apprenticeship Service; ICETEX, to fund Colombian students abroad and a smaller number of foreign students in Colombia; a financial corporation to mobilize Colombian private capital; regional development corporations; municipal power companies; a national geographic institute to survey Colombian resources; and perhaps most significantly, INCORA, the agrarian reform institute. In August 1961 funds from the Social and Economic Development Trust Fund were designated to assist the Colombian government in developing a comprehensive educational program, the main objective of which was to ensure that all children, regardless of means, received a minimum of five years of education.[20]

Colombian initiatives conformed to the alliance emphasis on self-help, and both Secretary of State Dean Rusk and the U.S. ambassador to the United Nations, Adlai Stevenson, singled out the Colombian programs for praise in 1961. Rusk also endorsed the community development work that would be carried out in Colombia by the Peace Corps. Stevenson was more preoccupied with the continuing communist threat and the fragility of the National Front government in Colombia, an arrangement he described as "curious." Stevenson noted that the country continued to face problems associated with Communist "infiltration," banditlike violence in the countryside, and economic dislocation, but he also expressed optimism about Lleras Camargo's reform program.[21]

Alliance programs in Colombia balanced economic, cultural, and social aspects with continued military aid. Even before the social and economic programs were approved in the course of 1961, the United States and Colombia concluded a bilateral military accord providing U.S. equipment. This perceived challenge to Colombian security, political stability, and the security of U.S. investment in Colombia were as important in shaping the bilateral relationship as the desire for economic and social reform. The possibility of turning the corner on development and political stability in Colombia led the Kennedy and Johnson administrations to make "substantial financial assistance available to Colombia." The Agency for International Development viewed Colombia in the mid-1960s as "one of the major hopes for rapid development." It had a democratic two-party system and progressive political leadership, was traditionally oriented toward sound financial policies and free enterprise, possessed a strong, forward-looking private sector, had varied natural resources, and had a market potential sufficient for advanced industrialization.[22]

U.S. officials also recognized Colombia's problems, however. The National Front governing alliance could not be a permanent solution to the long-term political problems, in part because it was unstable and contributed at times to political atrophy. It was soon evident that the National Front structure was more effective in reducing political conflict and perpetuating traditional elite rule than in achieving programatic results. Strong divisions within the Conservative and Liberal parties compounded the instability of the system. Conservatives were divided into three groups identified with former prominent Conservative leaders: Laureanistas, Ospinistas, and Alzatistas. The Liberal Revolutionary Movement (MRL) was divided into two main factions, one hard-line opponents of the National Front, the other more moderate. There was also an independent Liberal Movement (MIL) formed in 1963 by three Liberal senators. The absence of general political consensus within Congress stalemated legislation in the Valencia presidency.[23]

Political unrest from 1963 to 1965 compounded these problems, particularly a major strike in 1963 against the oil companies, which blamed communist agitators. By April 1963 the U.S.-owned Colombian Petroleum Company discontinued its operations, and by August damage to property was so extensive that President Valencia ordered in the army to maintain control. After the arrests of some thirty leaders and a week of nightly bombings in Bogotá, the strike was broken. There were large-scale student disorders in 1965 to protest the U.S. invasion of the Dominican Republic and the Colombian government's effort to suppress student "rights." U.S. officials were especially concerned because the Colombian Communist party's youth wing shared leadership of the National Federation of University Students.[24]

The Kennedy and Johnson administrations had to develop alliance programs in this troubled context. The major objectives of the alliance and USAID in Colombia throughout the decade were to assist Colombia in overcoming a severe balance of payments problem, strengthen and diversify agricultural production (especially to reduce dependence on coffee exports); to improve nutrition; and to modernize an educational system where one-third of people over seven years of age were illiterate. Between 1961 and 1965, Colombia received more than $833 million in loans and aid from the United States and international agencies. The Agency for International Development (AID) in 1961 and 1962 contributed $12 million for the construction of eighteen thousand home units and $8 million to the Caja Agraria to provide credit for small producers and farm tenants; during 1962 and 1963, $60 million was designated to support the initial phases of the Colombian development plan and $30 million to subsidize essential imports. The Peace Corps also entered Colombia in 1962. By the mid-1960s almost seven hundred Peace Corps volunteers were working in education, rural development, agricultural programs, and technical assistance.[25]

The Colombian Response

Colombia's reaction to the early Alliance for Progress programs was generally positive. There is little doubt that Kennedy was popular among Colombians, and the alliance was able to ride the crest of that appeal in a manner that Lyndon Johnson and Richard Nixon could never have achieved. Colombia's elite press supported Kennedy during the 1960 campaign, rapidly cooled toward the Fidelista revolution in Cuba, shared U.S. concerns about a "Communist" threat in the Caribbean and South America, and favored the alliance and its goals. The leading Liberal press of Bogotá, *El Tiempo* and *El Espectador*, endorsed the alliance emphasis on social and economic advance. The weekly magazine *Semana*, founded by Lleras Camargo, echoed that view, arguing that the domestic reforms required as a precondition for U.S. aid challenged the traditional policies of the conservative oligarchy. Medellín's leading Conservative daily, *El Colombiano*, portrayed the Punta del Este conference establishing the alliance as a watershed in hemispheric affairs and a decisive confrontation between communism and capitalism, between those who "profit from hunger but offer no solution" and those in whose interest it was to resolve the problems.[26]

Even before Kennedy's death, one of the main Latin American architects of the alliance, Lleras Camargo, expressed concern about the slowness of progress. Writing in *Foreign Affairs* in October 1963, he suggested that planners had been overly optimistic about the prospects for change in societies in which patterns of social, political, and economic relationships had been in place for generations. The rhetoric of reform, he concluded, had been far more radical than the will to change, as, for instance, in the areas of agrarian reform or taxation, where tax evasion by elites undermined the capacity of the alliance to achieve its goals, particularly a redistribution of wealth.

Carlos Lleras Restrepo, president from 1966 through 1970, also had reservations not only about the alliance but about the lending policies of the international organizations. Criticism from Lleras Restrepo was especially important given his close identification with the program and strong support for economic development; he was also highly regarded by the Johnson administration. Johnson's National Security Adviser McGeorge Bundy portrayed Lleras as the "man who glued Colombia together . . . forward looking, moderate and a firm supporter of the Alliance," although Bundy acknowledged that Lleras had earlier criticized the alliance.[27]

Lleras Restrepo's determination to take an independent stand on Colombian economic planning came to a head in 1966 when the IMF, AID, and the IBRD requested a devaluation of the peso in order to increase exports and improve the balance of payments. Lleras balked at the IMF demand, preferring to maintain the value of the peso and implement strict exchange controls. He recognized the problem, but feared the political repercussions of the domestic price increases that would accompany a devaluation. He also objected to the fact that the entire "USAID program hinged on being in full agreement with the IMF. We differed with the IMF on how technically to face the structural imbalance in our payments."[28] In this case Lleras's objections led the IMF and USAID to reverse its position. As Levinson and de Onís concluded, the history of subsequent Colombian exports proved Lleras correct.

Lleras's firm stand against the IMF was not an anti-American position. On the contrary, he worked closely with U.S. officials and employed a highly specialized Harvard team of economists to assist in designing the government's economic policies. Nonetheless, Colombian scholars see Lleras taking an increasingly independent position on trade policy and relations with the communist bloc. Trade diversification accompanied a movement toward the formation of more integrated markets (the first meeting of the Andean group took place in Chile in 1967), increased industrialization, and enhanced nontraditional exports.

Significantly, the softening of Colombian lines toward Soviet bloc nations in trade matters preceded the movement toward détente in the Nixon-Kissinger years. It was also a pragmatic rather than ideological move. The Foreign Ministry stressed in mid-1967 that the development of improved commercial relations with socialist nations did not imply "adhesion to their political ideas or their economic systems." With one billion people and increasing levels of industrial production, those nations represented valuable potential markets for Colombian products. In the 1950s Colombian trade with the socialist bloc was only 0.54 percent of total trade; by 1967 that had risen significantly to 5.12 percent. In June 1967 Lleras sent a trade delegation to the socialist countries, and in 1968 concluded a commercial agreement with the Soviet Union.[29]

With Kennedy's death, the Colombian elite press grew less sanguine about the Alliance for Progress and its future, lacking confidence in Johnson and in the success of the alliance itself. *El Siglo* editorialized that there was widespread concern about the future of the alliance, that it was too embryonic to have acquired its own momentum without a "driving spirit." Five years later, *El Siglo* concluded that its fears had been realized; the creation of the alliance had awakened "enthusiasm and hope," but the growing American commitment in Vietnam, U.S. balance of payments problems, and the rising cost of U.S. domestic programs had contributed to stagnation of the alliance. *El Tiempo* shared that view; an editorial cartoon on 17 August 1965, entitled "The Alliance for Progress," as the Johnson administration escalated the war in Vietnam, depicted a forlorn campesino seated on a sack of coffee, reflecting on Kennedy. The caption read "Going up in smoke?" The Bogotá leftist journal *Tercer Mundo* was more penetrating in its concern about the weaknesses of the alliance in its later stages and the principles on which the alliance had been established. The anonymous author of "A Leftist Viewpoint" concluded that the alliance was founded on the desire of U.S. capitalists to gain easier access to Latin American markets and resources as well as the U.S. fear of the implications of the Cuban Revolution.[30]

The Alliance Under Lyndon Johnson

Johnson attempted to counter the view that he was not committed to the Alliance for Progress. Secretary of State Dean Rusk remembered later that Johnson had spoken to him about his support for the alliance only a week after assuming the presidency, and he publicly reaffirmed the administration's commitment to the alliance, emphasizing that a strong alliance would be a living memorial to John Kennedy. In this White House address, with Jacqueline Kennedy present, Johnson stressed his own youthful appreciation of Mexicans and Mexican-Americans in Texas and his 1960 election campaign support for the principles of the alliance. It was significant that Colombian president Lleras Camargo, who had contributed significantly to the creation of the alliance, responded on that occasion to Johnson's assurances of continuity.[31]

Johnson's appointments reflected the ambiguity of the administration's commitment, selecting as his first assistant secretary of state for inter-American affairs Thomas Mann, a man from the past rather than the progressive future; he had held the post under Eisenhower and Kennedy, although his range of jurisdiction was now expanded. Mann held concurrent responsibilities as assistant secretary for Latin America, U.S. coordinator of the Alliance for Progress, and special assistant to the president. He remained in those positions until March 1965, when he became undersecretary of state for economic affairs, and was replaced as assistant secretary by Jack Hood Vaughn, former director of Peace Corps programs in Latin America, and who in 1966 returned to the Peace Corps as director. Vaughn's successors as assistant secretary were Lincoln Gordon, who had been a major figure at Punta del Este in drafting the alliance charter, and Covey T. Oliver, a former ambassador to Colombia. Oliver was chosen for the post in

May 1967 at least in part because Johnson was aware of the fact that Oliver was critical of the administration's lack of commitment and attention to the alliance's earlier emphasis on social and civic programs during its preoccupation with the war in Vietnam, which seemed to have almost totally absorbed the adminstration's energies by 1967. At the time of Oliver's appointment, Johnson instructed him to stress social as much as economic development and not to be "outflanked from the left rhetorically."

Administrative streamlining and rhetoric could not mask the decline in concrete commitment to the alliance and the issue of Latin American development, a situation that was not improved by the decision to send marines into the Dominican Republic in 1965. Covey Oliver as assistant secretary for inter-American affairs was well aware of the problems faced by the alliance and its supporters as the Johnson administration moved toward its own demise in 1968. There was an increasing diversion of funds and resources in general to the Vietnam war, congressional reticence to fund programs, and public impatience to see concrete results from the alliance, especially given the major balance of payments problems faced by the United States late in the decade.[32]

Johnson nonetheless believed the record was a positive one on balance. In 1966 the president outlined what he considered to be some of the main accomplishments of the alliance. He noted that Colombia had taken a leading place among the Andean countries, owing in part to the commitment of the National Front government to resolve problems of underdevelopment within a democratic framework. "If it could achieve a continued success," Johnson observed, "a strong impetus would be given the Alliance for Progress—a much needed demonstration effort, important to U.S. policy in this hemisphere." Johnson lamented the high degree of electoral absenteeism in Colombia, and, echoing Lleras Camargo earlier, warned that "unless significant progress is made toward realizing the political, economic and social aspirations, there is danger of their turning to extremist solutions."[33]

The Johnson administration shifted the rhetorical emphasis of the alliance to social and political development, but concrete changes were minor. The alliance reduced, for instance, the commitment to housing construction because of the view that it did not generate foreign exchange in Latin America, contribute directly to economic development, or increase U.S. trade; thus housing construction continued to lag behind population increases, and agrarian reform left many outside the modern agricultural economy. Nonetheless, Colombian economic growth was significant in the late 1960s, and there was reason for optimism about the future.[34]

In February 1969, as the first decade of the alliance drew to a close, the U.S. Senate Foreign Relations Committee released its staff study entitled "Colombia: A Case History of U.S. Aid." The report concluded that the alliance had fallen far short of objectives in the economic and social areas. Even AID concluded that the program in Colombia had suffered a "dreadful collapse" after its early identification as a "showcase of the Alliance." AID data indicated a GNP growth rate for Colombia of only 1.1 percent for the years 1961 to 1967, in spite of the fact that Colombia, with less than 8 percent of Latin America's population, had received over 11 percent of alliance funding. During the same period there had been no increase in tax revenues as a portion of GNP, and gross investment declined as a percentage of GNP. In agriculture, per capita production actually declined by slightly more than 8 percent between 1960 and 1968. The U.S. comptroller general's report in 1969 concluded that AID officials had been slow and negligent in undertaking performance evaluations of projects.[35]

Foreign Investment and Economic Development Since 1960

Alliance programs were designed to supplement not displace private sector investment. U.S. capital has continued to play a major role in the Colombian economy, although there has been diversification of investment since 1960, for instance, in the emergence of French and Japanese capital in the automobile industry. In 1959 Colombia ranked fifth in South America as a market for U.S. direct foreign investment (DFI), with $399 million. Of that total, the majority was in oil ($225 million), followed by manufacturing ($77 million), public utilities ($28 million), and trade ($39 million). In 1960 there were 195 U.S. firms or affiliates and branches in Colombia, ranking it fourth in South America. In the manufacturing sector, there were two large U.S. firms in textiles, but U.S. capital concentrated in the production of chemicals and allied products, followed by food products, paper products, rubber, fabricated metals, and electrical and other machinery. U.S. oil and manufacturing firms in Colombia generated most of their revenues from domestic sales rather than from exports. Overall, those firms paid $79 million in wages and salaries to some thirty-one thousand employees and paid $34 million in taxes. Significantly, and this was a factor that contributed to Colombian unemployment problems and the emigration to the United States of professionals and technicians, one-third of the supervisory and technical staff of those U.S. firms were from the United States.[36]

From 1970 to 1974, U.S. DFI in Colombia averaged $33.9 million per year; that level almost doubled between 1975 and 1979 to $72.3 million per year and then underwent a dramatic rise in the 1980s, averaging more than $367 million between 1980 and 1984. Manufacturing became increasingly important to the Colombian economy in the late 1970s and 1980s, with its value in terms of GDP rising from 367,000 pesos in 1980 to over 775,000 in 1984. In that year the growth rate for manufacturing was higher than it had been in the 1960s. The main areas of manufacturing increase were in sugar refining, beverages, tobacco, rubber, iron and steel, and metallurgical coke. Colombia, in fact, was the one exception to the general decline of U.S. DFI in Latin America during the 1980s. By 1982, the total assets of U.S. firms and affiliates in Colombia were $4.2 billion, employing over fifty-four thousand Colombians and paying wages and salaries of $679 million a year. In 1983, of more than fifty-five thousand Colombian employees in those firms, thirty-four thousand were in manufacturing, and fewer than four thousand in the oil industry. By 1985 employment in manufacturing had declined to thirty thousand, but the oil industry had made gains to forty-four hundred. That trend continued in the late 1980s. By 1987 the level of U.S. DFI in Colombian oil was twice that in manufacturing. In that year Colombia ranked fourth in South America as a market for U.S. capital, close behind Argentina and Venezuela but distant from the continental giant, Brazil.[37]

The oil industry expanded in the early 1960s with the successful Texaco-Gulf Orito well in the Putumayo in 1963. The companies directly exported the crude oil from that major development on the Ecuadoran border through the Pacific port of Tumaco, giving rise to complaints in both Colombia and Ecuador that they were draining the fields without contributing to the secondary economic development of the countries. Ultimately, in the 1970s, Gulf and Texaco sold their interest in the concession to ECOPETROL, which continued to operate the fields. By the end of the 1960s and early 1970s there was some decline in the industry. There were no new wells drilled in that period; this absence of new developments combined with continuing increased domestic consumer demand to shift the country in 1976 to net importer status. Revitalization late in the decade, led by ECOPETROL and Occidental Petroleum in the Arauca and Llanos, reversed that situation by 1985, although continued high demand for gasoline has necessitated imports in the late 1980s. By 1985 there were ten foreign companies active in Colombian oil, the majority of them U.S. affiliates: Occidental, International Petroleum Company, Texas Petroleum Company, Shell, Houston Oil, Chevron, Mobil, Triton, BHP, and ELF Aquitaine Colombie.[38]

In agriculture, one of the main areas of expansion of production and U.S. investment was in the rejuvenated banana industry during the 1970s and 1980s, as the industry shifted west from its traditional concentration near Santa Marta to the Gulf of Urabá. In the latter region, the international companies have concentrated on serving as marketing agents for the independent growers, much as the United Fruit Company had in the 1920s. The infusion of new capital and the efforts of INCORA to improve crop yields have resulted in expanded production and export. In 1978 alone the growth rate in banana production was over 21 perent.[39]

U.S.-Colombian Diplomacy After the Alliance

Colombian scholars identify the emergence in Colombian foreign policy in the early 1970s of an intensified policy of interdependence with increased autonomy from the United States. This orientation was strongly evident under Lleras Restrepo, especially in trade policy. The Foreign Ministry stressed in 1966 and 1967 that independence was the main characteristic of Colombian foreign policy toward the United States. In a message to Congress in July 1967, Lleras emphasized the necessity of establishing a more "universal" foreign policy and outlined the development of relations with the "Socialist" countries as well as with African and Asian nations, the role of Colombia within the UN and the OAS and the movement toward regional economic integration. He also advocated Colombian foreign investment, especially in mixed enterprises in Central America. Significantly, he criticized the U.S. role at the 1967 Punta del Este meetings, charging that the U.S. position had been overly vague, especially on the question of allowing aid credits to be spent in other Latin American countries. To Lleras, the United States had lost a valuable opportunity to make a political impact and to give eloquence to hemispheric solidarity. Lleras also expressed his opposition to interference in the internal affairs of other nations. When he addressed the first session of the UN in 1946 he had hoped that a real internationalism would emerge from the ashes of the war; clearly, that was still his aspiration in 1967.[40]

Lleras's foreign minister in 1969 to 1970, leftist Liberal Alfonso López Michelsen, viewed the Colombian role in international relations as that of a moderate middle power, faithful to the principles of the UN Charter and supporting the nonproliferation of nuclear weapons, control over the exploitation of the seas, decolonization, and racial nondiscrimination. In keeping with the functions of a middle power, Colombia played an important mediating role in the "Football War" between El Salvador and Honduras in 1969, with Colombian Carlos Holguín Holguín presiding over a consultatory group of the OAS.

In trade policy, the Lleras administration sought regional integration and diversified trade relations. During his official visit to meet
with President Nixon, Lleras urged the establishment of a system of
nondiscriminatory tariff preferences by developed nations for less-
developed countries. He believed that the existence of discriminatory
trade preferences against Latin America made it essential to establish a hemispheric system of preferences among the Latin American
nations. The administration perceived the main task for Latin America
in the 1970s to be improvement of the economic and social conditions
of the general population and more active participation in the world
economy, not simply as the supplier of raw-material exports.[41]

The Lleras administration, of course, adopted no public position on
the Nixon-Humphrey elections in 1968, but El Tiempo had supported
Humphrey over Nixon, fearing that the return of the Republicans
would undermine inter-American relations. Eduardo Santos Calderón
concluded that Nixon's election was a "calamity" for Latin America.
To Santos, Nixon was a declared enemy of the left, a devout believer
in the export of the "American way of life," and a political "reactionary." Appalled at Vice-President Spiro Agnew's lack of expertise in
foreign affairs, Santos also expressed concern that there would be
renewed support for the Latin American military, for "any restless
colonel South of the Rio Grande" who spoke against communism.[42]

Moderate Liberals revealed their temperate attitude toward the
United States in their response to the demonstrations that greeted
Nelson Rockefeller on his official fact-finding mission to Latin America
in 1969. El Tiempo faulted communist agitators for the demonstrations,
suggesting that Colombians could not fault the Nixon administration
for its policy of neglect and then attack U.S. emissaries when they
sought to improve relations. Conservative El Siglo was even more
laudatory, suggesting that diplomatic and cultural relations between
the United States and Colombia were "excellent" and that the Rockefeller visit provided an occasion to improve them.[43]

In spite of reservations about the Nixon administration, there were
some lines of affinity with the Conservative government in the early
1970s of Misael Pastrana Borrero (1970–74). Pastrana's Foreign Minis-

ter, Alfredo Vásquez Carrizosa, former Colombian ambassador to the OAS and an important delegate earlier to the Punta del Este conference, reflected the spirit of détente as early as 1971 or 1972 in accepting ideological pluralism and cautiously celebrating the end of the cold war. At the same time, consistent with differences between Liberal and Conservative politics, the Pastrana administration tended to be more favorably disposed toward the United States than the Lleras administration had been and also took more seriously the issue of collective security and the Cuban threat. Pastrana and Vásquez Carrizosa were entirely within the tradition of Marco Fidel Suárez earlier in the century in advocating a policy of harmony with the United States.

Not all Colombia's foreign policy concerns in these years involved the United States. In a televised interview in 1971 Vásquez Carrizosa identified the main issues confronting the administration as the two-hundred-mile offshore territorial limit, relations with the Vatican, development of a new Amazon policy, persistent problems in relations with Venezuela, and the future of the 1963 coffee pact, which had been renewed in 1968. Vásquez Carrizosa continued to develop his views on Colombian foreign policy during the following decade, in the early 1980s lending considerable support to the idea of nonalignment. This is not to downplay the importance of the United States in Colombian relations in this period but to emphasize that Colombian foreign policy had other preoccupations in the early 1970s.[44]

As president (1974–1978), the former foreign minister and leader of the more radical wing of the Liberal party, Alfonso López Michelsen might have been expected to pursue a more anti-American position. López Michelsen's appeals for policies based on pragmatic rather than ideological considerations and for mutual dependence or interdependence in relations with the United States were not radically distinct from the position of the preceding Pastrana administration, although there were marked differences on the place of Cuba in the inter-American system, on perceptions of the communist threat, and on the causes of drug traffic. López and Foreign Minister Indalecio Liévano Aguirre supported the return of Cuba to the OAS. They endorsed Panama's desire for a reversion of the canal to Panamanian control and insisted that the drug problem was primarily one for the consuming nations not the exporting countries such as Colombia.[45] This critical general stance did not prevent the López Michelsen government from cooperating with U.S. officials in attempting to close down Colombian processing plants for coca paste smuggled from Peru, Bolivia, and Ecuador. During this early stage of the war on drugs, the United States provided equipment and special training for the Colombian judicial police, the National Police, and customs officers.[46]

There were few signs of significant tensions between the two nations during President López's state visit with President Gerald Ford in September 1975. They discussed the Panama Canal treaties, the U.S. Trade Reform Act of 1974, progress on construction of the Darien portion of the Pan-American Highway, ongoing problems over the eradication of foot and mouth disease among Colombian cattle, the Colombian antinarcotics program, and the AID program. Marking a milestone in Colombian economic development, it was agreed to negotiate an end to AID assistance in recognition of Colombia's reduced dependency on external funding.[47] Subsequently, Peace Corps operations also ended in Colombia.

During Henry Kissinger's visit to Bogotá early the following year, the issues remained the perennial ones of continued support for the modernization of Colombian agriculture, narcotics control, human rights, and law of the sea negotiations. Following Kissinger's visit, the two nations concluded bilateral agreements providing for U.S.-funded loans to strengthen the rural cooperative program, to construct feeder roads to promote increased agricultural productivity, and technical assistance and research on small farmers. Later that year there was an expansion of assistance to Colombian antidrug operations.[48]

Narcotics, National Security, and the Guerrilla Movement

Although there may have been little optimism in Colombian political circles that Jimmy Carter as president would bring significant movement in U.S.–Latin American relations, Carter assured President López that Colombia's special rights in the use of the Panama Canal, as guaranteed in the 1921 Thomson-Urrutia Treaty, would be included in the Panama Canal treaties. The Carter administration also sent a presidential adviser and a senior official of the Drug Enforcement Administration (DEA) to Bogotá to meet with Colombian officials as part of what was described at the time as a "new initiative" on narcotics. Carter followed that mission with a major message to Congress on international cooperation to control drugs. Significantly, the Carter initiative coincided with the appointment of a new López ambassador to the United States, Virgilio Barco, who as president in the late 1980s escalated the war on the narcotics cartels. President López, without any visible pressure from the United States, established a select narcotics enforcement unit under the direct control of the attorney general, with financial assistance provided by the U.S. DEA. In the final year of López's presidency, Colombian seizures of cocaine nonetheless exceeded those in the U.S.[49]

From 1977, narcotics control assumed an increasing proportion of the energy, funding, and attention of the two nations. In his opening address to the nation in August 1978, President Turbay pledged that his government would do everything possible to combat drug trafficking, although he stressed that success depended on both U.S. financial support and U.S. efforts to curtail importation and consumption. The two nations already had in place a bilateral agreement, dating from 1961, that permitted cooperation on narcotics, and in the course of the next two years, Colombia negotiated agreements with Venezuela (1978), Ecuador (1979), and Peru (1979). In 1979 the United States and Colombia also began negotiations on a new extradition treaty, which became an issue of considerable political debate over the next decade, and signed a convention for cooperation in the development of an antinarcotics campaign. These initial measures had minimum impact. U.S. officials alleged that narcotics revenues exceeded that for coffee exports.[50]

U.S. funding for drug-related programs increased in the 1980s, for interdiction, crop eradication programs, legal training programs to

assist Colombian police and judicial authorities in enforcing existing laws, and for security support. The concentration on Colombia
logically followed from the fact that an estimated 79 percent of marijuana and 75 percent of cocaine consumed in the United States origi-
nated in or was processed in Colombia. The assistant secretary of
state for international narcotics matters informed the Senate Foreign
Relations Committee in early 1983 that U.S. funding and policy was
"predicated on Colombia undertaking a program for marijuana eradication while continuing and hopefully expanding its coca control program."[51] During the decade there were tensions over the issue of
extradition of Colombian drug figures, allegations from some political circles that the Colombian military was using its increased fire-
power on political opponents not simply the drug lords, and anxiety
that the level of economic power acquired by the drug industry had
permanently corrupted the Colombian political system. As the 1990s
dawned, the nation was embroiled in a seemingly unending war on
the drug industry as well as the political left.

The combination of leftist guerrilla activity with the narcotics industry by the 1970s and 1980s added a major dimension to what was
already viewed as a security threat in the 1960s. During the 1960s and
early 1970s U.S. officials treated the Colombian guerrilla movement
as a threat to national security for Colombia, the United States, and
the region as a whole. U.S. and Colombian officials from the early
1960s, viewed the guerrilla movements as Cuban-Soviet inspired. In
the 1960s, especially, they also understood that the problems of rural
violence and banditry were distinct from the guerrilla movement and
that the roots of such problems were indigenous economic and social
dislocation.[52]

Colombian authorities identified a link between Cuba and Colombian guerrillas in 1963, when they located a Cuban weapons cache near
the Venezuelan border.[53] Previously, weapons used in rural violence
and by guerrillas were mostly captured military weapons and older
weapons stolen from arsenals during the *Bogotazo* in 1948. U.S. officials
did not believe in the 1960s that a few thousand guerrillas constituted a significant threat to Colombian governments, but Washington

did provide military assistance, especially helicopters, throughout the decade. The supply of helicopters not only improved the capacity of the Colombian army to deal with the guerrilla movement but also to provide surveillance of the Caribbean coast against possible importation of arms from Cuba.[54] Official concern heightened in the 1970s and early 1980s, when there were apparent links between some of the guerrilla factions and the major narcotics cartels. Yet, the origins, history, and objectives of the guerrilla movements in Colombia are far more complex than this simplistic picture would suggest.

The guerrilla movement emerged at least in part out of the civil war between Liberals and Conservatives in the 1950s, a conflict in which the goals were ideological and economic in nature. The largest and most powerful organization for almost thirty years was the Revolutionary Armed Forces of Colombia (FARC), formed in 1966 as an instrument of the Colombian Communist party. Long led by Manuel Marulanda Vélez, FARC also built on the 1950s collaboration of convenience between Liberals and Communists in the countryside. From the 1960s FARC had its main strength in the Amazon region, the Llanos, and the eastern Cordillera. In the course of the 1980s it shifted away from armed struggle to participation in the political mainstream through the Patriotic Union party, which became the target of paramilitary death squads.

The main insurgent group inspired by the Cuban revolution was the National Liberation Army (ELN), formed in 1964. The ELN has been independent of the Colombian Communist party; but from the U.S. perspective this did not reduce its security threat. Intellectuals, students, and in more isolated instances individuals associated with the Roman Catholic Church, led the ELN. The most celebrated radical priest in the movement was Father Camilo Torres of the National University, who joined the ELN in 1966 only to be killed in combat a few months later. After Torres's death, the ELN continued to try to unite under a Christian-Marxist revolutionary ideology and emphasized armed struggle, obtaining support from Cuba through the 1970s. In the late 1970s and 1980s, the expansion of oil resources in the Arauca region in northeast Colombia, where the ELN had long been active, provided the organization with a new source of revenue from kidnapping and ransoming oil company personnel. The ELN has also caused massive ecological damage with its bombings of oil pipelines. In the early 1980s the ELN and the other Colombian guerrilla groups appeared to be gaining strength and moving toward the creation of a significant guerrilla front organization, the National Guerrilla Coordinating Body.

One smaller group, the M-19, became influential beyond its numbers in the course of the 1970s and 1980s. M-19 took its name from the 1970 presidential elections, in which former dictator Gustavo Rojas Pinilla (who campaigned against the ruling Liberal and Conservative mainstream on a populist platform), was allegedly fraudulently deprived of victory by the ruling parties. The M-19 identified itself with the populist and nationalistic image that the Rojistas were then cultivating among the Colombian masses, spurious as Rojas Pinilla's claim to such ideals may have been. In its early years M-19 engaged in spectacular acts to gain national attention—commandeering milk trucks to deliver milk to poor barrios, capturing large caches of government weapons in daring raids, and, in the most tragic, storming the Colombian Supreme Court in 1985 while it was in session. The Colombian government of Belisario Betancur retaliated with a massive military assault on the Court building, resulting in the death of the M-19 members and many of their hostages. In the aftermath, the M-19 also moved into politics, seemingly abandoning armed conflict as the means to social and political reform. In the 1989 presidential elections the party gained 13 percent of the popular vote, in spite of the assassination of its presidential candidate, Carlos Pizarro, one of three presidential candidates killed in the campaign. In coalition with several non–M-19 elements they also took first place in the constituent assembly elections in late 1990.

Guerrilla conflict, drug cartel–inspired violence, the belief by U.S. officials that the guerrilla movement and the drug cartels were tied, the transition to a more competitive political arena with the end of the National Front governments in the 1970s, and the continuing debate over social, political, and economic modernization provided the context for Colombian-U.S. relations in the 1970s and 1980s.

Colombia, Contadora, and the Central American Crisis

The crisis of the Somoza regime in Nicaragua, the victory of the FSLN in 1979, and the emergence of a U.S.-supported counterrevolutionary war did not alter the reality of the growing Colombian narcotics crisis, but it did provide an important vehicle by which Colombia became more involved in Central American affairs. The Colombian and the U.S. response to the Central American crisis, specifically the civil wars in Nicaragua and El Salvador in the post-1979 years, has underlined the extent to which Colombian leaders have linked domestic issues with international problems. President Turbay (1978–82) viewed the Colombian domestic insurgency in terms of international communist subversion rather than an indigenous response to social and economic injustices, and he was thus more inclined to interpret developments in Nicaragua and El Salvador within that framework. Ironically, Turbay's comparatively hard line against dissent and the adoption in 1978 of the Statute of National Security to combat urban and rural guerrillas brought the administration into conflict with the Carter administration's emphasis on human rights, but Turbay's perception of the insurgency in terms of the East-West conflict made him consistent with the views and policies of the subsequent Reagan administration. Thus, the Turbay administration suspended diplomatic relations with Cuba in 1981 following an M-19 offensive.[55]

The Turbay administration did not endorse the Somoza regime in Nicaragua during its final year. In late September 1978 Turbay joined with Venezuela in writing to the president of the UN General Assembly denouncing the government of General Anastasio Somoza Debayle for constant violations of human rights. They requested that the UN take measures to protect those rights. In the following months both the UN and the OAS censured the Somoza regime. The Cartagena declaration of Andean nation foreign ministers in late May 1979 appealed to the other American countries to formulate collective measures within a multilateral framework to resolve the Nicaraguan crisis. OAS foreign ministers in June 1979, on the eve of Somoza's demise, approved a resolution initiated by the Andean group, including Colombia, calling for the replacement of the Somoza regime, the installation of a democratic regime, including the main opposition groups, which would guarantee human rights and promise to hold free elections. That position was very close to that of the Carter administration. In July Colombian Foreign Minister Diego Uribe Vargas joined with counterparts from Venezuela, Ecuador, Bolivia, and Peru to urge Somoza to resign. With Somoza's departure, Colombia recognized the new Sandinista government.[56]

During the administration of Belisario Betancur (1982–86) there was a sharp reversal of the Turbay view that the crises in El Salvador and Nicaragua were part of the East-West struggle, although there was concern that Nicaragua had turned to the Soviet Union for economic and military assistance. Betancur was also convinced of the relationship between Colombia's domestic situation and the nature of the issues in Central America. He and his foreign minister, Rodrigo Lloreda Caicedo, perceived their peacemaking overtures through the Contadora process as an extension of the government's orientation toward amnesty with the domestic guerrilla movements and greater involvement with the Third World.[57] Concerned that the Central American situation would result in the escalation of a surrogate U.S. war or unilateral U.S. military intervention, or that the Cuban-Soviet presence would be expanded, Colombian officials joined with Mexico, Venezuela, and Panama in early 1983 on the island of Contadora off the coast of Panama in an effort to seek resolution to the Central American crisis.

Betancur was more active in Central America and the Caribbean than any of his predecessors. He offered to mediate the withdrawal of Cuban advisers from Grenada following the Reagan administration's landing of troops in 1983, and he joined the nonaligned movement.

In December 1982 Reagan and Secretary of State George Schultz met with Betancur and other Colombian leaders to discuss what Schultz characterized as the two nations' common interests, including their common democratic traditions, the Central American situation, narcotics, and the Caribbean Basin initiative.[58]

The United States appears to have sought to prevent the Betancur government from moving any further along its "divergent" foreign policy path. By the middle of his term Betancur's foreign policies had run into difficulties, in part because of the perceived neglect of the domestic and international drug crisis, where the administration reversed its original refusal to extradite those charged with international drug trafficking. The administration also faced a growing financial crisis and a need to negotiate IMF assistance. Perhaps the final development that shifted the administration toward a harder line was the evident linkage in the mid-1980s between FARC and the drug industry and the tragic confrontation between M-19 and the Colombian military in November 1985 in the Colombian Supreme Court.[59]

Throughout the Central American crisis, the Contra war in Nicaragua, the FMLN guerrilla insurgency in El Salvador, and the confrontation between the United States and General Manuel Noriega in Panama in 1989, Colombian governments consistently advocated negotiated multilateral solutions. Colombia played its traditional, positive role in the OAS (and United Nations) as part of the Nicaraguan election monitoring process in late 1989 and early 1990.

Yet, at the beginning of a new decade, with the cold war evidently over, with cooperation between East and West, and with Central America engaged in healing the wounds of war, in Colombian-U.S. relations the war on drugs remained at the core. The primacy of that issue for the Bush administration was symbolized in George Bush's meeting with Virgilio Barco in February 1990 in Cartagena, where the United States pledged additional assistance to aid Colombia and other affected countries to cope with what is unquestionably one of the most significant social, economic, political, and diplomatic issues of the century in U.S.–Latin American relations.

From the Alliance for Progress to the war on drugs, U.S. policy has sought to stabilize Colombian politics, to foster moderate economic reform in order to forestall more radical change, to assist Colombia in containing armed insurrection. Colombia for its part has emphasized the need to pursue a policy of "independence with dignity," recognizing the hegemony of the United States in hemisphere affairs but attempting to moderate the worst implications of U.S. unilateralism. It responded favorably to the alliance because it was multilateral in approach. Colombian leaders agreed with the containment of communism and rejected Fidel Castro as quickly as did the United States; but consistently they sought a multilateral solution to the problem of Cuba in the hemisphere. In world affairs, Colombia, like other small powers, has seen its interests in maintaining open channels, with the Soviet bloc during the cold war, with China, with the nonaligned movement, with the Third World. Too small a power to lead Latin America economically or militarily, Colombia has attempted to emphasize diplomatic moderation, negotiation, and conciliation in international relations.

Epilogue

The dust jacket of a recent study of Colombian foreign policy imaginatively conceptualizes Colombia's external relations as a paved highway leading from a quaint, colorful, agrarian society, through Washington's cherry blossoms, directly to the U.S. Capitol.[1] That artistic rendition effectively captures one dimension of the Colombian-U.S. relationship: the all-pervasiveness of the United States as a factor in Colombian foreign policy. That reality has been at the core of the history of interaction between the two nations in the past two hundred years. Above all, the preeminence of U.S. power in the hemisphere—economic, military, and political—has shaped relations. Had the power balance between the two nations been more equal, the history of the western hemisphere would have been very different, as each nation sought to pursue its national interests.

As much as there has been a degree of consensus, there have also been conflicts between the two nations in the years since each broke its colonial bonds in the late eighteenth and early nineteenth centuries. Those areas of tension, examined in this volume, reveal a great deal about the foreign policies and cultural values of Colombia and the United States. What was at the root of the conflicts? Was there a common thread which ran through the diplomatic disputes of the nineteenth and twentieth centuries? Have the countries held to divergent views of the world and their place within it? What have they had in common? Answers to such broad questions clearly risk excessive generalization; yet they must be addressed if one is to understand not only the detail but also the dynamic of Colombian-U.S. relations since independence.

What were the main areas of dispute in the nineteenth century? Actual treaty negotiations involved commerce, access to the Isthmus of Panama, control over isthmian transit, the resolution of claims by U.S. citizens arising from the wars for independence, freedom of religion, sovereignty, and the place of European nations in the western hemisphere. There were also issues and developments in which formal treaty negotiations were not involved: the role in Colombia of U.S. private foreign investment, slavery and race relations, immigration, the leadership of an inter-American movement, the nature of political institutions. These issues crossed the spectrum of cultural, ideological, political, and economic concern.

U.S. foreign policy objectives involving Colombia and those issues in the nineteenth century were consistent. At the basis of policy was a belief in the exceptionalism of the United States and its special role in the Western Hemisphere. During the Spanish-American wars for independence, the United States followed a cautious but realistic policy of neutrality in deed but rhetorical empathy for independence. There is little doubt that for ideological and practical reasons there was much that bound the United States to nations such as Colombia as they emerged from their colonial heritage. Rich in natural resources and with well-established populations, nations like Colombia promised to be fertile areas for U.S. trade. U.S. leaders anticipated that Colombia would cast off the shackles of European monarchism and authoritarianism and adhere to republican ideals. In trade, the United States sought to ensure access of its citizens' goods to Colombian markets, especially to counteract any preferences for European products and protection for domestic agriculture and industry. Such objectives ran counter to the Colombian desire to build an industrial base and protect its agricultural production in the nineteenth century, long before coffee came to dominate the nation's exports. The United States also consistently worked to prevent European powers from gaining additional influence and territory in Latin America. In the Colombian case, this meant keeping England and France from gaining control over isthmian transportation. Whether such an objective was strategic or economic in nature is a moot point, since U.S. policymakers in the nineteenth century saw control of the isthmus as essential to U.S. military and economic interests. In political terms, U.S. leaders continued to press Colombians to adhere to what they considered republican and democratic ideals and processes. By the late 1820s there was some disillusionment in U.S. circles with the direction of Colombian politics, with a perception that Colombia had not sufficiently eschewed its European, authoritarian, and militaristic Spanish heritage.

There were significant levels of misunderstanding in the course of the century. It was unfortunate and perhaps surprising that the United States, itself only a generation removed from colonialism, failed to appreciate Colombia's very different cultural and political traditions or the degree of difficulty that a colonial nation had in establishing new institutions. There was failure to equate the sectional crisis that tore the United States apart by 1861 with the regional tensions that hampered centralized authority in Colombia through much of the century. There was little appreciation for the Colombian tendency to place more emphasis on the role of the state in national economic development than was the case in the United States. There were differences over race relations and slavery. Colombia moved far more quickly than the United States to end the slave trade and to abolish slavery within its borders, and Colombians were proud of that fact. As much as racism may have lingered in Colombian society, Colombians continued to see themselves as more enlightened on matters of race than was the United States. This was especially important in the mid-nineteenth century, as increasing numbers of U.S. citizens came into contact with Colombians of African heritage, primarily in Panama and on the Caribbean coast. Certainly, racial factors contributed to grass-roots tensions in Panama between U.S. travelers and the local black population by the 1850s. Religion and the issue of religious freedom also grated in contacts between the two societies. The Protestant orientation—which had made Puritan New England less than tolerant in the colonial era and a seedbed of nativism and anti-Catholicism in the 1830s through the 1850s—led Americans to view Colombia as a backward, priest-ridden society, dominated by the Roman Catholic Church. That was an issue within Colombia itself in the nineteenth century, of course, but U.S. diplomats demonstrated little subtle appreciation of the degree of difficulty involved in resolving the problem. Colombian society had massive problems, to be sure, but there was little tolerance and less real understanding among U.S. representatives.

From the outset there was tension between the two nations over leadership in the hemisphere. In hindsight, given the very different subsequent histories of the two nations, this was a totally unequal contest. In the early nineteenth century, however, such was not the case. Bolívar's prestige, if not actual military power, certainly outweighed that of any U.S. leader in the Western Hemisphere by the 1820s. Colombians saw mutual interest, not a statement of U.S. hegemony, in the Monroe Doctrine. It was Bolívar not the United States who took the leadership in calling the first inter-American meeting in Panama in the 1820s. Colombians continued to perceive their role in the hemisphere in terms of potential eminence during the lengthy but unsuccessful effort to complete a Panama canal under Colombian control. This debate in the nineteenth century did not involve an abstract question of Colombian sovereignty but a concrete issue of Colombian economic and political power in the hemisphere. Had Colombians not seen their hemispheric role and national future in such positive terms in 1900, the debate over the "loss" of Panama would not have been the *cris de coeur* that it was. The Panama crisis was so painful because it effectively marked the end of a dream. The reality may have made that dream of Colombian leadership impractical well before the secession of Panama in 1903, but for a Colombian in the 1880s, watching Ferdinand de Lesseps's engineers make their first cuts in Colombian soil for the completion of a canal, it would have been irrational not to have shared in the dream.

Certainly, by the beginning of the twentieth century the unequal power relationship between the two nations was striking. The United States, beginning with James G. Blaine in the Harrison administration, had seized the initiative and leadership in inter-American affairs, and military victory over Spain in 1898 ended any lingering doubt there may have been over which nation would set the hemispheric agenda for the twentieth century.

The context in which policy evolved, if not the agenda and the objectives of Colombian-U.S. relations, altered significantly in the twentieth century. U.S. private investment in Colombia increased significantly by the 1920s. World War I emphasized the strategic importance

of Colombia's location astride northern South America in close proximity to the newly completed Panama Canal. Its possession of strategic natural resources, including oil and platinum, accentuated the
accident of location. World War I also brought the United States into
the arena of world affairs, marked the transition of the United States to
great-power status, and significantly shifted financial power to New
York from London, prefacing a major surge in foreign investment in
Colombia in the 1920s. The Russian Revolution provided an additional
major alteration in context and significantly influenced the nature of
U.S. policy toward Colombia and other Latin American nations in the
post-1919 years. Those strategic, economic, and ideological developments set the stage for the bilateral and multilateral relationship into
the cold war years, although there were threads of continuity from
the nineteenth century.

The rise of economic nationalism was not unique to Colombia in the
interwar years, but it was economic nationalism that triggered most of
the disputes between the two countries before World War II. Colombian efforts to impose restrictions on access to oil resources and to
regulate foreign enterprise in Colombia led to sustained diplomatic
negotiation. There was never any ambiguity in U.S. policy toward
U.S. private foreign investment in oil and other strategic commodities
in Colombia. Policymakers saw open-door access for American capital
to such commodities as vital to U.S. national security interests. They
also feared competition from other countries and sought to counteract
British foreign investment in Colombian oil. What was presented as an
open-door policy, premised on the idea of equality of access, was, in
the case of Colombian oil resources, a closed-door policy. The United
States placed less emphasis on the defense of commodities that lacked
the strategic dimension, such as bananas, in which the United Fruit
Company was the major investor, although there was the same policy
emphasis on ensuring that American capital was fairly treated, often
at the expense of Colombian competitors and Colombian labor.

Whether or not Colombia would have moved in different directions
in the interwar years without U.S. pressure is difficult to determine.
The economic nationalism of the 1920s and 1930s had widespread

support in Colombia. It crossed political party lines as well as class barriers, although regionally it was stronger in the interior than on the coast, where there was significant pressure to maintain access to less expensive U.S. manufactures. The major importance of coffee exports in the Colombian economy also tended to dull the edge of nationalism on one level, because of the perceived need to hold the U.S. market. Coffee exporters, for instance, were loathe to risk trade retaliation by the United States against coffee by raising Colombian tariffs to protect such infant industries as textiles. Colombia lacked leverage in achieving a balanced economic policy, encouraging new industries and agricultural diversification. Its oil resources, while important, paled in comparison with Venezuela's or Mexico's, and the development of major fields in the Middle East in the 1930s and 1940s further reduced Colombia's bargaining power. Consequently, much of the Colombian legislation of the 1920s and 1930s only nibbled at the edges of American economic power and presence in the country: restricting oil exploration periods; imposing production levels; regulating labor relations with foreign enterprise; attempting to stimulate some economic diversification.

Ideological opposition by the United States to statism further reduced the capacity of Colombia to move toward a greater degree of control over, for instance, natural resources. This was the case with the debate over the establishment of a government-owned and operated oil refinery in the López Pumarejo years, for example. Since major advocates of increased state involvement in oil development in the United States were unable to make significant progress against the free enterprise model, it was not surprising that Colombian policymakers were able to make only marginal strides until after World War II. The formation of ECOPETROL to operate the DeMares concession adhered more to the Latin American model of state oil enterprise (YPF in Argentina, YPFB in Bolivia, and PEMEX in Mexico) than to the U.S. approach; but it did not challenge the general principle of free enterprise nor threaten the presence of U.S. foreign investment, as had occurred in Mexico after 1938. Colombian policymakers in the

1930s and again in the 1960s specifically rejected nationalization of the oil industry.

U.S. policy was successful in the area of foreign investment in raw materials partly because of economic and political leverage, but also because many Colombian elites benefited from foreign investment and shared the goals of U.S. policymakers and corporate interests. Colombian leaders, however, would not tolerate U.S. power expansion beyond certain thresholds. As long as Colombian sovereignty and dignity could be preserved, there was little major conflict over foreign investment. This was one reason that both the United Fruit Company and Gulf Oil ran afoul of Colombian nationals in the 1920s and 1930s. As one Colombian said of Gulf Oil, its officials had a tendency to treat Colombians like their arch rivals the Venezuelans; such an approach was unacceptable to Colombians. Tropical Oil had less difficulty because its officials had learned the value of promoting cultural ties and engaging in constructive diplomacy. Thus, it survived in spite of its monopoly marketing controls in the 1930s. In the case of United Fruit, it ran aground on the shoals of Colombian commercial competitors, organized labor, and its own insensitivity to Colombian sovereignty and dignity in the interwar years. Yet, it too survived to expand after World War II.

In inter-American relations, Colombia followed a middle course in its response to U.S. policy initiatives. Less strident than Argentina in its critique of the United States, Colombian leaders nonetheless shared fully the Latin American opposition to U.S. military intervention and to interference in the internal affairs of Latin American nations. They sought those goals in common with other Latin American states at Havana in 1928, Montevideo in 1933, and Buenos Aires in 1936. They embraced the rhetoric of the Good Neighbor policy during the Roosevelt administration and applauded the decline in direct U.S. intervention during the Roosevelt presidency. Though the Good Neighbor policy may have been as much intended to contain Latin America as to encourage reform, no U.S. president was as popular as Franklin Roosevelt in Colombia until John Kennedy.

By World War II the pattern of economic and political interdependence was well entrenched. Colombia maintained its official "neutrality" in the conflict until 1943, but there was a significant degree of cooperation for hemispheric defense even before the U.S. declaration of war in late 1941. The war served to tighten the ties between the two countries, to underline the dependency of Colombia on U.S. markets for its exports and on U.S. manufactured goods, especially for the industrial sector. Again, the war occasioned considerable debate within Colombian political circles over the most appropriate stance for the nation to adopt. There was sympathy in some circles for the more corporatist model of fascism; in a few cases there were Nazi sympathies. In a broader cross section of Colombian society, however, there was basic empathy for the ideals contained in Churchill's and Roosevelt's Atlantic Charter: an open-door world; self-government; the renunciation of war; international organization. It was appropriate that leading Colombians such as Alberto Lleras Camargo should have played a role in the founding of the United Nations at San Francisco in 1945 and in the creation of the Organization of American States from the skeleton of the Pan American Union, because they shared those values with U.S. leaders.

Throughout the cold war years these shared values were more significant than the sources of conflict. Unquestionably, Colombian leaders, as with those elsewhere in the hemisphere, were highly critical of the Truman administration's policy of "benign neglect." They resented the failure of the United States to lend the same degree of support to Latin America as it did to Europe in the Marshall Plan years, rebuilding central and western Europe as a buffer against a feared Soviet expansionism. Colombians criticized the inadequacy of Point IV aid under Truman. They found the emphasis on private investment rather than foreign aid under Eisenhower as unpalatable as did U.S. critics of Eisenhower administration policies, and, like those critics, they pressed along with other Latin American nations for a new deal for Latin America.

Colombia's basic orientation was anti-Soviet and anticommunist throughout the pre-Castro cold war years. Both Conservative and Liberal governments required little prodding along those lines by the United States. They endorsed the cold war ideology, sent troops to Korea and sought to contain domestic communism. The Castro revolution in Cuba pushed Colombia further down a path on which it was already established. Colombian Liberals, if less so Conservatives, empathized with the Cuban desire for reform and a greater degree of control over foreign enterprise. They did not accept the movement of Cuba toward the Soviet Union, the suppression of civil liberties, and the export of revolution to other countries in Latin America. Yet, Colombians also continued to stress the need for a multilateral solution to the Castro revolution through the OAS, just as they condemned U.S. involvement in the Guatemalan intervention of 1954 and the Dominican Republic intervention in 1965.

Colombian leaders simultaneously embraced and criticized the Alliance for Progress. Conservatives feared its revolutionary potential, the idea of agrarian reform, tax reform, more universal education, and a higher degree of state intrusion into the private sector. Leftists and many Liberals did not believe the alliance reforms went far enough. They saw them as piecemeal reforms, when substantial change was necessary to preempt more radical change that would threaten class structures and traditional power in Colombian society. By the end of the 1960s both leading Colombians and Americans found the alliance a failure in terms of its objectives. Population growth, urbanization, high unemployment, inflation, disease, illiteracy, violence, and grinding poverty all continued to plague Colombian society.

In the 1970s and 1980s, as détente became a reality and the cold war issues abated, narcotics trafficking supplanted all other issues at the top of the agenda in Colombian-U.S. relations. Until the late 1980s, communism, the guerrilla movement, and the Central American crises exacerbated the drug crisis in inter-American relations. Guerrilla support for, or at least collaboration with, the major drug cartels (for profit if not ideological compatibility) and the massive social and economic damage drugs were causing in the United States made the Colombian cocaine industry appear to be an especially potent threat to the fabric of American society. The fundamental point of departure between

Colombian and U.S. leaders on the nature of the drug threat throughout the 1970s and early 1980s was the Colombian contention that U.S.
consumers were the problem and that, therefore, the problem was one
for the United States to resolve. The United States increased its technical and legal assistance to Colombia throughout these years in an
effort to encourage controls. It ultimately won its point in Colombian
government circles that the Colombian military had a responsibility to
act. Winning that point, however, in shifting Colombia toward the war
on drugs in 1989 cost thousands of Colombian lives and made little
impact on the drug industry, including consumption in the United
States. President Bush's war on drugs was fought on Colombian not
U.S. soil. Whether the war is winnable and its cost to civil liberties
and human life remain to be seen.

Many of the most fundamental social, political, and economic issues
in Colombian-U.S. relations in the past two hundred years have been
resolved amicably, in part because of shared values and in part because of the inequitable power balance between the two. There is some
irony in the fact, however, that the twentieth century is ending as the
nineteenth century began for both nations and their relations with
one another. Colombia has been undergoing a massive political crisis
occasioned by the drug wars and the failure to resolve basic issues of
governance. At the same time, Colombia has asserted some leadership
internationally, as in the Central American arena in the 1980s, in the
way Bolívar did in the 1820s. The U.S. situation has also become one
of greater uncertainty, as was the case in the early nineteenth century.
The cold war has ended, but the nation is in relative decline in the
world, challenged not only by some of the former major powers but
with new nations and economic power blocs emerging to challenge
the continuation of the American Century. The United States in the
Bush administration is thus reaching out once again to Latin America,
economically and politically, in the way in which the United States did
in the aftermath of its own independence and the post-Napoleonic
wars. Colombia specifically and Latin America generally may be the
beneficiaries of a relative decline of the United States, as it is forced
to seek a true internationalism in a world in which no other ratio-

nal course remains. If we learn anything from a study of the bilateral relationship between the United States and Colombia, it is the value of multilateralism and international organizations, the reality of interdependence, the need to respect the political and cultural differences of other nations and peoples. We also, however, witness the limited capacity of nations and their leaders to learn from the past.

Abbreviations

AMRE	Archivo del Ministerio de Relaciones Exteriores, Bogotá
ASS	Assistant Secretary of State
DC	Department of Commerce, United States
DS	Department of State, United States
DSB	Department of State, *Bulletin*
EPP	Dwight D. Eisenhower Presidential Papers
FMC	Foreign Ministry, Colombia
FO	Foreign Office, Great Britain
FRUS	U.S. Department of State, *Foreign Relations of the United States*
HSTL	Harry S. Truman Presidential Library
LBJP	Lyndon Baines Johnson Presidential Papers
LC	Library of Congress, United States
MRE	Ministro de Relaciones Exteriores, Colombia
NA	National Archives of the United States
NFTC	National Foreign Trade Council, United States
NSC	National Security Council, United States
NSF	National Security Files, Lyndon Baines Johnson Presidential Library
PAU	Pan American Union
PPF	President's Personal File
PRO	Public Record Office, Great Britain
PSF	President's Secretary File
RG	Record Group
SC	Secretary of Commerce
SN	Secretary of the Navy
SS	Secretary of State
TRP	Theodore Roosevelt Presidential Papers
WHTP	William Howard Taft Presidential Papers
WJBP	William Jennings Bryan Papers
WWP	Woodrow Wilson Presidential Papers

Notes

Introduction

1. Arthur Schlesinger, Jr., "Foreign Policy and the American Character," *Foreign Affairs* (Fall 1983); Robert Pastor, *Condemned to Repetition* (Princeton, 1987), 270–71; Akira Iriye, "Culture and Power: International Relations as Intercultural Relations," *Diplomatic History* (1979).

1. The First Half Century

1. Henry Clay to U.S. Minister in St. Petersburg, 10 May 1825, Hamilton Fish Papers, State Department Files, box 285, LC.
2. Manuel José Forero, *La primera republica, 1810–1816*, vol. 5 of *Historia extensa de Colombia* (Bogotá, 1966); Luis Galvez Madero, *La Gran Colombia, 1819–1830*, vol. 7 of *Historia extensa de Colombia* (Bogotá, 1970).
3. E. Taylor Parks, *Colombia and the United States, 1750–1934* (Chapel Hill, N.C., 1935), 75–76.
4. On Nariño and this early period, see Colombia, Biblioteca de historia nacional, *El precursor: Documentos sobre la vida pública y privada del General Antonio Nariño* (Bogotá, 1902), vol. 2. Parks, *Colombia*, 65–66, 74–75.
5. Cited in Parks, *Colombia*, 40–46. William S. Robertson, ed., *The Diary of Francisco de Miranda: Tour of the United States, 1783–84* (New York, 1928).
6. Parks, *Colombia*, 49–54. José Joaquín Caicedo Castilla, *Historia Diplomatica*, part 1, vol. 17 of *Historia extensa de Colombia* (Bogotá, 1974), does not mention Miranda and the Leander mission as part of the U.S. relationship with the independence movement.
7. Parks, *Colombia*, 63–67.
8. Parks, *Colombia*, 83.
9. 20 Mar. 1816, William R. Manning, ed., *Diplomatic Correspondence of the United States Concerning the Independence of the Latin American Nations*, 3 vols. (New York, 1925), 1:20–30.

10. De la Lasta to Monroe, undated (1812), in Manning, ed., *Diplomatic Correspondence*, 2:1165–66.
11. Palacio to SSUS, 26 Dec. 1812; Manning, ed., *Diplomatic Correspondence*, 2:1164–65.
12. Despatches from these and other Colombian representatives during this period are contained in Department of State, Despatches from The Colombian Legation in Washington to the DS (microfilm series 51), and the Ministry of Foreign Relations Archive, Bogotá.
13. Robertson to SS, 7 Oct. 1812, Despatches from the Colombian Legation to DS. García de Sena to SS, 28, 29 Mar. 1814; 1 Apr. 1814; 10 June 1814 (microfilm series 51, vol 1).
14. Zea memo, 14 Aug. 1819; Adams to Torres, 19 Nov. 1819, *Legacion en los EEUU*, vol. I, 1818–20, AMRE.
15. Torres to Adams, 20 May 1820 (Despatches from Colombian Legation to DS, Microfilm series 51, vol. 2).
16. FMC to Torres, 1 Sept. 1819; 2 Feb. 1820; 24 Feb. 1820; 12 Apr. 1820; 19 June 1820; 17 July 1820, *Legacion en Los EEUU*, vol. 1, 1818–20. Torres to FMC, 20 May 1820; 2 Aug. 1820, *Legacion en los EEUU*, vol. 2, 1820, AMRE.
17. Torres to FMC, 26 Dec. 1820, *Legacion en los EEUU*, vol. 2, 1820, AMRE; Parks, *Colombia*, 88–104; Monroe, *Writings*, S. M. Hamilton, ed. (New York, 1900), 6:97.
18. Anderson to Adams, 22 Dec. 1823, RG 84, NA. José M. Salazar to Adams, 2 July 1824 (Despatches from Colombian Legation to DS, microfilm series 51, vol. 1, part 2). Memo of meeting of Charles Todd, Miguel Peña, Colombian Supreme Court justice and former president of Cucuta Congress, and Santander, 16 June 1823, in Manning, ed., *Diplomatic Correspondence*, 2:1261–63; Santander to Monroe, 18 Mar. 1825, Monroe Papers, series 1, reel 9, LC. Parks, *Colombia*, provides a sound overview of the Colombian reaction to the Monroe message, 130–32, 139–40.
19. Parks, *Colombia*, 132–34.
20. Anderson to Adams, 18 Aug. 1824, Manning, ed., *Diplomatic Correspondence*, 2:1283, 1286–87.
21. Gual to Salazar, 7 Oct. 1824, Congreso de Panamá, vol. 1 (1825–28), AMRE. Clay to Anderson, 25 Nov. 1825; 15 Mar. 1826; Clay to Joel Poinsett, Mexico, 23 June 1826, Clay Papers, microfilm reel 7, LC. Bolívar to Santander, 17 Feb. 1826, Congreso de Panamá, vol. 1 (1825–28), AMRE.
22. Hurtado to Canning, 11 Jan. 1826; Canning to Hurtado, 23 Jan. 1826, Con-

greso de Panamá, vol. 1 (1825–28). Canning's views on Cuba are discussed in Parks, *Colombia*, 145–46.

23. Gual to Salazar, 10 Aug. 1825, Congreso de Panamá, vol. 1 (1825–28), AMRE.

24. Salazar to Clay, 30 Dec. 1825, 19 Mar. 1826; Anderson to Clay, 7 Feb. 1826; Anderson to Clay, 9 Mar. 1826; Revenga to Anderson, 17 Mar. 1826, in Manning, ed., *Diplomatic Correspondence*, 2:1288–96.

25. Clay to Middleton, St. Petersburg, 10 May 1825; 21 Apr. 1826, Hamilton Fish Papers, State Department Files, box 285, LC. Salazar to Clay, 30 Dec. 1825 (Despatches from Colombian Legation to DS, microfilm series 51, vol. 1, part 2).

26. Raimundo Rivas, *Relaciones internacionales entre Colombia y los Estados Unidos, 1810–1850* (Bogotá, 1915), 71.

27. Parks, *Colombia*, 154–57.

28. Moore to Van Buren, 7 May 1831, 7 June 1831, 14 Oct. 1831, 19 Jan. 1832, 2 Apr. 1832, 21 May 1832, in Manning, ed., *Diplomatic Correspondence*, 5:448–65.

29. William McGreevey, *An Economic History of Colombia, 1845–1930* (Cambridge, Eng., 1971), 36–37; Luis Eduardo Nieto Arteta, *Economía y cultura en la historia de Colombia* (Bogotá, 1970), 2:141.

30. The best analysis of Santander's views is contained in David Bushnell and Neill Macaulay, *The Emergence of Latin America in the Nineteenth Century* (New York, 1988); David Bushnell, *The Santander Regime in Gran Colombia* (Newark, Del., 1954).

31. Edward Livingston, SS, to McAfee, 30 Mar. 1833, Manning, ed. *Diplomatic Correspondence*, 5:338–40; McAfee to SS, John Forsyth, 6 Mar. 1835, Manning, 5:512–14; DS to McAfee, 20 July 1833, Diplomatic Instructions of the DS, 1801–1906, vol. 15, no. 6.

32. McAfee to MRE, 31 May 1834, U.S. Legation in Colombia, vol. 87 (1823–49), AMRE.

33. McAfee to DS, 13 Sept. 1833; SS to McAfee, 1 May 1835, Manning, ed. *Diplomatic Correspondence*, 5:484–85, 343–46. U.S.–New Granadan trade grew in the 1830s from $1.2 million with all of Gran Colombia in 1830 to $2.4 million with New Granada alone in 1835; the political crises of subsequent years, however, undercut those gains. In 1845, bilateral trade was a dismal $203,000.

34. McAfee to MRE, Lino de Pombo, 31 May 1834, Records of U.S. Legation

in Bogotá, RG 84.

35. Biddle to SS, 15 Nov. 1836, Manning, ed., *Diplomatic Correspondence*, 5:541–47; Forsyth to McAfee, 23 Sept. 1836, RG 84.

36. Blackford to Mariano Ospina, MRE, 20 May 1843, Manning, ed., *Diplomatic Correspondence*, 5:594–95; Webster to Blackford, 20 May 1842, Manning, ed., *Diplomatic Correspondence*, 5:353–54.

37. 20 May 1842, Diplomatic Instructions of the DS, vol. 15.

38. Acosta to Forsyth, 25 Feb. 1837 (Despatches from Colombian legation to DS, microfilm series 51, vol. 3).

39. 30 Sept. 1843; Blackford to Upshur, 8 Mar. 1844, Manning, ed., *Diplomatic Correspondence*, 5:595–96, 603–4.

40. Parks, *Colombia* 195–200.

41. Calhoun to Blackford, 15 Aug. 1844, Diplomatic Instructions of the DS, vol. 15; Buchanan to Bidlack, 30 May 1845, 23 June 1845, Diplomatic Instructions of the DS, vol. 15; 2 Jan. 1847, Manning, ed., *Diplomatic Correspondence*, 5:358–59.

42. Bidlack to Buchanan, 10 Dec. 1846, Manning, ed., *Diplomatic Correspondence*, 5:629–33.

43. Manning, *Diplomatic Correspondence*, 5:640, 649.

44. On the desire of the U.S. government to reduce Colombian coastal dependence on the goods of the Colombian interior, see SS John Clayton to Chargé Dr. Thomas M. Foote, Bogotá, 19 July 1849, Diplomatic Instructions of DS, vol. 15.

45. Treaty draft, Bidlack to Buchanan, 18 Dec. 1846, RG 84.

46. 20 July 1848, Diplomatic Instructions DS, vol. 15.

47. Clayton to Foote, 9 Jan. 1850, Diplomatic Instructions of DS, vol. 15.

48. Clayton to Foote, 19 July 1849; 15 Dec. 1849 (containing copy of a letter from Thomas Ludlow, President of the Panama Railroad Company then under construction), Diplomatic Instructions of DS, vol. 15.

49. Caicedo, *Historia diplomatica*, 1:261–62.

50. Herrán to MRE, 31 Jan. 1849, Legación de Colombia en Los Estados Unidos, vol. 24 (1847–48), AMRE.

51. Ludlow to Rivas, 31 Oct. 1849, Legación de Colombia en Los Estados Unidos, vol. 32, AMRE. These volumes contain excellent correspondence relating to the railroad negotiations as well as Colombian observations on the foreign policy implications of the project.

52. Parks, *Colombia* 272–73.

53. Clayton to Herrán, 2 Aug. 1849; Clayton to U.S. Chargé in Bogotá, 15 Dec.

1849; Clayton to Rafael Rivas, 29 Jan. 1850, Manning, ed., *Diplomatic Correspondence*, 5:364–66.

54. Rivas to MRE, 30 May 1850, Legación de Colombia en Los Estados Unidos, vol. 32, AMRE.

55. Rivas to MRE, 30 Aug. 1849, Legación de Colombia en Los Estados Unidos, vol. 32, AMRE.

56. Paredes to MRE, 15 Dec. 1853, Legación de Colombia en Los Estados Unidos, vol. 32 (1949–55), AMRE. Foote to SS, 29 Mar. 1850; 19 Dec. 1850, Manning, ed., *Diplomatic Correspondence*, 5:656–68.

57. Herrán to MRE, 21 Mar. 1848, Legación de Colombia en Los Estados Unidos, vol. 24 (1847–48), AMRE.

58. See vol. 32 (1849–55), Legación de Colombia en Los Estados Unidos, AMRE; for Rivas's attitude toward Britain, see for instance Rivas to MRE, 15 June 1850.

59. Corwine to Manuel Diaz, Governor of Panama, 3 Mar. 1851; Corwine to Webster, 30 June 1851, Despatches from U.S. Consuls: Panama, vol. 2, RG 59.

60. Foote to Clayton, 12 Apr. 1850, 5 July 1850; Paredes to Webster, 20 June 1852, Manning, *Diplomatic Correspondence*, 5:659–63; 672–75.

61. Corwine to SS, 14 Nov. 1851, Despatches from U.S. Consuls: Panama, vol. 2. Boyd to SS, 3 May 1856, Despatches from U.S. Consuls: Colón, vol. 1.

62. Paredes to MRE, 17 Jan. 1853; Paredes to General Tomas C. de Mosquera, 11 Jan. 1853; Mosquera to John Stapley, a New York lawyer, 4 Jan. 1853, Legación de Colombia en Los Estados Unidos, vol. 32, AMRE.

63. Marcy to Paredes, 20 June 1853; 12 Oct. 1853, Manning, ed., *Diplomatic Correspondence*, 5:369–72; Lino de Pombo, MRE, to Colombian Minister in Washington, 7 Mar. 1856, Correspondencia de la Secretaria de Relaciones Exteriores con los Ministros de Colombia en Washington, vol. 37, AMRE.

64. Bushnell and Macauley, *Emergence of Latin America*, 209–18.

65. Despatches from U.S. consuls in Colón (Aspinwall), vol. 1 (1852–57).

66. Report of Thomas Ward, U.S. Consul in Panama, 18 Apr. 1856, to SS, Despatches from U.S. Consuls: Panama, vol. 4.

67. Synopsis of the Papers filed at the DS in relation to the Occurrences at Panama April 1856, prepared by A. B. Corwine, 18 July 1856, Manning, ed., *Diplomatic Correspondence*, 5:393ff. William L. Marcy, SS, to Amos B. Corwine, 12 May 1856, Diplomatic Instructions of the DS, Special Missions, vol. 3.

68. Lino de Pombo to US Chargé, Bogotá, 28 June 1856, Manning, ed., *Diplomatic Correspondence*, 5:731–37. Lino de Pombo to Pedro Herrán, Washington, 10 June 1856, 22 Aug. 1856, Legación de Colombia en Los Estados Unidos, vol. 37, AMRE.
69. Bowlin to Lino de Pombo, 30 June 1856; Bowlin to Marcy, 1 August 1856, Manning, ed., *Diplomatic Correspondence*, 5:737–47.
70. Marcy to Bowlin, 4 June 1856, Diplomatic Despatches of the Department of State, vol. 15.
71. Marcy to Bowlin and Morse, 3 Dec. 1856, Diplomatic Instructions of the Department of State, vol. 15.
72. Lino de Pombo to Herrán, 12 Feb. 1857, Legación de Colombia en Los Estados Unidos, vol. 37, AMRE.
73. See the extensive correspondence and documentation in Manning, ed., *Diplomatic Correspondence*, 5:399–427.

2. An Era of Civil War and National Reconstruction

1. George Baker, ed., *The Works of William H. Seward* (New York, 1853–61), 4:311–12; Nuñez to the delegates at the November 1885 constitutional convention, translated from Luis Martinez Delgado, *La República de Colombia*, part 1 (1885–95), vol. 10 of *Historia extensa de Colombia* (Bogotá, 1970), 10:157.
2. Parks, *Colombia*, 298–300.
3. Seward to Rafael Pombo, Colombian Minister, 30 May 1861, DS Despatches to Colombian legation, vol. 6; Seward to Charles Francis Adams, U.S. Minister to London, 11 July 1862; Adams to Seward, 1 Aug. 1862; Dayton (Paris) to Seward, 29 Aug. 1862, copies in Legación de Colombia en Los Estados Unidos, vol. 49, AMRE.
4. Parraga to MRE, 8 May 1862; 8 June 1862; Murillo to MRE, 10 Sept. 1862, Legación de Colombia en Los Estados Unidos, vol. 49, AMRE.
5. Murillo to MRE, 9 Dec. 1862; 10 Feb. 1863, Legación de Colombia en Los Estados Unidos, vol. 49, AMRE. Seward to Murillo, 20 July 1863, DS Notes to the Colombian legation, vol. 6.
6. Seward to U.S. Minister in Bogotá, Allan Burton, 27 Apr. 1866, *FRUS* (1866–67), 522.
7. Rafael Pombo, *Notas de Derecho Universal y Norteamericano para la comi-*

sión mixta de reclamaciones, 1861–62, Legación de Colombia en Los Estados Unidos, vol. 48, AMRE.

8. Various issues of *El Tiempo* for 1864–65; on the suffrage question see 21 Dec. 1864; on the role of public opinion see 24 May 1865; on the relationship between political liberty and economic growth see 11 Oct. 1865.

9. *El Tiempo,* 24 May 1865, "Una calamidad americana."

10. Thompson to Parraga, 20 Sept. 1862; Parraga to Thompson, 26 Sept. 1862; Murillo to MRE, 9 Oct. 1862; Murillo to Governor of Panama, 10 Nov. 1862, Legación de Colombia en Los Estados Unidos, vol. 49, AMRE.

11. Parks, *Colombia,* 276–77.

12. Murillo to MRE, 11 Feb. 1863; 7 Apr. 1863; 29 May 1863; 2 July 1863; Seward to M. Romero, Mexican Minister in U.S., 20 Mar. 1863, Legación de Colombia en Los Estados Unidos, vol. 49, AMRE.

13. Parks, *Colombia,* 279–80.

14. Parks, *Colombia,* 281–84.

15. 1 Nov. 1872, Despatches from U.S. consuls: Buenaventura.

16. Murillo to MRE, 9 Oct. 1862, including Foreign Ministry marginal notes, Legación de Colombia en Los Estados Unidos, vol. 49; letter from French Society for the canal concession to President Gutierrez, 7 Jan. 1870 and Gutierrez's note, 16 Feb. 1870, Legacion de Colombia en Los Estados Unidos, vol. 100, AMRE.

17. See container 176, Caleb Cushing papers, LC; Santos Acosta to MRE, 25 Nov. 1868, Legación de Colombia en Los Estados Unidos, vol. 53, AMRE. Sullivan to Santiago Pérez, Secretary of Interior and Foreign Relations, 28 Apr. 1868, Legación de Los Estados Unidos en Colombia, vol. 100, AMRE.

18. Parks, *Colombia,* 345–46. Miguel Samper to Cushing, 17 Jan. 1869, Microfilm Reel 107, General Correspondence, William Seward papers, LC. Caicedo, *Historia diplomatica,* 310–19, neglects the 1869 treaty negotiations.

19. Fish to Hurlbut, 4 Sept. 1869; Fish to Santos Acosta, 30 Apr. 1869, State Department Files, box 237, Hamilton Fish Papers, LC. Acosta to MRE, 16 Jan. 1870, Legación de Colombia en Los Estados Unidos, vol. 53, AMRE.

20. Parks, *Colombia,* 348; Fish to Hurlbut, 19 Mar. 1870, 4 Apr. 1870, box 237, State Department Files, Fish Papers, LC. Hurlbut to MRE, 25 Nov. 1869, 1 Dec. 1869; Hurlbut memorandum, 17 Apr. 1870, Legación de Colombia, vol. 100; Acosta to MRE, 16 Jan. 1870, vol. 53, AMRE. Colombian Min-

ister Santiago Pérez to MRE, 4 Aug. 1870, 30 Sept. 1870, 20 Dec. 1870, Legación de Colombia en Los Estados Unidos, vol. 56, AMRE.

21. Acosta to MRE, 20 Apr. 1870, 15 May 1870, Legación de Colombia en Los Estados, vol. 53, AMRE. Colombian officials seem to have been as unhappy with the Dominican Republic adventure of the Grant administration as the U.S. Senate proved to be. See the unsigned memo in the records of the Colombian legation in Washington, entitled "El Tratado Dominicana—la Política del Destino Manifiesto," vol. 100.

22. Box 238, State Department Files, Fish Papers, LC.

23. Colombia, Debates del Senado de Plenipotenciarios, editions of 11, 13, 17, 18 May 1870, 30 July 1870, covering debates for March and April 1870. Senator Martín to MRE, 21 Dec. 1869; Senator Samper to Rojas, 14 Feb. 1870, Legación de Colombia en Los Estados Unidos, vol. 100, AMRE. General minutes of the negotiations are contained in vol. 100.

24. Long to SS, 30 Sept. 1877; 15 Jan. 1878, Despatches from U.S. Consuls: Panama, vol. 14.

25. John Wilson to SS, 2 Jan. 1889, Despatches from U.S. Consuls: Panama, vol. 14.

26. John Wilson to SS, 5 Dec. 1879, 6 Jan. 1880, Despatches from U.S. Consuls: Panama, vol. 14. *Panama Star and Herald*, 5 Jan. 1880.

27. Walter LaFeber, *The Panama Canal* (New York, 1978); Parks, *Colombia*, 356–59.

28. Dichman to SS Evarts, 19 July, 17 Oct. 1879, Despatches from U.S. Ministers in Colombia, vol. 33.

29. Arosemena to MRE, 23 Oct. 1879, Legación de Colombia en Los Estados Unidos, vol. 61, AMRE.

30. Arosemena to MRE, 13 Feb. 1880; 8, 9 Mar. 1880; Arosemena to de Lesseps, 2 Mar. 1880; Ramón Santo Domingo Vila (Colombian Minister, U.S.) to MRE, 10 Dec. 1880, Legación de Colombia en Los Estados Unidos, vol. 61, AMRE. New York *Tribune*, "Interamerican Questions," 31 Jan. 1880; New York *Herald*, "The United States and the Isthmus," 30 Jan. 1880.

31. Charles Williams, ed., *Diary and Letters of Rutherford Birchard Hayes* (Columbus, Ohio, 1922), 3:589; message to Congress, 8 Mar. 1880, James D. Richardson, ed., *Messages and Papers of the Presidents, 1789–1897* (Washington, D.C., 1898), 10:4537–38.

32. Richardson, ed., *Messages and Papers*, 10:4563. The Colombian minister in Washington transmitted the message verbatim to Bogotá; Domingo

Vila to MRE, 7 Dec. 1880, Legación de Colombia en Los Estados Unidos, vol. 61, AMRE.

33. Dichman to MRE, 6 Sept. 1880, Legación de Colombia en Los Estados Unidos, vol. 106, AMRE. Dichman to Evarts, 6 Nov. 1889, FRUS (1881), 337–38.

34. Wilson to ASS, 15 Mar. 1880, Despatches from U.S. Consuls: Panama, vol. 14. Becerra to *New York Times*, 16 Dec. 1884.

35. Arosemena to Evarts, 13 Feb. 1880; Evarts to Arosemena, 5 June 1880, Legación de Colombia en Los Estados Unidos, vol. 61, AMRE. Wilson to SS, 2 Apr. 1880, Despatches from U.S. Consuls: Panama, vol. 14. Wilson to Panama Secretary of State, 10 Mar. 1881, Despatches from U.S. Consuls: Panama, vol. 15.

36. Wilson to ASS, 16 July 1880, Despatches from U.S. Consuls: Panama, vol. 15.

37. R. Becerra to MRE, 20 Nov. 1884; Roldan to Becerra, 26 Nov. 1884, Legación de Colombia en Los Estados Unidos, vol. 62, AMRE.

38. Martinez Delgado, *Republica de Colombia,* provides not only the most thorough overview of the 1884–85 crisis but also of the ideological dimensions involved. Charles Bergquist, *Coffee and Conflict in Colombia, 1886– 1910* (Durham, N.C., 1978), provides a more analytical approach to the relationships between economic development, landholding patterns, ideology, class formation, and political change in this period. On Nuñez, see Indalecio Liévano Aguirre, *Rafael Nuñez* (Lima, 1944); on Miguel Antonio Caro, see Jaime Jaramillo Uribe, *El pensamiento colombiano en el siglo XIX* (Bogotá, 1964), 314–56. On trade relations, see Parks, *Colombia,* 264–66.

39. Becerra to MRE, 29 Sept. 1885, Legación de Colombia en Los Estados Unidos, vol. 62, AMRE.

40. Parks, *Colombia,* 228–30. Luis Martinez Delgado contends that Colombian forces were adequate to maintain order; *Republica de Colombia,* 93–94. Adamson to SS, 3 Feb. 1885, 23 Feb. 1885, 23 Mar. 1885, 6 Apr. 1885, Despatches from U.S. Consuls, vol. 17. Secretary of Navy to Commander B. McCalla, Panama, 24 Apr. 1885; Bayard to Adamson, 29 Apr. 1885, Despatches from U.S. Consuls: Panama, vol. 17. Britain also moved naval vessels into Cartagena, Panama, and Sabanilla and landed forces in late March at Panama.

41. Bayard to Becerra, 24 Apr. 1885, Legación de Colombia en Los Estados Unidos, vol. 62, AMRE.

42. Anderson to Assistant Secretary of State, 31 Jan. 1885, Despatches from U.S. Consuls: Panama, vol. 17.
43. Adamson to Assistant SS, 4 Aug. 1885, Despatches from U.S. Consuls, vol. 17.

3. Nations in Crisis: The Loss of Panama

1. Luis Carlos Rico, Colombian Foreign Minister, to SS, 12 Apr. 1904, translated from Caicedo, *Historia diplomatica,* 356.
2. For examples of U.S. investment see U.S. Legation in Bogotá, vol. 114 (1893–97), vol. 116 (1893–97), AMRE. For trade data and investment see Parks, *Colombia,* 271, 283; Colombian Legation in U.S., vol. 66, AMRE. On the American schools, see U.S. Minister Charles Hart to MRE, 27 Jan. 1900, Records of U.S. Legation in Bogotá, RG 84, NA.
3. Bergquist, *Coffee and Conflict,* provides an excellent analysis linking economic issues in the 1880s and 1890s with the War of a Thousand Days. On railroad development see the following diplomatic and economic reports: A. J. Cassatt (U.S. delegate on railroad commission) to SS Blaine, 5 May 1891; Federico Párraga to Antonio Roldan, MRE, 17 Jan. 1891, 5 May 1891; U.S. Minister, Bogotá, (Abbott) to MRE, 1 May 1890, U.S. Legation in Bogotá, vol. 112, AMRE.
4. Hurtado to SS, 25 Feb. 1892; Blaine to Hurtado, 7 Mar. 1892; 26-page "Observaciones" by Hurtado on McKinley Tariff, August 1891, Colombian Legation in U.S., vol. 66, AMRE.
5. Nuñez to Suarez, 16 Apr. 1892, 5 May 1892, 14 Jan. 1893; Hurtado to John W. Foster, SS, 5 Sept. 1892, Colombian Legation in U.S., vol. 66, AMRE.
6. Rengifo to MRE, 3 Apr. 1894, 29 Aug. 1894, 9 Nov. 1894; Hurtado to Rengifo, 5 Feb. 1894; Hurtado to MRE, 25 Sept. 1893, 13 Oct. 1893, 31 Oct. 1893, vols. 66, 67, Colombian Legation in U.S., AMRE.
7. Bergquist, *Coffee and Conflict,* 127–32.
8. U.S. Consul, Colón, to DS, 23 Dec. 1901, vol. 18, Despatches of U.S. Consuls: Colón.
9. The reports of the U.S. Consul in Panama City, H. A. Gudger, to SS, provide an important source of information on the internal Panamanian conflict: 6 Apr. 1900, 10 Apr., 24 Apr., 14 May, 18 June, 25 July, 26 July,

volume 23; reports of 14 Jan. 1901, 28 Jan. 1901, 1 Apr. 1901, 17 July 1901, 5 Aug. 1901, 20 Nov. 1901, 25 Nov. 1901, volume 24, Consular Despatches of DS: Panama, RG 59. U.S. Consul in Barranquilla, Shaw to SS, 7 Apr. 1900, Despatch Book 5034, RG 84 (Records of the American Legation at Bogotá). Gudger to Governor of Panama, 21 Nov. 1901, and Perry to U.S. Consul, 21 Nov. 1901, vol. 24, Despatches of U.S. Consuls: Panama, RG 59.

10. Gudger to DS, 12 Jan. 1902; 4 Mar. 1902; 17 Mar. 1902; 12 July 1902; acting consul to DS, 17 Sept. 1902, vol. 24, Despatches of U.S. Consuls: Panama.
11. Hay to Choate, 15 Jan. 1900, volume 2, Letterbooks, p. 321, Hay Papers, LC.
12. Hay to Martínez Silva, 12 Dec. 1901; Martínez to Hay, 7 Dec. 1901; Martínez to MRE, 23 Dec. 1901, Colombian Legation in U.S., vol. 69, No. 1, AMRE.
13. Uribe to Martínez, 12 Jan. 1901; Martínez to President of the New Panama Canal Company, 29 Apr. 1901; Martínez to MRE, 3 May 1901, Martínez to Rear Admiral John Walker of the U.S. Canal Commission, 3 May 1901, Martínez memorandum, 25 June 1901, Colombian Legation in U.S., vol. 69, No. 1, AMRE.
14. Martínez to Concha, 1 Apr. 1902, Colombian Legation in U.S., vol. 69, No. 2, AMRE.
15. Abadía to Concha, 22 Jan. 1902; 22 Feb. 1902; Concha to MRE, 5 Mar. 1902; Abadía to Concha, 17 Mar. 1902, Colombian Legation in U.S., vol. 69, no. 1, AMRE. U.S. House of Representatives, House Document 611, 57th Cong., 1st sess., 1902.
16. Concha to Hay, 31 Mar. 1902; Concha to Roosevelt, 20 Mar. 1902, Colombia Legation in U.S., vol. 69, no. 1, AMRE.
17. U.S. Congress, *Diplomatic History of the Panama Canal,* Senate document no. 474 (Washington, 1914), 261.
18. Henry Pringle, *Theodore Roosevelt* (New York, 1931), 311, and Howard Beale, *Theodore Roosevelt and the Rise of America to World Power* (Baltimore, 1956), 33. On Hay, see Tyler Dennett, *John Hay* (New York, 1933), 377.
19. An account of the Panamanian secession movement by the Panamanian senator to the Colombian Congress is José Agustín Arango, *Datos para la historia de la independencia del istmo* (Panama, 1905).
20. B-V to Marroquín, 23 Feb. 1902, box 20, Legal File, Sullivan and Cromwell Records, Bunau-Varilla Papers, LC. B-V, French version of *Panama,*

p. 400; the quotation is this author's translation from the French version, p. 391, box 14, Bunau-Varilla Papers, LC.

21. Colombia, Senado, Discurso pronunciado por el Dr. Luis Carlos Rico, sesión de 12 de Agosto de 1903 (Bogotá, 1903). Arosemena to Rico, 11 Nov. 1903, Documentos sobre la separación de Panamá, AMRE.

22. Contained in Roosevelt to Hay, 19 Aug. 1903, TRP, microfilm edition, reel 416, LC.

23. Bunau-Varilla, English manuscript version of *Panama*, pp. 150, 151, 155, 157, box 15, Bunau-Varilla Papers, LC. Roosevelt to Hay, 19 Aug. 1903, 15 Sept. 1903, Roosevelt-Hay Correspondence, reel 416, TRP, LC.

24. Bunau-Varilla, Manuscript draft (French) of *Panama, Creation, Destruction, Resurrection*, p. 444, box 14, Bunau-Varilla Papers, LC; Bunau-Varilla also met in September and October with ASS Francis B. Loomis, and with former ASS and Roosevelt confidant John Bassett Moore, p. 457. pp. 167–69, typescript of English draft.

25. Cables of 3, 4, and 5 Nov. 1903 to DS from U.S. Consul, Colón, vol. 19, Despatches from U.S. Consuls: Colón. Ortíz's statement is from the TRP, microfilm edition, Series 1, reel 38, LC.

26. Bunau-Varilla, *Panama*, English version, 169–73. Credit to Cromwell is given by William Harbaugh, *Power and Responsibility: The Life and Times of Theodore Roosevelt* (New York, 1961), 208–9.

27. Bunau-Varilla, *Panama*, English version, pp. 179–80, 181, 186–87, 190, box 14, Bunau-Varilla Papers, LC. See Charles Ameringer, "Philippe Bunau-Varilla: New Light on the Panama Canal Treaty," *Hispanic American Historical Review* 44 (February 1966), 28–52; Ameringer, "The Panama Canal Lobby of Philippe Bunau-Varilla and William Nelson Cromwell," *American Historical Review* 67 (January 1963), 346–63.

28. Letters of 6 Nov., 18 Dec. 1903, Documentos sobre la separación de Panamá, AMRE.

29. U.S. Consul, Colón, to DS, 24 Nov. 1903, vol. 19, Despatches of U.S. Consuls: Colón. William Thayer, *Life and Letters of John Hay* (New York, 1915), 2:319–27; *Public Opinion* 36 (3 Mar. 1904), 260. Roosevelt to Root, 16 Feb. 1904, box 163, Root Papers, LC. Commander of Caribbean Squadron to SN, 31 Mar. 1904, reel 43; Cromwell to Roosevelt, 12 Mar. 1904, 27 Mar. 1904, 31 Mar. 1904, reels 42, 43, TRP, LC.

30. John Barrett Papers, Speeches and Writings File, "Impressions on the River Magdalena," 10 Oct. 1905 to 14 Oct. 1905, box 104, LC.

31. Draft of Colombia-Panama agreement, 1906, DS 1502/4 1/2, RG 59; Enrique Cortes to William Nelson Cromwell, 8 July 1907, 1502/32–34; Cromwell to William Howard Taft, 5 July 1907, 1502/35–37; Cromwell to Taft, 6 Aug. 1907, 1502/54 1/2. On the Colombia-Panama boundary see Dawson to SS, 28 Oct. 1907 and 13 Apr. 1908, DS case file 9271, RG 59.

32. Reyes to President of Senate, 31 Aug. 1904, Documentos sobre la separación de Panamá, AMRE. Barrett sketch of Reyes, box 104, Speeches and Writings File, Barrett Papers, LC.

33. U.S. Minister to Colombia, James DuBois, to SS, 30 Sept. 1912, file 365, series 6, case files, WHTP, LC. Stibben to DS, 24 Dec. 1908, DS Numerical File 1502/107–9, RG 59; *El Nuevo Tiempo*, 23 Dec. 1908.

34. U.S. Minister T. C. Dawson, to SS, 24 Feb. 1909, Numerical File, 1502/169, RG 59. U.S. Minister, Elliott Northcott to Colombian Foreign Minister, 26 Oct. 1909, vol. 4921, RG 84 (Records of the U.S. Legation in Bogotá), NA.

35. Vice-Consul, Barranquilla, to DS, 16, 19 July 1909, file C8.7, Despatches from Barranquilla to DS, RG 84; Northcott to SS, 8, 19 March 1910, vol. 4921, RG 84.

36. U.S. Consular Report, Latin America, Colombia File, Barrett Papers.

37. Northcott, U.S. Legation, to SS, 12 Mar. 1910, DS 821.00, RG 59.

38. U.S. Legation to the Colombian Foreign Minister, 24 Sept. 1910, RG 84, Records of the Bogotá Legation.

39. Undated letter by Luis Barreto to the U.S. Minister, March 1910, DS 821.00, RG 59.

40. Legation to DS, 12 Mar. 1910, DS 821.00, RG 59.

41. DuBois to SS, 30 Jan. 1912; Taft to Knox, 30 Nov. 1912, series 6, case files, file 365, WHTP.

42. U.S. Chargé, Bogotá, to SS, 18 Nov. 1911, Bogotá Legation Records, RG 84. On Roosevelt's possible reentry into American national politics, see *El Liberal*, 28 May 1912. On the Colombian Senate see file 802.1, 1912, U.S. Legation in Bogotá, RG 84.

43. *Christian Science Monitor*, 20 Feb. 1912. The *Chicago Tribune* and *New York Sun* were both strongly critical of the Colombian position (20 Feb.). Huntington Wilson to DuBois, 18 Feb. 1912, series 6, case file 365, WHTP. DuBois to SS, 25 Mar. 1912, American Legation in Bogotá, RG 84. Knox to Taft, 20 Feb. 1913, Taft to Knox, 27 Feb. 1913, series 6, case file 365, WHTP. Report of the U.S. Minister in Bogotá to SS, 15 Dec. 1911, records of the

U.S. Legation in Bogotá, RG 84. Memo of instructions given DuBois by DS, 12 Dec. 1912, file 710, RG 84. The lengthy constitutional argument was presented by the SS to the House of Representatives and Senate in response to Senate resolution of 1 Mar. 1912; see U.S. House of Representatives Document 1444, 20 Feb. 1913. U.S. Chargé, Bogotá, to DS, 16 Apr. 1913; DuBois to SS, 17 Feb. 1913, file 710, RG 84.

44. The Mobile Address is in Arthur Link, ed., *The Papers of Woodrow Wilson* (Princeton, N.J., 1966 ff), vol. 28, 448–52. F. de P. Mateus, *Los Democratas, lo que significa para Colombia* (Bogotá, 1913).

45. U.S. Minister, Bogotá, to SS, 12 July 1913, RG 84.

46. Wilson To Bryan, 22 May 1914, DS Correspondence, box 43, Bryan Papers, LC.

47. Bryan to Thomson, 20 Aug. 1913, file 710, RG 84.

48. DuBois to DS, 5 Feb. 1913, U.S. Legation, RG 84.

49. Letter of Marco Fidel Suárez in *El Nuevo Tiempo*, 15 Mar. 1913.

50. Thomson to SS, 3, 24 Sept. 1913, U.S. Legation, Bogotá, RG 84. Henry Starrett, U.S. Consul, Cartagena, to DS, 5 Dec. 1913, file 710, RG 84.

51. Bryan to Wilson, Bryan to Thomson, 19 Sept. 1913, case file 826, WWP, LC.

52. Record to Tumulty and Wilson, 7 May 1914, case file 826, WWP.

53. Bryan to Wilson, 21 Nov. 1913; Wilson to Bryan, 17 Dec. 1913; Bryan to Thomson, 9 Mar. 1914, case file 826, WWP.

54. U.S. Legation, Bogotá, records for 1913–14, RG 84 contains the details of the various agreements.

55. Reyes to Wilson, 13 July 1914, case file 826, WWP.

56. Roosevelt claimed the treaty was "dishonorable" and "nothing but blackmail"; editor's note, Elting Morison, ed., *The Letters of Theodore Roosevelt* (Cambridge, Mass., 1954), 7:774; Roosevelt wrote Senate William Joel Stone, Chairman of the Senate Foreign Relations Committee, 11 July 1914, insisting that he be heard on the treaty, since, as he indicated, "I had full knowledge of everything of any importance that was done in connection with the transaction by any agent of the Government and I am solely responsible for what was done," a view with which Colombian officials would have heartily concurred. Morison, ed., *Letters*, 7:777–79.

57. Wilson to Thomson, 18 Feb. 1915, file 710, RG 84.

58. Thomson to SS, 26 Jan. 1916; Feb. 3, 1916; Suárez to Thomson, 25 Jan. 1916, U.S. Legation, Bogotá, RG 84.

59. Thomson to SS, 18 Feb., 10 Mar., and 22 Mar. 1916; see also Chargé Perry Belden to DS, 31 Mar. 1917, U.S. Legation, Bogotá, RG 84.

60. Case file 826, WWP. DuBois's pamphlet is in the file.

61. Lansing to Wilson, 23 Mar. 1917, Link, ed., *Papers of Wilson*, 41:456–57.

62. Roosevelt to Lodge, 13 Mar. 1917, Morison, ed., *Letters*, 8:1161; Roosevelt to Knox, 6 Dec. 1918, 8:1413–1414.

63. Minutes of meeting of 24 Dec. 1917, Records of the Comision Asesora, AMRE.

64. DuBois to SS, 30 Sept. 1912, file 365, case files, series 6, WHTP.

65. U.S. Chargé, Belden, to SS, 8 Sept. 1917, DS 821.6363 Barco/3, RG 59. U.S. Legation, Bogotá, to SS, 23 Apr. 1918, RG 84.

66. Bogotá Legation to DS, 8 Aug. 1914, 1 Feb. 1915, 22 July 1915, File 710, U.S. Legation, Bogotá, RG 84.

67. U.S. Chargé in Bogotá to Consul in Cartagena, 19 June 1913; John Bassett Moore, DS, to Berlin, 2 July 1913, Leishman to DS, 6 June 1913; U.S. Consul, Hamburg, to Leishman, 20 June 1913; U.S. Consul, Cartagena, to DS, 8 Dec. 1913; U.S. Vice-Consul, Cartagena, to DS, 20 Oct. 1913; Bogotá Legation to DS, 20 Sept. 1912, file 861.5, U.S. Legation, Bogotá, RG 84.

68. Bogotá Legation to DS, 17 Dec. 1914, 13 Oct. 1915, file 710, RG 84.

69. P. Belden to DS, 13 Feb. 1917; U.S. Minister in Panama to Belden, 26 Mar. 1917, file 710, U.S. Legation, Bogotá, RG 84.

70. Lansing to U.S. Minister, 26 Feb. 1916, file 863; DS to Bogotá, 17 Apr. 1917; William Redfield, Secretary of Commerce, to Lansing, 10 Apr. 1917; Lansing to Bogotá, 4 Jan. 1918; 5 June 1918; Bogotá to DS, 10 Aug. 1918, U.S. Legation, Bogotá, RG 84.

71. U.S. Consul, Medellín, to Belden, 11 Oct. 1917; Franklin Polk, DS, to Belden, 19 Oct. 1917, file 710, U.S. Legation, Bogotá, RG 84.

72. U.S. Minister, Bogotá, to SS, 18 Nov. 1918, U.S. Legation, Bogotá, RG 84.

73. Case file 826, WWP. Lansing Desk Diaries for 26 Jan. 1917, 29 Jan. 1917, Lansing Papers, LC.

74. U.S. Chargé, Belden, to SS, 29 July 1918, U.S. Legation, RG 84. For comments on the positive approach of the Suárez administration and the need to resolve the Panama dispute, see the Weekly Intelligence Summary, series 6N, week ending 30 Nov. 1918, WWP.

75. Report of Trade Commissioner, 3 June 1920, DS 821.00/459, RG 59; Philip to SS, 3 Oct. 1921, DS 821.00/474, RG 59.

4. The New Era

1. Colombia, *Informe de la comisión nombrada para estudiar el conflicto surgido entre la United Fruit Company y la Cooperativa Bananera Colombiana* (Bogotá, 1930).
2. On "progressive Pan-Americanism" see Robert Seidel's doctoral thesis by that title (Cornell University, 1973).
3. 25 Apr. 1921, Legación de Los EEUU en Colombia, AMRE.
4. Rodrigo Pardo and Juan G. Tokatlian, *Politica exterior Colombiana: De la subordinación a la autonomía* (Bogotá, 1988), 96–98.
5. On Rendón, see the annotated collection of his political cartoons on the period by Germán Colmenares, *Ricardo Rendón, una fuente para la historia de la opinión pública* (Bogotá: Fondo Cultural Cafetero, 1984). Representative works of other writers of the period include Luis López de Mesa, *La tragedia de nilse* (Bogotá, 1928); Baldomero Sanín Cano, *Letras colombianas* (Mexico, 1944).
6. *El Espectador*, 21 Mar. 1921; 6 Apr. 1921; Colmenares, *Rendón*, 183–87; *El Tiempo*, 19 Sept. 1927.
7. For trade data see U.S. Bureau of Foreign and Domestic Commerce, *Commerce Reports* (8 Apr. 1939) 330–33; Colombia, Departamento Administrativo Nacional Estadística, *Anuario de Comercio Exterior* (1938), 3.
8. U.S. Bureau of Foreign and Domestic Commerce, *Commerce Reports* (8 Apr. 1939), 330–33; Colombia, Departamento Administrativo Nacional Estadística, *Anuario de Comercio Exterior* (1938), 3.
9. Pan American Union, *Bulletin* 65 (1931), 1069. The most reliable source for corporate listings in Colombia is Colombia, Ministerio de Gobierno, *Legalizacciones de companías*, vol. 15 (1920), vols. 16, 17 (1921), vols. 18, 19 (1922), the last volume in the set; Archivo Nacional de Colombia, Bogotá.
10. *El Espectador*, 14 Apr. 1923, 17 July 1928.
11. U.S. Chargé, Bogotá, to MRE, 12 May 1921; Philip to MRE, 8 Nov. 1921, Legación de los EEUU en Colombia, AMRE.
12. See for instance *El Diario Nacional*, 10 Apr. 1922, "New Investments."
13. Riley to Kellogg, 3 Sept. 1927, DS 821.77/451. One of the strongest statements along these lines was by the U.S. commercial attaché, Carlton Jackson, to the Bureau of Foreign and Domestic Commerce, 31 Mar. 1924, when he reported that there was no doubt that U.S. locomotive, rolling stock, and steel companies were being discriminated against by the Colombian government deliberately in order to keep too high a percent-

age of Colombian business from going to the United States. He urged that Colombia be reminded of the fact that the United States purchased 90 percent of Colombian coffee. DS 821.77/253, RG 59, NA. The reference to the Belgian interests is from Philips to SS, 22 Apr. 1922, DS 821.00/500.

14. Examples contained in 1921–22 correspondence packages, Legación de los EEUU en Colombia, AMRE.

15. There is a more detailed account of Colombian oil developments and U.S. diplomacy in S. J. Randall, *The Diplomacy of Modernization: Colombian-American Relations, 1920–1940* (Toronto, 1977).

16. Randall, *Modernization*, 94–95; Philip to SS, 26 Sept. 1919, DS 821.6363/77; 8 Nov. 1919, DS 821.6363/86; 18 Dec. 1919, DS 821.6363/95; for law 145, 26 Nov. 1888, see DS 821.6363/92, RG 59, NA.

17. Fall to Long, 11 Oct. 1919, DS 821.6363/76, RG 59, NA.

18. 25 Nov. 1919, DS 821.6363/82, RG 59, NA.

19. Manning memorandum, 30 July 1920, DS 821.6363/128; Philip to SS, 28 Oct. 1920, DS 821.6363/128.

20. Randall, *Modernization*, 95.

21. These negotiations are more fully documented in Randall, *Modernization*, 90–128. See also Felix Mendoza and Benjamín Alvarado, *La indústria del petróleo en Colombia* (Bogotá, 1939).

22. Caffery's paraphrase of Chaux's comment is in Caffery to SS, 19 Sept. 1932, DS 821.6363 Barco/643, RG 59, NA.

23. See Catherine LeGrand, *Frontier Expansion and Peasant Protest in Colombia, 1830–1936* (Albuquerque, N. Mex., 1986).

24. James DuBois, Bogotá, to SS, 12 Mar. 1912, DS 821.77/18, RG 59; Robert Lansing (former Secretary of State) and Lester Woolsey, law firm representing United Fruit, to SS, 10 June 1921, and legal brief of 20 June 1922, DS 821.77/85 and DS 821.77/139. Charles Evans Hughes to Legation, Bogotá, 4 June 1921, DS 821.77/81.

25. Judith White, *Historia de una ignominia: La United Fruit en Colombia* (Bogotá, 1978), 123.

26. Colombia, *Revista de industrias* (enero de 1929), 240. One of the best examinations of the rural protest dimensions of the company–Colombian worker relationship in Magdalena is Catherine LeGrand, "Colombian Transformations: Peasants and Wage-Labourers in the Santa Marta Banana Zone," *Journal of Peasant Studies* 11, no. 4 (July 1984): 178–200. See also White, *Historia de una ignominia*.

27. Charles Kepner and Jay Soothill, *The Banana Empire* (New York, 1935), 70;

U.S. Consul, Santa Marta, Lawrence Cotie, to SS, 9 Mar. and 21 Aug. 1928, RG 59 821.6156/63.
28. Caffery memorandum, 10 Sept. 1930, RG 59, 821.6156/83, /87, /92. See Colombian press accounts in *El Tiempo*, 18 June 1930; *El Espectador*, 15 and 17 June 1930.
29. LeGrand, "Colombian Transformations," 183–85.
30. Colombian press accounts include: *Vanguardia Obrero*, 10 Nov. 1928; *El Diario Nacional* (Liberal-Socialist), 15, 22 Nov. 1928. See Ministerio de Industria, *Informe rendido . . . sobre el movimiento obrero occurrido en el departamento del Magdalena, Memoria de 1928–29* (Bogotá, 1929), 172–209. Caffery to SS, 3 Dec. 1928, RG 59, 821.5045/36.
31. Caffery to SS, 11 Dec. 1928, RG 59 821.5045/40; 5 Dec. 1928, 821.5045/24; Cotie Memo, RG 84: Santa Marta Consulate, 850.4. *El Tiempo*, 26 Dec. 1928; 9 Mar. 1930.
32. Caffery to SS, 2 Sept. 1929, RG 59 821.00 Amnesty/678; Miguel Urrutia, *The Development of the Colombian Labor Movement* (New Haven, Conn., 1969) 105–9; Antonio García, *Gaitán y el problema de la revolución colombiana* (Bogotá, 1955), 256–57.
33. This development is most fully documented in Randall, *Modernization*, 146–61.
34. *El Tiempo*, 22, 28 Nov. 1927; *El Diario Nacional*, 23, 24 Nov. 1927. U.S. Chargé in Panama, John Martin, to SS 19 Nov. 1927, RG 59 821.796 Sca 2/134; U.S. Minister, Samuel Piles to SS, 23 Nov. 1927, RG 59 821.796 Sca 2/131.
35. Piles to SS 28 Nov. 1927, 30 Nov. 1927, RG 59 821.796 Sca 2 /135/143.
36. White Memo, 19 Dec. 1927, White MSS, Hoover Library.
37. *FRUS*, 1928, 1:593; Sixth International Conference of American States, *Final Act* (Havana, 1928); *Report of the Delegates of the United States of America to the Sixth International Conference of American States* (Washington, 1928), 33–35.
38. *FRUS*, 1928, 1:786–88; 1929, 3:728–29; Secretary of War Davis to SS, 21 July 1928, RG 59 821. 796 Sca 2/171. Acting Secretary of the Navy to SS, 6 Aug. 1928, RG 59 821.796 Sca 2/177.
39. White to Caffery, 14 Nov. 1929, White MSS, Hoover Library; *FRUS*, 1929, 1:601; RG 810.79611 Pan American Airways/1000/10001. José Coronado, Colombian Chargé in Washington, to SS, 19 Mar. 1931, RG 59 821.796 Sca 2/314; H. Freeman Matthews, Assistant Chief, Latin American Divi-

sion, memo RG 59 821.796 Sca 2/321; Colombia, Ministro de Relaciones Exteriores, *Memoria* (Bogotá, 1932), 75.

40. Marco Fidel Suárez to Wickliffe Rose, IHB, 27 Mar. 1920; Schapiro to Heiser, IHB, 31 Jan. 1920, Folder 1314, box 95, series 1.2, RG 5, RA (Rockefeller Foundation Archives, Pocantico Hills, New York). There is also material on the health campaign in Department of State files; see for instance DS 158.219/12, RG 59, NA.

41. William P. McGreevey, *Statistical Series on the Colombian Economy* (Berkeley, Calif., 1964), table 1A.

42. George Miller, "The Evolution of the Hookworm Campaign in Colombia," 2 June 1928, and Dr. B. Wilson IHB to Rd. Russell, IHB, folder 70, box 7, series 311, RG 1.1, Rockefeller Foundation, RA.

43. Eder letter, 21 Nov. 1928; Frederick Strauss of J. W. Seligman & Company, to George Vincent, Rockefeller Foundation, 22 Nov. 1928, folder 70, box 7; see also Eder letter to Vincent, 24 Nov. 1930, and F. Russell reply, 28 Nov. 1930, folder 71, box 7; George Bevier to Howard, 5 Aug. 1930, folder 71, box 7; Bevier to Howard, 26 Jan. 1931, folder 311 H 1931, box 71, series 311 Colombia, RG 1.1, RA.

44. Bevier to H. Howard, 11 July 1930, folder 71, box 71; Bevier to Howard, 12 Jan. 1932, folder 73, box 7, series 311 Colombia, RG 1.1, RA.

45. Folder 85, National Institute of Hygiene, box 9, series 311 Colombia, RG 1.1, RA.

46. Dr. Alan Gregg, "Medical Education in Colombia," 1923, folder 17, series 311, RG 1.1, RA.

47. Folders 74 and 80 contain extensive correspondence and copies of malaria reports on this period, box 7, series 311 Colombia, RG 1.1, RA.

48. Hull letter of 12 Sept. 1938, folder 74, box 7, series 311, RG 1.1, RA.

49. See folders 91, 96, and 98, boxes 10 and 11, series 311 Colombia, RG 1.1, RA.

5. Depression and Reform

1. Jesús María Henao and Gerardo Arrubla, *A History of Colombia*, translated by J. Fred Rippy (Chapel Hill, 1938), 540–48; *El Tiempo*, 30 Jan. 1930; *New York Times*, 27 Jan. 1930, 7:4; 23 Feb. 1930, 10:1; M. Monsalve Martínez, *Colombia: Posesiones presidenciales, 1810–1954* (Bogotá, 1954).

2. Joan Hoff Wilson, *Herbert Hoover, Forgotten Progressive* (Boston 1975); Herbert Hoover, *The Cabinet and the Presidency 1920–1933* vol. 2 of *The Memoirs of Herbert Hoover,* (New York, 1952), 333; Herbert Hoover, *The State Papers and Other Public Writings of Herbert Hoover,* edited by William A. Myers (New York, 1934), 1:27–31.

3. Colombia, Departamento Administrativo Nacional de Estadística, *Anuario de comercio Exterior,* 1938, 3.

4. Luis Ospina Vásquez, *Industria y Protección en Colombia, 1810–1930* (Medellín, 1955), 458–59; Caffery to SS, 29 Aug. 1930, RG 59 621.003/92 and /95; U.S. Department of Commerce, *Commerce Reports,* 26 Jan. 1931, 250; Caffery to SS, 25 Feb. 1931, RG 59 821.5123/33.

5. NFTC Report, RG 59 611.2131/23. Colombia, *Diario Oficial,* 24 Sept. 1931; Pan American Union, *Bulletin,* 66 (1932), 732; U.S. *Commerce Reports,* 12 Oct. 1931, 112. Caffery to SS, 15 Dec. 1931, RG 59 621.003/176.

6. On coffee statistics, see William McGreevey, *Statistical Series on the Colombian Economy* (Berkeley, Calif., 1964); *New York Times,* 4 June 1930, 11; Caffery to SS, 30 Mar. 1933, RG 59 611.213/13; Dawson to SS, 22 May 1933, RG 59, 611.213/15. Dawson served as chargé after Caffery's departure from Bogotá on 20 May 1933.

7. Treaty negotiations are more fully discussed in Randall, *Modernization,* 28–34.

8. Seventh International Conference of American States, *Minutes and Antecedents, Ninth Committee* (Montevideo 1933), 91–92, 101–3.

9. Memo of 2 Feb. 1932, RG 151:640 Colombia.

10. *New York Times,* 17 July 1929, 26.

11. Howard Jefferson, former Federal Reserve Bank of New York official, to Kemmerer, 29 Mar. 1930, Kemmerer Papers, Letter Files: Colombia.

12. Kemmerer Diary, entries for 13 and 19 Sept., 16 Oct. 1930; Kemmerer address, "Currency Stabilization in Latin America," Fourth Pan American Commercial Conference, *Proceedings* (Washington, D.C., 1931), 1:24–30; RG 59 821.51A Kemmerer Commission.

13. Caffery to SS, 17 Mar. 1931, RG 59 821.51/872.

14. Caffery memos, RG 59 821.51/933; /980; /998. Caffery to SS, 10 Sept. 1931 and attached note to Matthews, 16 Sept. 1931, RG 59 821.516/143; /144; Stimson to Caffery, 2 Oct. 1931, RG 59 821.51/1100A; Caffery to SS, 4 Oct. 1931, ibid., /1101; Stimson to Caffery, 6 Oct. 1931, ibid.

15. U.S. Senate, Finance Committee, *Hearings,* part 3, 1700–2000; Department

of State, *Review of Questions*, vol. 2. Stimson Diary, entry for 12 Jan. 1932, vol. 20.

16. For Colombian press coverage of the financial developments, see *El Colombiano* and *El Tiempo*, 5–15 April 1932; Guillermo Suro, "Financial Measures Taken in Colombia to Meet the Economic Crisis," Pan American Union *Bulletin*, 66 (1932), 819; Colombia, *Diario Oficial* 23 Apr. 1932, 211. Reports of Commercial Attachés, R. Macgowan to Secretary of Commerce, 30 July 1932, RG 151. Caffery to SS, 15 Sept. 1932, RG 59 821.516/350; Acting SS to Chargé A. Dawson, 12 June 1933, RG 59 821.51/1658A; *New York Times*, 13 Nov. 1933, 10.

17. Samuel F. Bemis, *The Latin American Policy of the United States* (New York, 1943), 268–71. Bryce Wood, *The United States and Latin American Wars* (New York and London, 1966), 169–244.

18. Information relating to the Colombian reaction to the Nye Committee enquiry is drawn from the records of the Colombian Legation in Washington; see specifically Alberto Pumarejo, Minister of War, to MRE, 17 Aug. 1934; A. Gonzalez Fernandez to MRE, 3 Aug. and 18 Sept. 1934, AMRE.

19. H. Freeman Matthews to White, 16 May 1930, RG 59 821.6363 Barco/277; /278. Matthews to White, 3 June 1930, RG 59 821.6363 Barco/279.

20. White to Rublee, 23 May 1930, RG 59 821.6363/848A; White to Caffery, 1 Aug. 1930, White Papers: Correspondence File; Rublee memoir, Columbia University Oral History Project.

21. Caffery to SS, 10 Sept. 1930, RG 59 821.6363 Barco/398; 17 Sept. 1930, ibid., /399; 14 Oct. 1930, ibid., /404; 13 Oct. 1930, RG 59 821.6363/916.

22. 31 Dec. 1930, FO 371 A/981/65/11.

23. *FRUS*, 1931, 2:19–23.

24. *FRUS*, 1931, 2:25. See various Caffery despatches: RG 59 821.6363 Barco/ 480; /489; /490; /502; /503; /605; /608. For the legislation see Colombia, *Anales de la camara de Representantes*, 4 July 1931, no. 311, 2435 for law 80 of 1931. Colombia, Ministerio de Industrias y Trabajo, *Contrato Chaux-Folsom y documentos relacionados con esta negociación* (Bogotá, 1931).

25. Eduardo Zuleta Angel, *El Presidente López* (Medellín, 1966).

26. Zuleta Angel, *Presidente López; El Tiempo*, 31 May 1928; Seventh International Conference of American States, *Minutes and Antecedents, Ninth Committee* (Montevideo, 1933), 90–103; Sheldon Whitehouse to SS, 19 June 1934, RG 50 821.51/832. James Dunn to Marvin McIntyre, 15 June 1934, Roosevelt Papers, PPF 313 Colombia.

27. For the Roosevelt visit see Irwin Gellman, *Good Neighbor Diplomacy* (Baltimore, 1979), 38.

28. For López's ideas see Miguel Urrutia Montoya, *The Development of the Colombian Labor Movement* (New Haven and London, 1969), and Vernon L. Flaherty, *Dance of the Millions: Military Rule and the Social Revolution in Colombia* (Pittsburgh, 1957).

29. *Annual Report of the British Legation for 1936*, 18 Jan. 1937, FO 371; see also Sheldon Whitehouse to SS, 17 May 1934, RG 821.6363 Tropical Oil/116.

30. *New York Times*, 23 June 1934, 20; RG 59 821.6363 Tropical Oil/119.

31. U.S. Chargé, Bogotá, to SS, 10 Dec. 1934, RG 59 821.6363 Tropical Oil/120; Chargé to SS, 8 Apr. 1935, RG 59 821.6363 Tropical Oil/121; for the dispute over taxes, see RG 59 821.51/1862.

32. U.S. Minister, William Dawson, to SS, 21 Nov. 1935, RG 59 821.6363 Tropical Oil/127. On the oil workers, see Urrutia, *Colombian Labor*; Almario, *Trabajadores petroleros* (Bogotá, 1984).

33. Colombia, *Anales de la Cámara de Representantes*, no. 148, 24 Jan. 1936; *El Tiempo*, 17, 19, 29 Jan. 1936; Dawson to SS, 26 Jan. 1936, RG 59 821.6363 AN 2/91; British Minister, M. Paske-Smith to FO, 5 Dec. 1935, 17 Aug. 1936, FO 371 A/7014/1081/11, and A/10160/1081/11.

34. M. Paske-Smith to Foreign Office, 9 Dec. 1935, FO 371 A/10160/1081/11. This summary of the law is based on a memo by W. W. Waring of Tropical Oil, February 1937, Petroleum Legislation Binder, records of ESSO Inter-America; undated memo in same binder by Eduardo Esguerra Seranno; interview by the author with L. P. Maier (in 1936 vice-president of Andean National Corporation), Coral Gables, 23 March 1971; Colombia, *Leyes de 1936* (Bogotá, 1950), 389–99. Austin Foster of Socony to Cordell Hull, 4 Jan. 1938, RG 59 821.6363 Barco/670.

35. Félix Mendoza and Benjamín Alvarado, *La indústria del petroleo en Colombia* (Bogotá, 1939), 206–7.

36. See Almario, *Trabajadores petroleros*; data on employment is from Colombia, DANE, *Anuario* (1938), 44; Henrietta Larson, *New Horizons, 1927–50* (Cambridge, Mass., 1971), 819, 375.

37. Almario, *Trabajadores petroleros*, 104–7.

38. *El Tiempo*, 14 June 1938.

39. José Garcés Navas, "La administración López y la indústria bananera del Magdalena," *Acción Liberal* (August 1938); S. W. Washington to SS, 17 Dec. 1934, RG 59 821.5045/149; 3 Jan. 1935, RG 59 821.6156/204.

40. Colombia, *Anales de la Camara de Representantes,* 21 Dec. 1934; Ministro de Industrias, *Memoria,* 1934, 1:141–44.
41. LeGrand, "Colombian Transformations," 190–92.
42. Dawson to SS, 20 Oct. 1936, RG 59 821.504/82, /84; SS to American Minister, 20 Apr. 1937, RG 59 821.6156/218; Duggan to G. H. Butler (division of American republics), 27 Aug. 1937, RG 59 821.6156/231.
43. Colombia, *Anales de la Camara de Representantes,* 21 Nov. 1936; Dawson to SS, 20 Oct. 1936, RG 59 821.504/82; /84; Ministro de Industrias, *Memoria,* 1938, 1:147; RG 59 821.6156/208; /210; /211. For more general analysis of the constitutional and agricultural reforms of the López years, see: Albert Hirschmann, *Journeys Towards Progress* (New York, 1963), 93–158.
44. Spruille Braden, U.S. ambassador, to SS, 21 and 29 Sept. 1939, RG 59 821.6156/267, /268.
45. RG 59 321.1121 Bennett, George/37; U.S. Chargé Winthrop Greene to SS, 1 Feb. 1938, RG 59 821.6156/256; Herbert Feis memorandum of a conversation with United Fruit chairman, 5 May 1938, RG 59 810.712/2.
46. William Phillips to S. Walter Washington, 24 Aug. 1934, RG 59 611.2131/205B.
47. There is a full discussion of the negotiations and consequences of the agreement in Randall, *Modernization.*
48. Hull to Roosevelt, 28 Sept. 1938, Roosevelt Papers, PPF. 313 Colombia. On the Santos transition see David Bushnell's, *Eduardo Santos and the Good Neighbor, 1938–42* (Gainesville, Fla., 1967), and Spruille Braden's memoir, *Diplomats and Demagogues* (New Rochelle, N.Y., 1971).

6. War, Diplomacy, and Hemispheric Integration

1. By far the most insightful treatment of this period is David Bushnell, *Eduardo Santos and the Good Neighbor 1938–42* (Gainesville, Fla., 1967).
2. *El Siglo,* 6 Dec. 1939.
3. Bushnell, *Santos,* 34–35.
4. Braden to SS, 15 Sept. 1940, *FRUS* 5 (1940), 81.
5. Bushnell, *Santos,* 10–13 and passim, provides the definitive treatment of Colombian political thought during the war. Frederick Pike and Thomas Stritch, eds., *The New Corporatism: Social-Political Structures in the Iberian World* (Notre Dame, 1974).

6. Cable of 7 Dec. 1941; Colombian Ambassador to MRE, 19 Dec. 1941, *Legación de Colombia en los Estados Unidos*, binders for 1941, Archivo del Ministerio de Relaciones Exteriores (AMRE), Bogotá.

7. Colombian Ambassador to Hull, 22 Dec. 1941, *Legación de Colombia en Los Estados Unidos*, binder for 1941, AMRE.

8. Colombian measures in support of the American war effort are outlined in Ambassador Braden to Welles, 27 Jan. 1942, DS 821.00/1394, RG 59; Colombia, Ministro de Relaciones Exteriores, *Memoria* (1942); Colombia, *Decretos de caracter extraordinario* . . . (Bogotá, 1942), 17, 42–48, 64–69.

9. *New York Times*, 3 Jan. 1941, 6. The *New York Times* carried frequent reports in 1941 of alleged Nazi activities in Colombia and of Colombian authorities' efforts to contain them. See for instance 16 Aug. 1941, 6; 20 Aug. 1941, 10; 30 Aug. 1941, 4; 5 Aug. 1941, 9.

10. For the Lend-Lease agreement see DS 821.24/219 B, RG 59, and U.S. Department of State, *FRUS* 6 (1942), 189–92. Colombia requested little actual assistance under the Lend-Lease agreement before the end of the war.

11. On the blacklists and the freezing of Axis assets, see Colombia, Ministro de Relaciones Exteriores, *Memoria*, (1942), xvii–xix; and *Decretos de caracter extraordinario* . . . (1942), 376–78. There is a clear statement of U.S. policy on the Proclaimed List in SS to Lane, 31 Mar. 1943, DS 740.00112A European War 1939/23233, RG 59. For controls imposed on Axis nationals, see as well the *New York Times*, 25 Jan. 1942, 16; 10 Mar. 1942, 6; 6 Apr. 1942, 4. Several hundred Axis nationals were sent to the U.S. for internment during the war; from June 1942 Axis subjects were barred from residence in coastal regions as well as Magdalena River ports. See *New York Times*, 27 June 1942, 4. On the Antioquia bank see *FRUS* 6 (1943), 56.

12. Braden to Secretary of State, 2 Dec. 1941, DS 821.20/186.

13. U.S. Ambassador Arthur Bliss Lane to Secretary of State, 19 Aug. 1942, DS 821.20/212. For an expression of concern about German submarine activity along the Guajira coast of Colombia see U.S. military attaché to Secretary of State, 24 Aug. 1942, DS 821.20/220. For a general statement on Colombian cooperation see B.C. Davis memo, Office of American Republic Affairs, 7 Feb. 1945, box 34, RG 59.

14. Bushnell, *Santos*, 113–14; *El Siglo*, 28–29 Dec. 1941, 23–24, 27 Jan. 1942. *El Colombiano*, 17–18 Dec. 1941. On the Condor Legion see Department of State memorandum by B. Brindage, 15 Nov. 1945, box 34, Records of the Office of American Republic Affairs, RG 59. The Spanish legation in Bogotá allegedly made a small contribution to the organization.

There were reportedly other falangist cells, besides that in Cali, in Bogotá, Medellín, Buga, and Bucaramanga. In Bogotá there was a youth and a women's wing of the organization. On attitudes toward *El Siglo* see J. H. Wright (American Republic Affairs) memo to Alger Hiss, Laurence Duggan, and the Bogotá embassy, 19 Aug. 1942, Office of American Republic Affairs, Box 34, RG 59.

15. See U.S. Ambassador Arthur Bliss Lane to SS, 2 May 1942, DS 821.00/ 1411, RG 59; *El Liberal*, 27–28 Apr. 1942; *El Siglo*, 28 Apr. 1942; Bushnell, *Santos*, 115–16.

16. *New York Times*, 6 July, 1942, 5; 7 July 1942, 5, 18; 8 July, 1942, 12; 12 July 1942, 14. Bonsal to Welles, 15 July 1942, box 33, lot file 55D216, RG 59. For the position of the Colombian government at the time of the Chapultepec meeting of American states, see John Wiley, U.S. Ambassador, to SS, 20 Jan. 1945, DS 710. Conference W and PW/ 1-2045, RG 59.

17. For previsit preparations for U.S. discussions with Alfonso López see Lot File 55 D 216, box 23, Philip Bonsal memo for Welles, 15 July 1942; on the United Fruit withdrawal from Magdalena see State Department memorandum, 21 Sept. 1942, Records of the Office of American Republic Affairs, box 34, RG 59. On military relations see Lane to Welles, 22 July 1942, lot file 55 D 216, box 33, RG 59.

18. *New York Times*, 21 July 1942, 5. For López's message to Roosevelt, see DS *Bulletin* 10 (June 1944), 416.

19. The Colombian Senate approved the administration initiative in late November 1943; see the *New York Times*, 28 Nov. 1943, 1; 29 Nov. 1943, 18 (editorial).

20. *New York Times*, 1 Jan. 1944, 4; 14 Dec. 1944, 7.

21. Lane to SS, 3 Mar. 1943, DS 840.51 Frozen Assets / 9798, RG 59. W. E. Dunn, counsellor of Bogotá embassy, to SS, 22 Jan. 1945, DS 740.21112A / 1-2245, RG 59.

22. *New York Times*, 4 Dec. 1942, 9. For the perspective of the labor federation, see the *New York Times*, 24 Aug. 1942, 4.

23. Winthrop S. Greene to SS, 26 April 1938, DS 810.79611 Pan American Airways/1622. Braden to SS, 31 Dec. 1939, DS 821.796 Avianca /20. There are interesting and important accounts of these developments in Braden, *Diplomats and Demagogues* (1971), 196–261. Herbert Boy, *Una historia con alas* (2nd ed., Bogotá, 1963), 239–42; Bushnell, *Santos*, 18–20; Randall. *Modernization*, 146–61.

24. SS to Braden, 2 February 1940, *FRUS* 5 (1940), 730–33; *FRUS* 5 (1940),

729–30; *El Tiempo*, 9 June 1940; Marshall to D. L. Stone, Canal Zone, 16 September 1939, File 2538-31/43, RG 165.

25. Braden to SS, 30 Mar. 1939, DS 821,796 Sca 2/408, RG 59. For a list of twenty-five SCADTA pilots and their political affiliation and linkages with the Axis, see DS 821.796/9-1846. Some of these men were arrested and interned or deported during the course of the war.

26. Braden to SS, 20 Mar. 1940, DS 821.00N/55, RG 59; SS to Braden, 6 Feb. 1940; Braden to SS, 14 Feb. 1940 and 22 Feb. 1940, *FRUS* 5 (1940), 723–26; 728–29; 730–33.

27. Bushnell, *Santos*, 23.

28. Wiley to President Ospina, 19 Sept. 1946, DS 821.796/9-1846; Wiley to SS, 26 Sept. 1946, DS 821.796/9-2846, RG 59. On Hoffman see DS 821.796/5-2147, RG 59.

29. Acting SS to Wiley, 23 Oct. 1946, DS 821.796/9-1846, RG 59.

30. Waynich to Miller, 5 Nov. 1952, box 4, lot file 53D26 (Records of the Office Files of the Assistant Secretary of State for Latin American Affairs), RG 59.

31. Colombia, *Memoria de Relaciones Exteriores* (1942, 1943, 1945).

32. Colombian Ambassador to Colombian Minister of Finance and Public Credit, 12 Dec. 1941; Ambassador to Minister of Foreign Relations, 29 Dec. 1941, 1941 binders, *Legación de Colombia en Los Estados Unidos*, AMRE.

33. Department of State Research and Analysis Branch, Report 2099, "U.S. Investment in Colombia, 1943," RG 59.

34. B. C. Davis, Office of American Republic Affairs, 1918–1947, memorandum of 7 Feb. 1945, box 34, RG 59.

35. For a more thorough treatment of this subject see S. J. Randall, "Colombia, The United States and Raw Materials Control During World War II," paper presented to the International Congress of Americanists, Amsterdam, July 1988. On the raw materials issue, see War Production Board, Army and Navy Munitions Board, Part I, "Industrial Mobilization Plan, 1939," File 865, IX, RG 179 (records of the War Production Board). Board of Economic Warfare, Enemy Branch, "Materials Inventory of the European Axis: Platinum Group Metals," 5 Dec. 1942, U.S. Commercial Company, box 154, RG 253.

36. C. B. Spaeth (assistant coordinator, Council of National Defense) memo for W. Averell Harriman, 6 Feb. 1941, file 121, Preclusive Buying, RG 179. The South American Gold and Platinum Company was controlled by the Lewisohn interests of New York.

37. See American Hemisphere Exports Office, "Contributions of the Other American Republics to the War Effort," 31 Dec. 1942, War Production Board, File 870, Foreign War Economy, RG 179.

38. U.S. Ambassador, Arthur Bliss Lane, to Acting Colombian Foreign Minister, 29 Mar. 1943, Preclusive Operations File, U.S. Commercial Company, box 153, RG 234.

39. U.S. Legal Attaché, Bogotá, to Department of State, 1943 (no date), Platinum-Colombia File, U.S. Commercial Company, box 154, RG 253. U.S. Commercial Company, Foreign Minerals Survey, "Economic Program With Reference to Colombia," 1 Aug. 1944, U.S. Commercial Company, box 137, RG 253.

40. Lane to SS, 27 Nov. 1943, U.S. Commercial Company, box 153, RG 234. Several sources discuss the smuggling problem; among the more useful are the following: executive director, Bureau of Supplies, memo, 27 Jan. 1944, box 153, Preclusive Operations File, U.S. Commercial Company, RG 234. David Adler, Preclusive Operations Division, report on Colombian platinum, 29 Sept. 1943, U.S. Commercial Company, box 154, RG 253. Stettinius to U.S. Embassy, 9 Nov. 1943, Colombia Folder, U.S. Commercial Company, box 154, RG 253.

41. Albert La Spina, FEA, report of February 1944, U.S. Commercial Company, box 153, RG 234. On the Rubber Reserve Company see SS to the U.S. Chargé, George Keith, 23 Mar. 1942, DS 811.20 Defense (M) Colombia / 42A.

42. FEA, Foreign Minerals Survey, "Economic Program with Reference to Colombia," 1 Aug. 1944, U.S. Commercial Company, box 137, RG 253.

43. Board of Economic Warfare, Office of Exports, Current Controls Bulletin No. 20 (30 Apr. 1942) and DS 821.24/235, RG 59.

44. U.S. commercial attaché, Bogotá, to SS, 4 May 1942, DS 821.24/227; U.S. Ambassador A.B. Lane to SS, 11 May 1942, DS 821.24/232, RG 59.

45. The best discussion of this period in the oil industry's situation is Bushnell, *Santos*, 99–102.

46. This charge was advanced by *El Siglo*, 11, 24, 26, June 1940; Ambassador Braden confirmed that there had been hostilities and casualties in the Barco concession area. See Braden to SS, 26 June 1939, DS 821.6363/ 1313, and 4 Sept. 1940, DS 821.6363/1363.

47. *New York Times*, 4 Aug. 1948; 3 Jan. 1951; 13 July 1951; Harvey O'Connor, *Empire of Oil* (New York, 1955), 245, 250.

48. For the work of the Children's Bureau see the records of the Interdepartmental Advisory Council on Technical Cooperation, 1938–53, box 43, RG 353.

49. Undated memorandum by the Interdepartmental Advisory Council on Technical Cooperation, box 49, RG 353, NA.

50. Undated document, Informational and Educational Activities in the American Republics, HSTL. For a general overview of the situation in 1947, see Information and Cultural Program Folder, Records of the deputy assistant secretary of state for Inter-American Affairs, 1945–56, box 3, lot file 57 D 598, RG 59, NA.

51. DS, *Bulletin* 10 (May 1944), 416.

7. Cold War and Containment

1. Lleras Camargo to Eisenhower, 24 Nov. 1958, Colombia folder 3, box 7, Whitman File, International Series, EPP.

2. Forrestal to Marshall, 1 Mar. 1948, DS 710.J/3-148; Forrestal to Marshall, 16 Mar. 1948, DS 710.J/3-1648; Arthur Hill, National Security Resources Board to Marshall, 4 Mar. 1948, DS 710.J/3-448, RG 59, NA.

3. Report of the NFTC, 10 Mar. 1948, and covering letter from Council Chairman, Robert Loree, 10 Mar. 1948, DS 710.J /3-1048. Rubin Memorandum, 3 Mar. 1948, DS 710.J /3-348; Laylin memorandum, 11 Mar. 1948 and 7 Apr. 1948, DS 710.J /3-1148, RG 59.

4. Organization of American States, *Novena Conferencia* (Washington, D.C., 1950), 1:191–97.

5. On the *Bogotazo* and Gaitán, see John D. Martz, *Colombia* (Chapel Hill, N.C., 1962); J. L. Flaherty, *Dance of the Millions* (Pittsburgh, 1957). The best assessment of the violence that followed in the course of the decade is Gonzalo Sánchez, Ricardo Peñaranda, comps., *Pasado y Presente de la Violencia en Colombia* (Bogotá, 1986). On Gaitán, see Herbert Braun, *The Assassination of Gaitán: Public Life and Urban Violence in Colombia* (Madison, Wis., 1985), and Richard Sharpless, *Gaitán of Colombia: A Political Biography* (Pittsburgh, 1978). For a U.S. retrospective view of the riots see the memorandum by assistant secretary of state for Inter-American Affairs, Roy Rubottom, 22 May 1958, box 5, lot file 60 D 553, RG 59.

6. Rubottom memo for SS, 22 May 1958, box 5, lot file 60 D 553 (Records of the Assistant Secretaries of State for Inter-American Affairs), RG 59. For

Truman's recollection, see p. 10, Latin America, Foreign Policy, Manuscript version of HSTL Memoirs, HSTL. At his press conference of 15 Apr. 1948, Truman indicated that U.S. officials had anticipated demonstrations but they had not expected a political assassination that would touch off massive rioting. *Public Papers of the Presidents*, 215–16. For an internal Colombian comment on U.S. views, see the Colombian Consul in Washington to MRE, 22 Apr. 1948, Legación de Colombia en los EEUU, AMRE.

7. Colombia, Records of the Comisión Asesora, AMRE. The exchange between Piedrahita and the CIA was in May 1950.

8. DS news summary prepared for the SS, 20 Apr. 1948, DS 710.J / 4-2048, RG 59.

9. Rubottom Memo, 22 May 1958, box 5, lot file 60 D 553, RG 59, NA.

10. Rubottom to SS, 22 May 1958, box 5, lot file 60 D 553, RG 59. Communists certainly were involved in taking over several radio stations once the rioting had begun and urging attacks on the political and business establishment. A prominent example was Diego Montaña Cuellar, legal counsel to a number of oil unions, over *Radiodifusora Nacional*. William Sanders, Oral History Transcript, HSTL. Sanders was a co-ordinator of the Conference.

11. Memorandum of 22 Apr. 1944, box 34, lot file 55 D 216, Records of the Office of American Republic Affairs, RG 59.

12. U.S. Department of Commerce, Bureau of Foreign and Domestic Commerce, "Economic Review of Colombia, 1949" (June 1950).

13. U.S. Council on Foreign Economic Policy, "Investments in Less Developed Countries," 12 Dec. 1955, Report Series, box 3, EPP. April 1953 Report on U.S. Interests in Latin America, U.S. Department of Commerce, Office of Business Economics, box 50, RG 43, NA. Samuel Pinzer and Frederick Cutler, "The Role of U.S. Investments in the Latin American Economy," *Survey of Current Business* (January 1957): 2–12.

14. Briefing papers for Dulles, July 1956, box 5, lot file 53D26, RG 59, NA.

15. Briefing Papers for John Foster Dulles trip to Bogotá, 1956, box 5, lot file 53D26, RG 59. The quotation on the implications of Colombian political instability is from Office of Intelligence Research, DS, Report 5120, 19 Sept. 1950, RG 59.

16. "Conditions and Trends in Latin America Affecting U.S. Security," National Intelligence Estimates, 12 Dec. 1952, CIA Reports, Intelligence File, PSF, HSTL.

17. Memorandum of 4 Nov. 1950, box 4, Briefing papers for SS, lot file 53 D

26, RG 59. The mutual security program objectives are from Mutual Security Program, Fiscal Year 1958 (1), confidential files, subject series, box 42, White House Central Files, EPP.

18. DS, Office of Intelligence Research, Report 5120, 19 Sept. 1950, RG 59. Conferencia dictada por Eduardo Zuleta Angel, 12 Sept. 1950. Colombian ambassador to Panama to MRE, 6 Nov. 1950, 1950 documents of the Comisión Asesora, AMRE.

19. On Korea and Colombia, see DS memo of meeting of the Colombian ambassador with department officials, 14 Dec. 1950, box 4, lot file 53 D 26, RG 59, and a press release announcing the commitment of Colombian troops, same source. Urdaneta meeting with DS officials, Miller memorandum, 5 Feb. 1951, box 4, lot file 53 D 26; Miller memorandum, 15 Dec. 1952 on Colombia and Korea, box 4, lot file 53 D 26, RG 59.

20. For NSC 56/2 see *FRUS* (1950), 1:626–37.

21. Copy of the Military Plan for Colombia, 43 Feb. 1952, DS 721.5-MSP /2-652, RG 59.

22. Beaulac to SS, 19 June 1951, DS 721.5-MAP /6-1951, RG 59.

23. DS memo for Edward Miller, 7 Apr. 1952, DS 721.5-MSP /4-752; Acheson to Bogotá Embassy, 2 Apr. 1952, DS 721.5-MSP /3-2852, RG 59.

24. Memo of meeting, 19 June 1952, box 4, lot file 53 D 26, RG 59.

25. Mann memo, 23 June 1952, box 1, lot file 57 D 598, Records of the Deputy ASS for Inter-American Affairs, 1945–56, RG 59. The Colombian battalion and one frigate cost the United States $7.6 million to maintain and supply from June 1951 to February 1953. Waynich memo, 19 June 1952, box 1, lot file 53 D 26. Colombian ambassador to SS, 4 Aug. 1952, DS 721.5-MSP/ 8-52; DS memo, October 1953, DS 721.5-MSP/10-953. Waynich memorandum for SS, 24 Sept. 1952, DS 721.5 MSP/9-2452.

26. Waynich to SS, 8 July 1953, DS 721.5-MSP/7-853, RG 59. DS to Bogotá embassy, 7 Sept. 1955, DS 721.5-MSP/6-1755, RG 59.

27. Gerberich memo of conversation with Chaves, 8 Oct. 1953, DS 721.52/ 10-853, RG 59.

28. Box 7, lot file 60 D 553, RG 59, NA.

29. Briefing memo for ASS, Roy Rubottom, 24 Feb. 1958, Colombia folder, lot file 60 D 553, RG 59; Cabot to SS, 26 Aug. 1958, DS 721.5-MSP/ 8-2658; Cabot to SS, 3 Sept. 1958, DS 721.5-MSP/9-358, RG 59. The often extremely violent persecution of Protestants and of American Protestant missionaries in Colombia was an area of considerable importance in Colombian-U.S. relations during the 1950s. It had long predated the cold

war issues, however, and hence is not treated in this paper, although one could draw a tangential connection between extreme Roman Catholic conservatism, especially in the smaller towns, and strong anticommunism.

30. Cabot to SS Herter, 25 Apr. 1958 and Herter to Cabot, 5 May 1958, DS 721.5 MSP /4-2558; Cabot to Herter, 23 Apr. 1959, DS 721.5- MSP /4-2359, RG 59. By 1959, 18 to 20 percent of the Colombian budget was allocated to the armed forces; of that amount, 35 percent was designated for the Military Assistance Program forces; 65 percent was for traditional forces.

31. Bogotá Embassy to DS, 7 July 1948, DS 821.6363/7-748, RG 59.

32. Bogotá Embassy to DS, 3 Aug. 1948, DS 821.6363/8-348; SS to Bogotá Embassy, 11 Feb. 1950; Lleras to John Fishburn, DS, 16 Feb. 1950, DS 821.062/2-1150, RG 59. Beaulac, Bogotá, to SS, 26 Apr. 1950, DS 821.062/4-2650, RG 59; *El Tiempo*, 25 Apr. 1950. The ICFTU was established in London in 1949.

33. Beaulac to Miller, ASS, 14 Nov. 1950, box 4, lot file 53D26, RG 59. The DS felt that the communists were losing influence in the Colombian labor movement at this stage. See briefing report for the SS, 4 Jan. 1950, box 4, lot file 53D26, RG 59.

34. U.S. Labor Attaché, Bogotá, to DS, 23 Oct. 1952, DS 821.062/10-2352; Embassy to DS, 3 Sept. 1952, DS 721.001/9-352; Ambassador to SS, 17 Oct. 1952, DS 721.00 (w)/10-1752; 6 Sept. 1952, DS 721.00 (w)/9-552; U.S. Labor Attaché, Bogotá, to DS, 27 Mar. 1953, DS 721.001/3-2753; DS 721.00 (w)/5-2253, RG 59. In the 1951 congressional elections the Communist party polled approximately 4,400 votes, most of them being cast in the Viotá region. In 1945 the party had attracted over 26,000 votes. DS memo, 19 June 1953, box 2, lot file 57D634, RG 59.

35. R. Lankenau, Labor Attaché, to DS, 23 Oct. 1952, DS 821.062/10-2352; labor attaché to DS, 15 Jan. 1953, DS 821.06/1-1553; Embassy to SS, 2 Apr. 1952, DS 821.062/4-852. U.S. Consul, Barranquilla, to DS, 23 Apr. 1952, DS 721.001/4-2352, RG 59.

36. U.S. Consul in Barranquilla to DS, 12 Nov. 1953, DS 821.06/11-1253; also 821.06/5-2654, RG 59. In April and May 1953 the Archbishops of Colombia issued a statement on the role of the Church in organized labor in which they claimed that "it is the mission of the Church to say what is legitimate and what is not in the demands of labor and what means it is legitimate to employ to make them effective." Significantly, the Church hierarchy did not support the Peronist CNT.

37. *El Tiempo*, 2 July 1954; 3 July 1954; *El Espectador*, 2 July 1954.

38. NSC meeting, 10 May 1957, Whitman File, NSC Series, box 8, EPP. Eisenhower to Major General Gabriel Paris Gordillo, 5 May 1958, International Series, Office of the Staff Secretary, box 3, White House Office Files, EPP.
39. Embassy to DS, 13 Dec. 1957, DS 821.062/12-1357; 821.062/11-2657; Embassy to DS 13 Nov. 1857, DS 721.001/11-1357; DS 821.062/2-2058; 821.062/4-2459. For the situation in the oil industry, see Embassy to DS, 1 Oct. 1958, 24 Oct. 1958, DS 721.00 (w)/10-158. Labor Attaché to DS, 26 Nov. 1958, DS 821.062.002/11-2658.
40. Embassy to DS, 13 Dec. 1957, DS 821.062/12-1357; 821.062/2-2558; Embassy to DS, 28 May 1958, DS 821.062/5-2858; 3 Oct. 1958, 821.062/10-358. George Meany to Rubottom, 5 May 1958, box 7, lot file 60 D 553; B. Stephansky memo on Latin American Labor situation, 10 Oct. 1958, same file. On the CTC elections in late 1958 see DS 721.00 (w)/12-1958. On the reaction to the Cuban Revolution see the CTC publication, *Revista*, January 1959, and Embassy to DS, 9 Mar. 1959, DS 821.062/3-959.
41. On Lleras see the briefing papers prepared for Eisenhower, Colombia folder, Whitman File, International Series, box 7, EPP.
42. Ibid.
43. Final Act of the Fifth Meeting of Consultation of Ministers of Foreign Affairs of American States, Santiago, Chile, 12–18 Aug. 1959, Herter Folder, Dulles-Herter Series, Whitman File, box 9, EPP.
44. Lleras Camargo to Eisenhower, 28 May 1960; Eisenhower to Lleras, 19 May 1960; Herter to Eisenhower, 31 Mar. 1960; International Series, box 7, Whitman File, EPP. For Lleras's views on China, see U.S. Ambassador to Colombia memo, 26 May 1960, Colombia Folder, International Series, box 3, Office of the Staff Secretary, White House Office Files, EPP.

8. Decades of Optimism and Crisis

1. The most thoughtful analysis of the main trends in Colombian external relations is Rodrigo Pardo and Juan G. Toklatlian, *Politica exterior colombiana: De la subordinación a la autonomía?* (Bogotá, 1988).
2. OAS summit meeting, April 1967, National Security File, National Security Council History, Chronology, LBJ Papers.
3. On coffee exports and the international agreement, see Colombia, Ministro de Relaciones Exteriores, *Memoria* (1963), 457–59. On the sugar issue

see Colombian ambassador to Misael Pastrana Borrero, Minister of Development, 28 July 1960, AMRE.

4. DS, *Bulletin* 43 (1960), 540; *New York Times*, 3 Sept. 1960, 4; 6 Sept. 1960, 1. On Lleras Camargo see *El Pensamiento de Alberto Lleras Camargo* (Bogotá, 1960). On coffee see a document prepared in the Western Hemisphere Department of the IMF, 16 May 1960, attached to Sanz to MRE, 23 May 1969, AMRE.

5. For the International Coffee Agreement, see Colombia, Ministro de Relaciones Exteriores, *Memoria* (1963), 418–21.

6. *New York Times*, 12 Sept. 1960, 1; Oct. 23, 1960, 50.

7. DS, *Bulletin* 43 (October 1960), 820; 44 (6 Feb. 1961), 201.

8. Bello to Colombian Ambassador, 14 Feb. 1961, Correspondencia Diplomatico, enero-marzo de 1961, AMRE.

9. L. Ronald Scheman, ed., *The Alliance for Progress* (New York, 1988), 8–9.

10. Murray Lawson, Administrative History of the USIA, vol. 1 (1968), box 1, USIA files, LBJ Papers.

11. Murray Lawson, Administrative History of the USIA, vol. 1 (1968), box 1, LBJ Papers. Data on foreign assistance provided courtesy of Michael Betcher, Public Affairs Officer, United States Consulate General, Vancouver, Canada.

12. Murray Lawson, Administrative History of the USIA, vol. 1 (1968), box 1, LBJ Papers.

13. On immigration see: U.S. Department of Commerce, Bureau of the Census, *County and City Data Book* (Washington 1978), 636, 720; U.S. Bureau of the Census, *Statistical Abstract of the United States, 1989*, 12; *1970*, 92; Colombia, DANE, *Encuestra de hogares* (Bogotá, 1971), table 3.

14. Jorge Eliecer Ruiz, *Cultural Policy in Colombia* (Paris, 1977).

15. Harley Oberhelman, "William Faulkner and Gabriel García Márquez," in George McMurray, ed., *Critical Essays on Gabriel García Márquez* (Boston, 1987); Florence Delay and Jacqueline Labriolle, "Márquez, est-il le Faulkner Colombien?" *Revue de Littérature Comparée* 47 (1973): 88–123; Raymond Williams, *Gabriel García Márquez* (Boston, 1984).

16. I thank Zapata Olivella for his generosity in sharing his ideas and Kurt Levy for introducing me to Zapata Olivella almost twenty-five years ago.

17. Ministro de Relaciones Exteriores, *Memoria* (1960–61), 104–8.

18. Mensaje del Presidente de la Republica al Congreso Nacional, 20 de julio de 1960 (Bogotá: Oficina de la Presidencia, 1960), 5–6. Jerome Levinson

302 Notes to Pages 232–235

and Juan de Onís, *The Alliance that Lost its Way: A Critical Report on the Alliance for Progress* (Chicago, 1970), 7.

19. Carlos Sanz de Santamaria (Colombian ambassador to U.S.) to MRE, 20 Dec. 1960, Legación de Colombia en los Estados Unidos, AMRE. Sanz was one of six Latin American ambassadors to the United States and the Latin American ambassadors to the United Nations who met on 3 Nov. 1960 with Thomas Mann for a "private, frank" discussion of the Cuban situation. Dempster McIntosh, U.S. Ambassador, to Turbay, 13 Sept. 1960, AMRE. On Punta del Este, see José Joaquín Caicedo Castillo, *Conferencia sobre la política internacional de Colombia* (Bogotá, 1963); Caicedo Castillo, *El Panamericanismo* (Buenos Aires, 1961). MRE, *Memoria 1966–67*, 27.

20. LBJ to President Guillermo Valencia, 9 Aug. 1966, Confidential File, box 7, File CO 51 Colombia; Administrative History of the Department of State, vol. 1, chapter 6, LBJ Papers. DS, *Bulletin* 44 (21 Aug. 1961), 349.

21. For Rusk's testimony to the House Foreign Affairs Committee and Stevenson's analysis see DS, *Bulletin* 44 (26 June 1961), 1005; (24 July 1961), 141.

22. Administrative History of the Department of State, vol. 1, LBJ Papers; DS, *Bulletin* 44 (25 Dec. 1961), 1069. For the investment convention see Colombia, Ministro de Relaciones Exteriores, *Memoria* (1963), 474–76. Agency for International Development and Alliance for Progress, Project and Program Data Related to Proposed Programs, FY 1965, Agency File, National Security File, LBJ Papers.

23. Director of Central Intelligence, Prospects for Colombia (July 1963), box 8-9, National Security File, National Intelligence Estimates, LBJ Papers.

24. Central Intelligence Agency, "Survey of Latin America," Latin America, vol. 1, NSF Country Files, LBJ Papers.

25. MRE, *Memoria 1965*, 293–99. Administrative History of the Department of State, vol. 1, chapter 6, "Inter-American Relations," LBJ Papers. Agency for International Development and Alliance for Progress, Project and Program Data Related to Proposed Programs, FY 1965, NSF, Agency File, LBJ Papers.

26. *El Tiempo*, 7 Nov. 1960; *El Espectador*, 5 Aug. 1961, 9 Aug. 1961; *La Republica*, 13 Jan. 1964; *Semana*, 14 Aug. 1961; *El Colombiano*, 7 Aug. 1961, 9 Aug. 1961. For an overview of the Colombian press during the cold war years, see Graeme S. Mount and Stephen J. Randall, "The Colombian Press and the Cold War, 1945–1968," *North/South: Canadian Journal of Latin American Studies* 8, no. 16 (1983): 21–42.

27. Administrative History, vol. 1, chapter 6, section F, "Inter-American Relations." LBJ Papers.

28. As quoted in the Senate Foreign Relations Committee review of the alliance programs.

29. Levinson and Onís, *Alliance*, 208–9; U.S. Senate, Committee on Foreign Relations, *Survey of the Alliance for Progress in Colombia: A Case History of USAID*, prepared at the request of the Subcommittee on American Republic Affairs (Washington, D.C., 1969), 45. Pardo and Toklatlian, *Politica exterior*, 103. MRE, *Memoria, 1967–68*, 281–84, 299–302.

30. *El Siglo*, 25 Nov. 1963, 23 June 1968; *Tercer Mundo*, January–March 1967, February–April 1968.

31. White House Central File, File CO 51 Colombia, 1963–1966, box 23, LBJ Papers; Dean Rusk Oral History, LBJ Presidential Library.

32. Oliver to House of Representatives Committee on Foreign Affairs, 21 Mar. 1966.

33. Letter of 9 Aug. 1966, Confidential File, box 7, File CO 51 Colombia, LBJ Papers.

34. Administrative History, vol. 1, chapter 6, "Inter-American Relations," LBJ Papers.

35. "The Failure of the Alliance for Progress in Colombia," *Inter-American Economic Affairs* 23 (Summer 1969): 87–86.

36. U.S. Department of Commerce, Office of Business Economics, *U.S. Investments in Foreign Countries* (Washington, D.C., 1960), 89, 95, 119–22.

37. United Nations, *Foreign Direct Investment in Latin America: Trends, Prospects and Policy Issues* (New York, 1986), 1, 11. U.S. Department of Commerce, *U.S. Direct Investment Abroad:* Operations of U.S. Parent Companies and Their Foreign Affiliates (Washington, D.C., 1986), 91; United Nations, ECLA, *Economic Survey of Latin America, 1980* (Santiago, 1980), 142. U.S. Bureau of the Census, *Statistical Abstract of the United States*, various years.

38. Embassy of Canada, "Report on the Colombian Oil and Gas Industry" (Bogotá, 1990).

39. ECLA, *Economic Survey of Latin America* (Santiago, 1980), 140.

40. MRE, *Memoria 1966–67*, 24; Mensaje del Senor Presidente del la Republica de Colombia, Doctor Carlos Lleras Restrepo, al Congreso Nacional, 20 de Julio de 1967, AMRE. DS, *Bulletin* 55 (1966), 97–98.

41. MRE, *Memoria, 1969–70*, 1:5–21; 2:299. *El Tiempo*, 11 June 1969.

42. *El Tiempo*, 1, 3, 5, 7 Nov. 1968.

43. *El Tiempo*, 3, 11, 14 June 1969; *El Siglo*, 27 May 1969, "The Marxist Dialect and Mr. Rockefeller."

44. MRE, *Memoria, 1970–71*, 7–22, 179–84. Vásquez Carrizosa, *Los no alineados: Una estategía política para la paz en la era atómica* (Bogotá, 1983).

45. Pardo and Tokatlian, *Politica exterior*, 104–5; Alfonso López Michelsen, *El gobierno del Mandato Claro*, vol. 3 (Bogotá, 1976).

46. DS, *Bulletin* 72 (1975): 108–13.

47. DS, *Bulletin* 73 (1975): 588–94.

48. DS, *Bulletin* 74 (1976): 343–45, 768; 75 (1976), 187, 284, 489–93.

49. DS, *Bulletin* 77 (1977): 380–82; 78 (1978), 42–46.

50. Colombia, MRE, *Memoria, 1978–79*, xxviii; *Memoria, 1979–80*, 49; DS, *Bulletin* 78 (1978), 42–46.

51. DS, *Bulletin* 83 (1983): 67–68.

52. Central Intelligence Agency, "Survey of Latin America," Latin America, vol. 1, NSF Country Files, LBJ Papers.

53. Memo by Thomas Hughes, Bureau of Intelligence and Research, 29 Nov. 1963, Country File: Latin America, Box 1, National Security Files, LBJ Papers.

54. Freeman to Mann, 28 Feb. 1964, File 11/63-6/64, Box 1, NSF Country File, Latin America, LBJ Papers.

55. Fernando Cepeda Ulloa and Rodrigo Pardo García-Peña, *Contadora: Desafío a la diplomacía tradicional* (Bogotá, 1985), 28. Pardo and Tokatlian, *Politica exterior*, 107, 135.

56. MRE, *Memoria, 1978–79*, 9–16, 49–54.

57. Cepeda Ulloa and García-Peña, *Contadora*, 28. Pardo and Tokatlian, *Politica exterior*, 107, 135.

58. DS, *Bulletin* 83 (1983): 5–17.

59. Pardo and Tokatlian, *Politica exterior*, 186–87.

Epilogue

1. Gabriel Silva Lujan, *Política exterior* (Bogotá, 1985).

Archival Sources

Colombia

Foreign Ministry Archives
Records of the Comisión Asesora, 1913–
Records of the Colombian Legation in Washington
Records of the United States Legation in Bogotá

National Archives
Records of the Ministry of Government

United States

National Archives
Record Group 43—Records of International Conferences
Record Group 59—General Records of the Department of State
   Diplomatic Instructions of the Department of State, 1801–1906
   Despatches from U.S. Ministers in Colombia, 1820–1906
   Central Decimal Files, 1910–
   Numerical and Minor Files of the Department of State, 1906–10
   Despatches from U.S. Consuls (Panama, Colón, Cartagena, Sabanilla, Barranquilla)
   Notes from the Colombian Legation in Washington to the Department of State, 1811–1906
Record Group 59 Lot Files
   Records of the Office of American Republic Affairs, 1918–1947
   Records of the Bureau of Inter-American Affairs
      Records of Assistant Secretary Edward Miller
      Records of Assistant Secretary John Cabot
      Records of Assistant Secretary Henry Holland
   Records of Deputy Assistant Secretaries of State for Inter-American Affairs, 1945–56
   Office of Inter-American Regional Economic Affairs

Record Group 80—Records of the Department of the Navy
Record Group 84—Records of United States Foreign Service Posts
Record Group 40—General Records of the Department of Commerce
Record Group 151—Records of the Bureau of Foreign and Domestic Commerce
Record Group 165—Records of the War Department
Record Group 169—Records of the Foreign Economic Administration
Record Group 253—Records of the U.S. Commercial Company
Record Group 353—Inter-American Affairs Committee, 1945–70

Library of Congress
Presidential Papers
  John Quincy Adams
  Grover Cleveland
  Calvin Coolidge
  James A. Garfield
  Ulysses S. Grant
  Benjamin Harrison
  Thomas Jefferson
  William McKinley
  James Monroe
  James K. Polk
  Theodore Roosevelt
  William Howard Taft
  Woodrow Wilson
Papers of Secretaries of State
  James G. Blaine
  William Jennings Bryan
  Henry Clay
  Bainbridge Colby
  John C. Calhoun
  Hamilton Fish
  John Hay
  Charles Evans Hughes
  Cordell Hull
  Philander C. Knox
  Robert Lansing
  William Marcy

Richard Olney
Elihu Root
William Seward
Daniel Webster
Personal Papers
  John Barrett
  Philip Bunau-Varilla
  M. Murillo

Presidential Libraries
Herbert Hoover Presidential Library, West Branch, Iowa
Lyndon Baines Johnson Presidential Library, Austin, Texas
Franklin D. Roosevelt Presidential Library, Hyde Park, New York
Harry S. Truman Presidential Library, Independence, Missouri

Manuscript Division, Princeton University Library
Edwin Kemmerer Papers

Rockefeller Archives Center, Tarrytown, New York
Records of the International Health Board
Papers of the American Institute for Free Labor Development

Yale University: Manuscripts Division, Sterling Memorial Library
Frank Polk Papers
Henry Stimson Papers

Great Britain: Public Record Office
F.O. 371—Colombia—General Correspondence, Political

Bibliographical Essay

Considering the important contacts between these two nations, the volume of historical literature on Colombian-U.S. relations is slight, especially in English; readers will wish to sample the more extensive materials on Colombian foreign and domestic politics and economy available in Spanish, some of the most important of which are noted here.

Because of the comparative dearth of secondary materials and in an effort to ensure that the volume would be a contribution to scholarship as well as a more popular understanding of Colombian-U.S. relations, I early on determined that this volume would be written essentially from archival materials in the United States and Colombia not readily available to students or, in some instances, many professional historians. The footnotes and the list of archival sources will be of value and interest to those who may wish to delve further into an aspect of the larger story. Given the nature of this series and the existence of a general overview volume by series editor Lester D. Langley, I have excluded discussion of general literature in U.S. domestic politics or foreign policy unless it impinged very directly either on the interpretative dimensions of this study or on Colombian-U.S. relations.

For readers unfamiliar with Colombian society and culture, the best place to begin is with the novels and short stories of Nobel Prize winner Gabriel García Márquez, especially *One Hundred Years of Solitude,* and the many general studies by Germán Arciniegas, a former director of *El Tiempo* and president of the Colombian Academy of History. A textbook overview in English is provided by Jesús Maria Henao and Gerardo Arrubla, *A History of Colombia,* translated and edited by J. Fred Rippy (Chapel Hill, N.C., 1938). The only modern survey in English is provided by Harvey F. Klein, *Colombia: Portrait of Unity and Diversity* (Boulder, Colo., 1983). For those who read Spanish the multivolume *Historia extensa de Colombia* covers cultural, political, diplomatic, and economic history from the colonial period to the present. One should be cautioned that the publications of the Academy of History do not in general address the historiographical innovations in social and economic history of the past thirty years in western Europe and North America. Far more promising are the just published volumes in the Historia moderna series. An important but dated reference work is Joaquín Ospina, *Diccionario biográfico y bibliográfico de Colombia,* 3 vols. (Bogotá, 1927–39).

On foreign relations, the essential starting point remains E. Taylor Parks, *Colombia and the United States, 1765–1934* (Chapel Hill, N.C., 1935); although now very dated methodologically, this work was thoroughly researched and will likely continue to be the standard study of the nineteenth century. In Spanish the essential study of foreign relations is Antonio José Uribe, *Anales diplomático y consulares de Colombia,* 6 vols. (Bogotá, 1900–1920). The *Historia extensa* series is comprehensive, but the foreign policy volumes cited in the footnotes are generally nonanalytical. Less concerned with foreign policy but more satisfactory from the perspective of professional historians are the excellent volumes edited by Jaime Jaramillo Uribe, *Manual de historia de Colombia,* 3 volumes (Bogotá, 1984). Chronologically following Parks's volume, Richard Lael's *Arrogant Diplomacy* (Wilmington, Del., 1988), my own *Diplomacy of Modernization: Colombian-American Relations, 1920–1940* (Toronto, 1977), and David Bushnell's, *Eduardo Santos and The Good Neighbor, 1938–42* (Gainesville, Fla., 1967) provide scholarly and detailed analyses through World War II. There is no comprehensive study in English of the cold war era, the years of the Alliance for Progress and the National Front, or the emerging narcotics crisis of the 1970s and 1980s, although there is extensive monograph and periodical literature, which is mentioned below.

Raimundo Rivas provides a detailed account from a Colombian perspective on the critical first half of the nineteenth century in *Relaciones internacionales entre Colombia y los Estados Unidos, 1810–1850* (Bogotá, 1915); David Bushnell's *The Santander Regime in Gran Colombia,* 2d edition (Westport, Conn., 1970), and Bushnell and Neill Macaulay, *The Emergence of Latin America in the Nineteenth Century* (New York, 1988), although not dedicated to foreign policy questions, provide insight into the political context in which early diplomacy was conducted, as does Catherine LeGrand, *Frontier Expansion and Peasant Protest in Colombia, 1830–1936* (Albuquerque, N.Mex., 1986); The independence period is well served by John Lynch, *The Spanish-American Revolutions, 1808–1826* (New York, 1973). Important for Colombian context are several other standard volumes, including: Tulio Halperin-Donghi, *The Aftermath of Independence in Latin America* (New York, 1973); *From Independence to 1870,* vol. 3 of the *Cambridge History of Latin America,* (Cambridge, Eng., 1985); Harold Davis et al., *Latin American Diplomatic History: An Introduction* (Baton Rouge, La., 1977). Javier Ocampo López, "La agitación revolucionaria en el Nuevo

Reino de Granada y el ejemplo de la independencia de Estados Unidos," *Revista de Historia de América* (July–September 1976), addresses the issue of early U.S. intellectual-political influence. William R. Manning's multivolume edition of diplomatic correspondence is an indispensable source for the early years: *Diplomatic Correspondence of the United States Concerning the Independence of the Latin American Nations*, 3 vols. (New York, 1925); but see also for discussion of Colombian issues Arthur P. Whitaker, *The United States and the Independence of Latin America, 1800–1830* (Baltimore, 1941). The domestic political history of Colombia in the early period is most extensively told in Carlos Restrepo Canal, *La Nueva Granada*, part 1 (1831–1840), vol. 8 of *Historia extensa de Colombia* (Bogotá, 1971). Given the importance of several of the early leaders in both the United States and Colombia, one should consult standard studies of Simón Bolívar by Augusto Mijares, *The Liberator* (Caracas, 1983); of John Quincy Adams by Samuel Flagg Bemis, *John Quincy Adams and the Foundations of American Foreign Policy* (New Haven, Conn., 1949), and Bradford Perkins, *Castlereagh and Adams, 1812–1823* (1964); of Thomas Jefferson by Merrill Peterson, *Thomas Jefferson and the New Nation: A Biography* (1970).

The economic history of nineteenth and early twentieth century Colombia is vital to an understanding of the evolution of foreign policy. William McGreevey, *An Economic History of Colombia, 1845–1930* (Cambridge, Eng., 1971), is the basic starting point, but should be supplemented by Marco Palacios, *Coffee in Colombia, 1850–1970: An Economic, Social, and Political History* (Cambridge, Eng., 1980); José Antonio Campo provides insight into the relationship between exports and economic development in *Colombia en la economía mundial* and in "Desarrollo exportador y desarrollo capitalista colombiano en el siglo xix," *Desarrollo y Sociedad* 8 (May 1982): 37–75; major works in the field are Luis Ospina Vásquez, *Industria y protección en Colombia, 1810–1930* (Bogotá, 1955); *Historia económica en Colombia; Un debate en marcha* (Bogotá, 1979); Diego Pizano Salazar, *La expansión del comercio exterior de Colombia, 1875–1925* (Bogotá, 1981). A detailed overview of Colombian economic history is Abel Cruz Santos in the *Historia extensa* series, *Economía y hacienda publica*, 2 vols. (Bogotá, 1965–66). Malcolm Deas, "The Fiscal Problems of Nineteenth Century Colombia," *Journal of Latin American Studies* 14 (November 1982); Orlando Fals Borda, *Historia de la cuestión agraria en Colombia* (Bogotá, 1975); Robert Beyer, "Transportation and the Coffee Industry in Colombia," *Inter-American Economic Affairs* 2 (1948): 17–30, all provide important context for an understanding of the relationship between economic development and external relations; Jorge Orlando Melo, "La economía Colombiana en la cuarta década del siglo xix," *Sobre historia y política* (Bogotá, 1979), is a very professional analysis; his *Historia de Colombia: El establecimiento de la dominación española* (Medellín, 1977) should be read by those interested in an earlier era. Luis Eduardo Nieto Arteta, *Economía y cultura en la historia de Colombia*, 6th ed. (Bogotá, 1975), is a widely read classic in the field. Alvaro Tirado Mejía provides several studies on this period that require consideration: *Introducción a la historia económica de Colombia*, 3d ed. (Bogotá, 1974), and *Colombia en la repartición imperialista, 1870–1913* (Bogotá, 1976). The most accessible statistical series has been published by Miguel Urrutia and Mario Arrubla, eds., *Compendio de estadísticas históricas de Colombia* (Bogotá, 1970); Frank Safford's *The Ideal of the Practical: Colombia's Struggle to Form a Technical Elite* (Austin, 1976) is one of the most original enquiries on economic culture for the nineteenth century; one should also see his "Social Aspects of Politics in Nineteenth Century Spanish America: New Granada, 1825–1850," *Journal of Social History* 5 (1972): 344–70.

Domestic Colombian politics in the second half of the nineteenth century are carefully delineated by Helen Delpar, *Red Against Blue: The Liberal Party in Colombian Politics, 1863–1899* (Alabama, 1981); Gerardo Molina's two volumes explore a similar theme, *Las ideas liberales en Colombia, 1849–1914* (Bogotá, 1970), and *Las ideas liberales en Colombia, 1915–1934* (Bogotá, 1974). A standard source is J. León Helguera, "The Problem of Liberalism versus Conservatism in Colombia, 1849–85," in Frederick Pike, ed., *Latin American History: Select Problems* (New York, 1969). Charles Bergquist's *Coffee and Conflict in Colombia* (Durham, N.C., 1978) is essential reading for the relationship between economic and political change and their foreign relations implications. See the detailed analysis in Luís Martínez Delgado, *La República de Colombia*, part 1 (1885–95), vol. 10 of *Historia extensa de Colombia* (Bogotá, 1970).

Other than the emerging crisis over Isthmus of Panama affairs, Colombian-U.S. relations from the 1850s to the 1880s has received scant attention, except for Parks's general study. Important studies of U.S. policy in these years provide context, including Walter LaFeber, *The New Empire* (Ithaca, 1963); Milton Plesur, *America's Outward Thrust* (New York, 1971); Robert Beisner, *From the Old Diplomacy to the New* (Arlington Heights, Ill., 1975); David M. Pletcher, *The Awkward Years: American Foreign Relations Under Garfield and Arthur* (Columbia, Mo., 1962).

Relations at the turn of the century have been better served in the literature because of the dramatic nature of the events. On the fight over the control of the isthmus, see Dwight Miner, *The Fight for the Panama Route* (New York,

1940); Walter LaFeber, *The Panama Canal* (New York, 1978); Sheldon Liss, *The Canal* (Notre Dame, Ind., 1967); David McCullough, *The Path Between the Seas* (New York, 1977). There is a broader perspective in Germán Arciniegas classic account, *Caribbean: Sea of the New World* (New York, 1954); for a Panamanian perspective see Ernesto J. Castillero Reyes, *Episodios de la independencia de Panamá* (Panama City, 1957), Ricardo Alfaro, *Medio siglo de relaciones entre Panamá y los Estados Unidos* (Panama City, 1959), and D. A. Arosemena, ed., *Documentary History of the Panama Canal* (Panama City, 1961). On the foreign policies of Theodore Roosevelt toward Colombia, see Lael's work cited in the notes; William Harbaugh, *Power and Responsibility: The Life and Times of Theodore Roosevelt* (New York, 1961); John M. Cooper, Jr., *The Warrior and the Priest: Woodrow Wilson and Theodore Roosevelt* (Cambridge, Mass., 1983). Walter and Marie Scholes provide a thorough account of the Taft years: *The Foreign Policies of the Taft Administration* (Columbia, Mo., 1970). Important articles include Charles Ameringer, "The Panama Canal Lobby of Philippe Bunau-Varilla and William Nelson Cromwell," *American Historical Review* 67 (January 1963), and "Philippe Bunau-Varilla: New Light on the Panama Canal Treaty," *Hispanic American Historical Review*, 64 (February 1966), 28–52. The multivolume Roosevelt papers and letters edited by Elting R. Morison are invaluable (Cambridge, Mass., 1954), as is Roosevelt's *Autobiography* (New York, 1913). Robert Bacon's *Latin America and the United States: Addresses by Elihu Root* (Cambridge, Mass., 1917) deals with one of the most important figures of the period. An important study for its insights on the period from progressivism to World War II is Emily Rosenberg, *Spreading the American Dream: American Economic and Cultural Expansion, 1880–1945* (New York, 1982).

J. Phanor Eder, *Colombia*, 5th ed. (London, 1921), provides useful insight into Colombia from a member of one of the major families in the development of the Cauca Valley at the turn of the century. Other less accessible works that advance a Colombian perspective include: Diego Martinez, *On the Treaty Between the United States and Colombia* (Washington, 1916); Diego Mendoza, *El canal interoceanico y los tratados* (Bogotá, 1901); Marco Fidel Suárez, *Tratado entre Colombia y los Estados Unidos* (Bogotá, 1914); Miguel Antonio Caro, *Discursos y otras intervenciones en el Senado de la República, 1903–04* (Bogotá, 1979), is the view of the leading contemporary conservative. The most professional, objective account, though badly dated, is Antonio José Uribe, *Colombia y los Estados Unidos de América: El canal interoceánico* (Bogotá, 1925), and *Las modificaciones al tratado entre Colombia y los Estados Unidos* (Bogotá, 1921).

On the Woodrow Wilson era see the recent work by Mark Gilderhus, *Pan*

American Visions: Woodrow Wilson in the Western Hemisphere, 1913–1921 (Tucson, Ariz., 1986), which contains a thorough bibliography on U.S.–Latin American relations in this period. There is again a striking absence of material on Colombia in English except Lael's recent work mentioned earlier. Arthur Link's multivolume edition of the Woodrow Wilson papers provides critical original documentation, 55 volumes (Princeton, N.J., 1966–), and his *Woodrow Wilson and a Revolutionary World, 1913–1921* (Arlington Heights, N.J., 1979) is essential reading.

On the Colombian side much of the work is dated. The most recent treatment of the foreign policy of the period is José Joaquín Caicedo Castillo, *Historia diplomatica*, part 1, vol. 17 of *Historia extensa de Colombia*, vol. 17 (Bogotá, 1974). The biography of the major figure in the development of Colombian foreign policy in these years, by Bernardo Blair Gutiérrez, *Don Marco Fidel Súarez, su vida y su obra* (Medellín, 1955) is of limited value for those interested in foreign relations. This is also true of Eduardo Lemaitre, *Rafael Reyes: Biografía de un gran colombiano*, 3d ed. (Bogotá, 1967); Baldomero Sanín Cano, *Administración Reyes, 1904–1909* (Lausanne, 1909); one should consult Rafael Reyes, *The Two Americas* (New York, 1914). Carlos E. Restrepo provides personal reflections on his era in *Orientación republicana*, 2 vols. (Medellín, 1917–30), as does José Manuel Marroquín Osorio, *Don José Manuel Marroquín intimo* (Bogotá, 1915). The excellent general study by Alonso Aguilar, *Pan Americanism from Monroe to the Present: A View from the Other Side* (New York, 1969), provides insight into the Latin American perspective on the Pan-American idea as does the strongly pro-Bolívar study by Indalecio Liévano Aguirre, *Bolivarismo y Monroismo* (Bogotá, 1987).

The best starting point for postwar U.S. policy in Latin America is Joseph Tulchin, *Aftermath of War: World War I and U.S. Policy Toward Latin America* (New York, 1971), although it covers only the early years in the decade; there is insight into the Anglo-American relationship in Latin America in Michael Hogan's, *Informal Entente* (Columbia, Mo., 1977). Extremely important for the relationship between the U.S. political economy and foreign policy in this period are works by Ellis Hawley, *The Great War and the Search for a Modern Order: A History of the American People and Their Institutions, 1917–1933* (New York, 1979); Carl Parinni, *Heir to Empire* (Pittsburgh, 1969); Melvyn Leffler, "1921–1932: Expansionist Impulses and Domestic Constraints," in William Becker and Samuel Wells, Jr., eds., *Economics and World Power* (New York, 1984). See as well Leffler, "Herbert Hoover, the New Era and American Foreign Policy, 1921–1929," in Ellis Hawley, ed., *Herbert Hoover as Secretary of*

Commerce (Iowa City, Iowa, 1981). Kenneth Grieb, *The Latin American Policy of Warren G. Harding* (Fort Worth, Tex., 1976) places Colombia in perspective. Michael Krenn provides an important recent contribution in his one chapter on Colombia in *U.S. Policy Toward Economic Nationalism in Latin America, 1917–1929* (Wilmington, Del., 1990). The most recent Colombian overview of this period is Carlos Uribe Celís, *Los Años veinte en Colombia, ideología y cultura* (Bogotá, 1985). Fernando Botero and Alvaro Guzmán, "El enclave agrícola en la zona bananera de Santa Marta," *Cuadernos Colombianos* 11 (1977): 309–90, provides essential insight into the agricultural developments in the area dominated by the United Fruit Company, as does Catherine LeGrande's work cited above; Judith White, *Historia de una ignominia: La United Fruit en Colombia* (Bogotá, 1978), is a critical, comprehensive study; Charles Kepner and Jay Soothill, *The Banana Empire* (New York, 1935), is very badly dated but worth consulting. The major investment surge of the decade is traced by Paul Drake, "The Origins of United States Economic Supremacy in South America: Colombia's Dance of the Millions, 1923–33," Mimeograph, Woodrow Wilson International Center, Washington, D.C., 1979. Cleona Lewis, *America's Stake in International Investments* (New York, 1938) remains the standard work on the period, but see as well Joelle Diot, "Colombia económica 1923–1929: Estadísticas historicas," *Boletín Mensual de Estadística (Departamento Administrativa nacional de Estadística)* 300 (July 1976): 122–35, and Max Winkler, *Investment of United States Capital in Latin America* (Boston, 1929); work on the oil industry and energy development continues to be critical of foreign investment; see René De la Pedraja, *Energy Politics in Colombia* (Westview, Conn., 1989), a well researched study, which should be consulted for the full range of U.S. investment activity in the Colombian energy sector in the twentieth century; more polemical and less well-researched is Jorge Villegas, *Petroleo colombiano, ganancia gringa*, 4th ed. (Bogotá, 1976). Still useful on foreign investment in this period is J. Fred Rippy, *The Capitalists and Colombia* (New York, 1931), and *Latin America in the Industrial Age*, 2d ed. (Westport, Conn., 1971); there is insight and overview in George Philip, *Oil and Politics in Latin America: Nationalist Movements and State Companies* (Cambridge, Eng., 1982). Bernardo Tovar Zambrano, *La intervención económica del estado en Colombia, 1914–1936* (Bogotá, 1984), and Jesus Antonio Bejarano, *El capital monopolista y la inversión norteamericana en Colombia*, 2d ed. (Bogotá, 1978), address issues of considerable debate in modern Colombian politics. Gustavo Humberto Rodriguez provides a good introduction to the most important political figure of the late 1920s in *Olaya Herrera, político, estadista y caudillo* (Bogotá, 1980).

The depression years have been well served in the English literature, although considerably more work needs to be done on the Colombian side. In addition to Randall and Bushnell noted earlier and in the notes, there is material of varying utility on Colombia in the following: Alexander DeConde, *Herbert Hoover's Latin American Policy* (Stanford, Calif., 1951); David Haglund, *Latin America and the Transformation of U.S. Strategic Thought* (Albuquerque, N.Mex., 1984); Bryce Wood, *The Making of the Good Neighbor Policy* (New York, 1961), and Wood, *The United States and Latin American Wars* (New York, 1966), which treats the Leticia conflict with Peru; Dick Steward, *Trade and Hemisphere* (Columbia, Mo., 1975); Irwin Gelman, *Good Neighbor Diplomacy: United States Policies in Latin America* (Baltimore, 1979); David Green, *The Containment of Latin America* (Chicago, 1971). On the Colombian side, one should begin with volume 17 of the Historia extensa series, by José Joaquín Caicedo Castilla.

For an introduction to postwar Colombian politics see John D. Martz, *Colombia, a contemporary political survey* (Chapel Hill, N.C., 1962); on the Rojas Pinilla era, see the now dated study by Vernon L. Flaherty, *Dance of the Millions: Military Rule and the Social Revolution in Colombia* (Pittsburgh, 1957); more recent on the period are James D. Henderson, *When Colombia Bled, A History of the Violencia in Tolima* (Tuscaloosa, Ala., 1985); Silvia Galvis and Alberto Donadio, *El Jefe Supremo: Rojas Pinilla en la Violencia y en el poder* (Bogotá, 1988). There is no study of the Truman presidency and Latin American relations, although a good introduction is David Green, "The Containment of Latin America," in Barton Bernstein, ed., *The Politics and Policies of the Truman Administration* (Chicago, 1970); R. Harrison Wagner, *United States Policy Toward Latin America* (Stanford, Calif., 1970) provides a glimpse into the Truman years; major biographers of secretaries of state George Marshall and Dean Acheson indicate that Latin America was of little interest to the Truman administration in comparison to Asia and Europe; see Gaddis Smith, *Dean Acheson* (New York, 1972), and Robert H. Ferrell, *George C. Marshall* (New York, 1966). The best study available of the Eisenhower years in Latin America is Stephen Rabe, *Eisenhower and Latin America* (Chapel Hill, N.C., 1988), although Colombia receives little attention. On the Kennedy administration and the Alliance for Progress, see the now standard study by Jerome Levinson and Juan De Onís, *The Alliance that Lost its Way* (Chicago, 1970); L. Ronald Scheman, ed., *The Alliance For Progress* (New York, 1988).

On recent Colombian developments and U.S. policy, Bruce M. Bagley's work is an important contribution to our understanding of the social and political context for foreign policy: see Bagley, "Power, Politics, and Public Policy in Colombia: Case Studies of the Urban and Agrarian Reform During the National Front, 1958–74," Ph.D. dissertation, University of California, Los Angeles, 1978. See also Gonzalo Sánchez G., "La Violencia en Colombia: New Research, New Questions," *Hispanic American Historical Review* 65 (November 1985), 789–807. The best overviews and analyses of Colombian politics after 1945 include Robert H. Dix, *Colombia: The Political Dimensions of Change* (New Haven, Conn., 1967); Jesus Bejarano, *El régimen agraria de la economía exportadora a la economía industrial* (Bogotá, 1979). R. Berry, ed., *Essays on Industrialization in Colombia* (Tempe, 1983); Berry, "Rural Poverty in Twentieth Century Colombia," *Journal of Interamerican Studies and World Affairs* 20 (November 1978): 355–76. World Bank, *Economic Growth of Colombia: Problems and Prospects* (Baltimore, 1972), provides critical information on economic changes since World War II and their implications for Colombia's place in international economic affairs.

Colombian analysts have overwhelmingly concentrated their work on the post-1945 foreign policy developments. On Colombian foreign policy in the post-1945 years the best analysis is provided by Rodrigo Pardo and Juan G. Tokatlian, *Política exterior colombiana* (Bogotá, 1988), and G. Drekonja Kornat, *Colombia política exterior* (Bogotá, 1982). For an incisive recent overview of the political conditions, see Bruce M. Bagley, Francisco Thoumi, and Juan G. Tokatlian, eds., *State and Society in Contemporary Colombia* (Boulder, Colo., 1988). The most active work has been completed on the post-1960s, including Tokatlian's, Bruce M. Bagley, "La política exterior de Colombia durante la década de los 80: Los limites de un poder regional," in Monica Hirst, comp., *Continuadad y cambio en las relaciones América Latina-Estados Unidos* (Buenos Aires, 1987). Useful for historical perspective is Marta Ardila, "Caracterización de la política exterior colombiana," *Magazin Diplomático y Negocios Internacionales*, no. 8 (1987). On the role of Colombia in the Contadora peace process in the Central American crisis see Fernando Cepeda Ulloa and Rodrigo Pardo García, *Contadora: desafío a la diplomacía tradicional* (Bogotá, 1985). Malcolm Deas and Mark Chernick, *Colombia durante el gobierno del Presidente Betancur: Las relaciones entre política exterior, crisis Centroamericana y proceso de paz nacional*, Documentos Ocasionales, septiembre–octubre 1988, Centro de Estudios Internacionales de la Universidad de Los Andes (Bogotá, 1988); Malcolm Deas, "The Colombian Peace Process, 1982–85, and its Implications for Central America," in Giuseppe Di Palma and Laurence Whitehead, eds., *The Central American*

Impasse (New York, 1986); Bruce Bagley, "La ley anti-narcóticos de 1988 en Estados Unidos y su impacto para Colombia," *Colombia Internacional*, no. 4 (octubre–diciembre 1988); Ana Mercedes Botero, "Colombia ante la enmiedas a la ley de comercio exterior de los Estados Unidos," *Colombia Internacional*, no. 4 (octubre–diciembre, 1988); Alfredo Vásquez Carrizosa, "La política exterior de la administración Barco, 1986–1988," *Colombia Internacional*, no. 3 (julio–septiembre 1988). A former foreign minister, Vásquez Carrizosa's more general study of the nonaligned movement is important for an understanding of Colombia's search for alternative foreign policies in the post–cold war years: *Los no Alineados: Una estrategía política para la paz en la era atómica* (Bogotá, 1983). Important recent literature on the Colombian-U.S. relationship in the context of the drug crisis includes Richard Craig, "Colombian Narcotics and United States–Colombian Relations," *Journal of Inter-American Studies and World Affairs* 23 (1981), 243–70; Daniel Premo, "Colombia: Cool Friendship," in Robert Wesson, ed., *U.S. Influence in Latin America in the 1980s* (New York, 1982). One of the most promising lines of analysis on Colombian foreign policy emphasizes its role as a middle and regional power: see Bruce Bagley. "Regional Powers in the Caribbean Basin," Johns Hopkins SAIS, occasional paper no. 2 (Washington, 1982); Rodrigo Pardo, "Impact of the Debt Crisis on a Regional Power: The Case of Colombia," *Texas Journal of Political Studies* 9 (Fall–Winter 1986–87), 11–33. Ultimately, the considerable scholarly productivity of the past decade will require a new synthesis of Colombian-U.S. relations in the post-1960s.

Index